The Golden Sky

EC Stilson

Literati Publications
www.literatipublications.com
P. O. Box 453
Pocatello, ID 83201

The Golden Sky
Copyright© 2011 EC Stilson

The views herein are the responsibility of the author and do not necessarily represent the position of Literati Publications. Names have been changed to protect those written about in this memoir.

Cover design and artwork by Ruby Morris.
@RubyHirsch

Visit the author at www.ECWrites.net.

ISBN-13: 9781460961971

Printed in the United States of America.

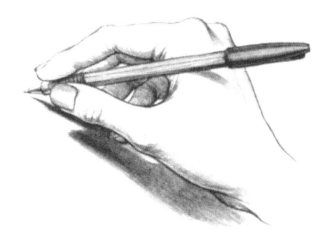

Note to my readers

Before taking this journey, know that you hold my journal in your hands. It's raw and real. Every word is precious to me, written through the honest eyes of youth. At the age of nineteen I turned to pen and paper, my only confidants. I then reread my journal and perfected it, by making minor revisions, when I was in my 20s.

Yes, I was young. Yes, it was hard, but still, I was about to begin the journey of a lifetime…and see that after every storm there is a golden sky.

—Elisa (EC Stilson)

Praise for
"The Golden Sky"

EC Stilson has opened her heart and life to us through the "entries" in this book. She takes us step by step through the joys, challenges, and heartbreaks of being a wife and mother. It is a powerful message of hope, not only to those who have lost a baby born with defects, but to everyone who has had their dreams shattered and had to find a way to put life together again.

–Bob Deits Author of "Life after Loss."

EC Stilson's "The Golden Sky" is one of the most beautiful books I have read in a long time. Perhaps the word "beautiful" seems an odd choice given that the book journals the details of the death of her baby boy and its aftermath—but it's not just a book about that terrible loss. It is a testament to courage, it is poignant and honest, it is funny, and it is sad. Ultimately it is a story of transformation, growth and healing—of herself, her marriage, her family and her relationship with God. EC's style of writing is conversational and captivating, and with each turn of the page this book will touch your heart.

–Pamela D. Blair, Ph.D. Co-Author of the bestselling classic, "I Wasn't Ready to Say Goodbye: Surviving, Coping and Healing After the Sudden Loss of a Loved One"
I was immediately drawn into the story of "The Golden Sky." Having, myself, suffered the death of an infant son, I can say that EC Stilson has portrayed, amazingly well, the emotions of a grieving mother. Anyone who has lost a child will relate; others will gain a deeper understanding about the length and depth of the mourning process. All readers will be edified.

–Nannette Monson Kern Author of "Come Autumn."

Reading "The Golden Sky" made my days shine as bright as the Sahara sun. How EC Stilson can make the reader shine with such a sad book is beyond belief. It's all within her, the strength that she shows in her book bring out the warmest sunshine rays.

–Dimitri Sarantis Author of "Deep Blue Eyes on the Greek Isles"

This story opened my eyes to the hardships that are caused by the loss of a child. It is so well written that I felt as if going through the situation alongside the author. There is so much hope by the end of the story that this is sure to help many families that have gone through similar experiences.

–Candiss West
Your experiences really struck a chord with me, and it felt good to read another mother's experiences.

–Shana Judkins (mother of loss)

Reading EC Stilson's journal was almost as if exploring a secret attic and uncovering a lost notebook full of a young woman's journey through the loss of a child. I never expected to laugh as much as I did—laugh through the tears—and smile at "The Golden Sky."

–D.S. Tracy

Throughout time millions of women have lost infant children. But when it happens to you, you feel uniquely alone. How could God let this happen and how could these poignant feeling of lonely despair rip through me? With naked honesty, EC Stilson has documented the range of emotions, the tearing at family relationships, the social ignorance, and the ultimate arrival at "The Golden Sky" that came through her journey of losing Zeke. We all must process grief in our own way. This book dignifies the sharing of grief: an essential process to our own individual healing.

–Burke and Rose Larsen (parents of loss)

Elisa's reflections from her journal in this book are poignant, insightful, and often very humorous. Her sense of hope and great love of life made what could have been a tale of tragedy into a love story. It is the story of a mother's love for her child. It is also, and perhaps even more importantly, the story of the love between two parents who grieved separately for the loss of their son and yet were tied together forever by their life-changing experience. We would encourage anyone to read this book who would like to better understand how losing a baby can transform the life of a couple.

–Carolyn Kasteler & Kay Tanner (Angel Watch Counselors)

Dedication

This book is dedicated to Zeke (the brave soul), my amazing brother (Shane) and his sweetheart (Kazuna), my sweet mom, generous dad, and inspiring sister (Julie), as well as my dear friends: Angela, Candiss, Dee, Diana, Fran, Jamie, Joshua, Kristin, Romi, and Susan among others who are too numerous to name. Thank you for giving me the strength to reread my journal.

The Golden Sky
Contents

Part I
Searching

A path leading to nowhere and one leading to all....
They are one and the same.

I am lost on this path called life.
And I desperately need answers.

Entry #1

Being pregnant isn't the greatest thing since sliced bread. On the days I don't feel like I have Alzheimer's, I'm like Hercules journeying from Hell. Here I am at the age of nineteen, with a seven-month-old girl and another kid on the way.

God doesn't have life end up the way we plan. He throws us in weird situations, where we don't always get what we want, but we get what we need. Last year, before we had a kid, my husband Cade and I were street musicians in Hawaii. It was really sweet when we weren't cold and hungry. Now I'm a homemaker and Cade works to provide for us. He's an amazing guy, and we've been through a bunch together, but it's still hard sometimes.

I get lonely and when Ruby's asleep, I sit and cry. Not all the time, only sometimes. It's hard seeing people my age doing whatever they want and here I am, a young mom. Don't get me wrong. I wouldn't trade Ruby for anything, but I should have waited.

Old women in the grocery store always gawk at me, Ruby, and my blossoming belly. I'm actually a fairly nice person even though they can't see past this watermelon-stomach and how young I am. They must think I'm a loser, but I'm not; they don't care though. Their eyes tell more than I want to know, and their condemnation sucks! To their credit, it doesn't help that I look like a twelve-year-old. Once a lady asked me what it was like having such a young sister—before I was showing with this kid. I just laughed. What a joke, Ruby being my infant sister, and she's my own kid and all! Now that I really look pregnant—and twelve—enough said.

I'm not the coolest kid or the smartest, but I try hard. Whatever I lack I make up for in effort and determination. I play six instruments, and that took years of practice. Music comes naturally to me, and I'm quite good, even if I act like I'm not. It's no surprise though; I've been learning music since I was five.

I performed at an airport once, before September eleventh

happened and you could still play in the airports. A reporter saw me and thought I was talented. He put my picture in the Colorado newspaper. I acted like it wasn't a big deal, but it really was. A few colleges contacted me about it, but I didn't go to any of them. Instead, I graduated from high school a year early and ran away at seventeen.

I seem smart, once you get to know me, but I can be dumb. Well, maybe not completely dumb, just impulsive. I guess that's why I have one kid and another on the way. I wanted to pursue music but screwed up. Ruby is what I needed though; she straightened me out. I was a wild kid. After all, what kind of seventeen-year-old runs away and wants to be homeless? I could have gone to Julliard, no kidding! They would've wanted me. I just wasn't up for it, that's all.

But I still cry when it's quiet because life is hard and there's no going back. There's a bright side, I guess. Cade's the only person I'd ever want to marry, even if it was sooner than later, and I'm glad I have the energy to take care of Ruby. It's better than being a forty-year-old mom, right? I'll just keep saying that.

Entry #2

I went to my five-month checkup. The heartbeat sounds great, and according to the doctor, my tummy's the right size. But if you ask me, when a man looks you in the face and says your forty-foot-wide stomach is "just right," he either needs new glasses or to stop taking prescription drugs. Hey, can doctors write their own prescriptions? Anyway, sorry for getting off the subject, I'm just like that, faster than sound—always.

The doctor wants me to get an ultrasound, but I really don't want to. With Ruby I was excited to find out her sex. I knew she would be a boy, just like I knew all four of my sister's girls would be boys. Yes, I do have an uncanny sense for these things. What can I say?

It's not that I'm disinterested. I'm interested, really. Things would be better if I didn't know. I just have a bad feeling. Cade

11

wants me to get an ultrasound. He's as excited as hell about this kid. He wants to find out the sex, and make sure everything's okay. Not me, man; I don't want that stinking ultrasound.

Entry #3

Ruby is so funny! Sure, everyone says that about their kids, but she really is. We play this stupid game she thinks is the best thing ever. We lie on the bed and pass each other the binky. She starts by sucking on it. I close my eyes, and she puts it in my mouth. Today we did that a couple of times, but on the third time, she stuck her foot in my mouth. I was so grossed out! It's been a couple days since she had a bath (if you know what I mean). But Ruby, she thought it was really something. She laughed, and I giggled so hard hot tears streamed from my eyes. My tummy is huge, and it shook like Jell-O. To watch it jiggle made it even funnier. That kid is a real ham—she really is.

Entry #4

Everybody talked me into getting an ultrasound, and I'm supposed to go in a few days. Even though I didn't want to, I'm excited now. I hope we'll have a boy. I know it shouldn't matter, but I've always wanted a son—a rowdy little kid, running around the house, pretending he's an airplane. I hope he'll have brown hair and be strong like his daddy. If we have a boy, we can be done having kids. We already have beautiful Ruby, and a little boy would even us out. Like that song says, "a boy for you, and a girl for me." That's what I want, a boy for me. I'll be happy with another girl too, but I really want a boy.

Entry #5

I'm finally feeling better. Can you believe it took me over five months to stop throwing up? Pregnancy—not only do you get to enjoy your food going down, you get a second taste as it comes back up. I tell ya, there's nothing like second chances.

Entry #6

Well, you'll never believe it, but we're having a boy. He looked so precious on the ultrasound. Those tiny fingers! I can't wait to see him in person! Cade is still out of town. We only get to see each other about four days a month, but it sure beats being homeless and hungry.

I called Cade to tell him the great news. We both cried. Can you believe it, Cade crying and all? When you first meet him, you'd never imagine him crying. He's a construction worker and looks tough, but he cries at sappy movies. I don't think life could be any better. We have a wonderful little girl and a baby boy on the way. Cade has a good job, and we just bought a house. After I had Ruby, we had a hard time adjusting to responsibility, but now things are getting better.

Entry #7

I can't stop thinking about the baby. I'm so happy he's okay. I had the weirdest feeling something was wrong, but he's all right and I worried over nothing! I can't wait to feed him and hold him.

Ruby will be such a great big sister. I told her today that she's going to have a lifelong friend. I hope they'll be close for the rest of their lives. My dad has these amazing, ice blue eyes. I wonder if my baby will get them. He'll be so cute, and I can already tell he's a sweetheart. If he gets my dad's eyes and my brother's personality, then he'll be extra amazing. Man, I can't wait to meet him. The holiday spirit mixed with the euphoria of having a great life—I'm walking on air today!

Entry #8

Well, I don't know what to say. I just got a call from the doctor. I answered the phone, and after realizing who it was, I prayed to God. I didn't even listen for a second, and prayed instead, "Please let him be calling to tell me our baby is a genius or something. Don't let it be bad news! I'm not strong enough. I want my baby to be okay!" When a doctor calls you, personally, out of the blue, it's bad news. They don't call with good news, just bad news. It's in their damn job description.

The doctor said there were abnormalities in the ultrasound. I guess the ultrasound tech didn't feel competent enough to voice his fears. Instead, he told us everything was okay, and turned things over to the doctor, who took two whole days to call! Two days when I was happier than crap!

So, we're going to the university hospital in a day. They will tell us what's going on. The doctor suspects there's a hole in his diaphragm, a cleft lip, heart problems, etc. Could we start with what looks okay? For crying out loud, the list would be shorter! I can't believe this is happening. This stuff doesn't happen to people I know, let alone me. Take it a day at a time, you say! Well, guess what, if you ever go through this, then you can try that, okay?

Entry #9

I'm getting ready to go to the hospital. Ruby knows something is wrong. I can tell she wants to make things better. I keep crying on and off, and she doesn't understand why. Maybe this was some huge mistake. The baby might be fine. Who knows, hopefully that ultrasound machine wasn't clear, and they assumed bad things were there. It's better to err on the side of caution, right? I always try looking at the bright side, so let's see, today I can be happy because I get to see my baby on the ultrasound again. Cade is home, and I'm glad he'll be with me.

None of this seems real. God, does my baby really have problems? Even if things aren't perfect, He can heal the baby, right? God, please help me get through this.

That was something, calling everyone and telling them what's going on. I didn't want to tell my parents and Cade's parents. When I talked to my sister, she said doctors have told people their kids would have Downs, and then the kids were born fine. When I told my mom, she bawled on the phone. She called my mother-in-law afterward, and they talked for hours about what was happening. My mom said the mail lady came to her door after she got off the phone. She tried acting like she hadn't cried, and her grandson might not die.

Entry #10

What a freaking great day! There's nothing like going to the doctor and getting the worst news of your life. I feel bad for the people who work there. They must see depressing things all day. Yet their lives continue normally, and mine just ended. I want to fall into a dark hole and never come out.

Our baby only has a partial diaphragm, and a bunch of his organs are up in his chest. It will be a miracle if he develops half his lungs. He has a cleft lip and palate, a heart defect, and part of his cerebellum is missing. I guess the cerebellum is what helps us move.

They did the ultrasound and walked from the room without telling me a damn thing. After a while they returned with an "expert." Okay, if those people didn't feel competent enough to do it right the first time, why do it at all? Where was the "expert" the first go around? Freaking fabulous! The "expert" sat down and told Cade and me about our son's problems. She constantly referred to him as "the fetus," and then proceeded telling me I should abort the pregnancy. I must have seemed so delusional. I stopped her and said, "Well, can't you fix him?"

"You mean, the fetus?" she asked.

"My baby. Can't you fix my baby? You're an "expert." Do something! Can't you fix him?" She shook her head. I said, "Pull his organs down, patch the hole; his lungs will have room to grow, and we'll call it good."

She told me I needed time to think, then led Cade and me to a different room where my parents sat waiting. My dad really wants the abortion. He said he'll pay for it and everything, seeing as how we don't have insurance. He means well and all. He went on and on about fixing the situation; he's a real "can do" man. I love that guy, but this is my baby.

My poor mom cried in the corner. She doesn't know what to do or say, but she did exactly what I needed by just being there. I have so much swimming in my head. Cade grew quieter than death on Memorial Day and turned yellow. I tried finding one happy thing to hold onto, but all hope is leaving. Please God, give our son hope!

The "expert" of practically nothing returned to the room. She answered our questions; and there were a lot. She was actually nice, considering how she'd just ruined my life and all. She kept coming back to "the fetus" and abortion, though, and that wasn't cool with me.

God, when you handed me this lovely situation, what were you doing? Is there a plan in this, or should I just go suck crap now? Anyway, I'm getting off track, and this stupid eraser bites worse than my life does. It's all permanent in here, baby.

The "expert" said there's a slim chance our boy will live a normal life. The key word in that phrase is "normal." What's her definition of "normal," anyway? I hope it means good. I can't take that away from my son. If there is a chance, I want him to have it.

She said they can do an amnio test. It will let us know if he has some form of trisomy. If he does, he'll only live a little while before death claims him. My dad jumped on that like butter on bread. He wanted me to have the test done and my mom thought it was a good idea, too.

The "expert" said an amnio test could cause a miscarriage, and for a fleeting moment, I wished I would have one. I only thought it for a second, how it would make things easier, so much simpler, but now I'm mad at myself for being so stinking weak. I'm learning a lot about my faults today.

I talked to Cade and decided to have the test done. One step at a time. If the baby has trisomy, I might consider an abortion. I don't want him to suffer through surgeries if he'll die soon anyway, but I want him to have a chance at life no matter how small it may be.

Entry #11

So, I went into a room and sat back in this really comfy looking seat which appeared way better than it felt. I found myself thinking, "This seat is a lot like me." The room was decorated in a sickeningly-sweet flower theme—as if anyone who goes in there (to get an amnio test) wants to feel all flowery and happy. Just before I could rip the border off the wall, a very plump nurse entered the room.

She totally lacked empathy, and I felt worse sitting in her presence. She sucks as a nurse and should really find a job at a hair salon where people aren't pregnant with complications.

She'd done her hair up, and I bet she'd make one hell of a beautician. She said how sweet and refreshing I am, but my tear-streaked face didn't believe her as she laughed and talked, on and on. She said she wanted to be honest, since I'm a smart kid. Then she told me how I should end the pregnancy because I need to do what's best for me, like I'm so freaking amazing or something. She asked if I'm married and how old I am, as if the baby didn't matter.

I told her I want to have the baby unless he has trisomy, and she said he'll probably die shortly after being born anyway. I seriously thought about walking out until she produced a needle, like a magician discovering a rabbit in his hat. That needle was the size of Milwaukee!

It takes a lot to scare me, it really does. I went through a natural childbirth with Ruby and was quiet the whole time. Not that it didn't hurt, but my family taught me how to be tough. I've got a relentless pain tolerance, but that ungodly needle—of all things—took me off guard. I stopped Miss Sunshine right there and asked if she wanted to kill me. It seemed like a poorly written horror film where the baby will die so they kill off the mother, too.

She laughed and told me to relax. I wanted to say, "Over my dead body," but decided she might take the advice. She didn't really care about me anyway. That nurse was a textbook definition of self-absorption. She said if I moved, the needle could hit "the fetus." She didn't want to get in trouble or something—forget she might hurt my son.

The needle punched through my skin. It didn't hurt as much as I'd expected, as far as needles the size of Milwaukee go. I saw my baby on the ultrasound, and the needle the nurse used. I held still, not wanting that stupid thing to touch my son. He kicked a couple of times. Poor little guy, he doesn't know there's anything wrong with him. Anyway, they said the results will come back soon. It won't be soon enough, though. When God made me, He didn't throw patience into the deal.

So, we still don't know if our baby has trisomy. I'll get back to you on that later, but right now...I need to go cry.

Entry #12

I watched a chick flick tonight, to get my mind off it all. I might go crazy, no kidding, just like the homeless balloon makers in Hawaii. The people who made balloon animals were always the worst. I swear it was the first sign of their insanity.

Anyway, I couldn't pay attention to much of the movie, except the end. A bride stood at the altar. She cried, even though nothing was wrong; her son didn't have birth defects or anything. That's where the movie ended.

I'm really glad it's over. I watched the thing thinking it would distract me, but now I feel worse. How come movies usually end when the couple gets married? Do writers think life after marriage sucks?

Maybe it honestly can. Look at my life right now—and I'm married.

Entry #13

He doesn't have trisomy! Can you believe it? He might be okay. I thanked God, and even told Him I'll go to church if He'll fix my boy. It's a lifetime of church with droning voices and old people with bad breath, but it will be worth it. I'll do it for my son. I hope God heard me. I knelt down and everything. I used to do that all of the time, a few years ago, when I was religious. I had so much faith it could have filled a steeple.

Sometimes how I acted makes me sick. Not the faith part, just some other things. I told people they were going to Hell. I thought I was being helpful, really. One time someone stole my Bible. I'd read it so much the cover fell off, and I duct-taped the thing so it would stay together. It seemed ironic since the Bible says not to steal and all. I finally got my Bible back, and a new kid joined a Bible study I held during lunch. I wondered if he stole my Bible, but the Bible says not to judge, so I tried not to think about it.

I swear I thought God wanted me to be some sort of Nun. You know, the kind who devote their lives to God, except I could have gotten married and everything. Weird, but I believed it. I thought the more I read my Bible, the closer I would be to God, and the more He might notice me. Now I just hope He loves me for who I am, and will take some of those years into account, and help my son. I must sound like a nut trying to make a deal with God. He knows I'm good for it, if He's watching. I never break a promise, never.

Entry #14

My sister had a beautiful baby girl today. I'm so glad everything is all right. She could have bled to death; she had placenta previa. That's when the placenta is in the wrong spot. Anyway, she realized she was bleeding, and left for the hospital as fast as she could. She made it in time and is doing okay now. I love my sister. She's such a strong person. I'm sure you'd like her, too, if you met her. She's really beautiful and nice. Not many people are like that, good looking and kind. She is, though.

Anyway, she had her baby today. My niece came early, but she's healthy. I went and saw them earlier. Her skin looked see-through, but she's still gorgeous.

My parents said I shouldn't visit; they think it's too hard for me. But it's not. I'm just happy for my sister and glad her baby is healthy.

I came home and opened my Bible to Psalms 34:19, "Many are the afflictions of the righteous, but the Lord will deliver them out of them all." I know God is looking out for us, too.

Entry #15

It's late, but I had to tell you about tonight. It was amazing! I attended church, and a neat person spoke. He told stories about healing, and I found myself grasping onto every word. At the end of the service, he called me to the front of the room. He didn't even know me, just pointed, and told me to stand. He said God gave him a message meant for me. He said, "Many are the afflictions of the righteous, but the Lord will deliver them out of them all." Chills ran up and down my body before I started crying.

Entry #16

Some nice counselors visited our house today. One of the ladies had a baby who died. She told us all about it, and even seemed happy to answer my questions. I hope they'll come back. I felt better talking with someone who's gone through this. She didn't know her baby had problems when she was pregnant; instead, they found out when the baby was born. It happened a long time ago, and they could have saved her baby in modern times. It wasn't like the lady was super ancient. I mean, she was old, not ancient, but at least forty.

I told them how I had this crazy dream of giving birth to a

fish. I don't know what's wrong with me. They said I'm probably just scared and don't know what to expect. I'm too upset to tell them I hate fish. I don't want them disliking me for dreaming I gave birth to something I hate. I just don't know what to expect—like they said—but why can't I dream of birthing something cool, like a tiger, or something? I'm plagued by that dream. I love my son, and he is not a fish!

I don't know why, but Cade told them how we met. He can be so sweet. I guess he fell in love with me the first time we played our instruments together. Cade is a phenomenal rhythm guitarist. He told them the whole story, and they seemed enthralled. Then, they asked if we could play a song for them. We performed a couple songs, and Ruby got into it. She loves our music.

One of the counselors liked it so much she asked us to play at her son's wedding in a couple of weeks. We said we'd do it, and Cade seems pretty excited.

Anyway, they told me there's a girl who had a baby with problems like our baby has. She lives fairly close and wants to meet someone who's gone through something similar. They asked if they could give her my number, and I said I'd be up for it. I wonder if she'll call me; I hope she will.

Entry #17

I talked to one of my best friends from high school. He was a cool kid. We both worked at a diner, and he would drive me there after school. I remember this one time: a huge line of cars waited to leave the parking lot, and my buddy didn't want to wait in line. He drove right over a huge, grassy hill and through a white-picket fence. I thought it was great at the time. We laughed so hard. The school wanted to know who did it, but no one ever told on him.

Anyway, he called to see how I'm doing. I don't know what he did with his cool side, but it's hidden somewhere. I told him about my baby boy, and hoped my old friend would surface, but he didn't. You know what he did? That kid cried on the phone, just like a baby. Can you believe it? I've got enough to deal with without helping that guy. He called to see how I'm doing, and then cried like I'm a damn shrink or something. He didn't cry long, but it seemed like forever. Then, when he talked again, his voice sounded strange.

He went on for a bit, telling me how sorry he is, and how, way back when, he wanted to marry me. He thought he could have prevented this if I'd married him. It made me feel weird, so I said I had to go, but he wasn't done. I didn't feel like making the kid cry again. I just couldn't take any more of him bawling and confessing. Krap, with a capital "K."

"I've turned Mormon, and I'm living right, Elisa," he said. "I'd like to give your baby a blessing."

I didn't want him blessing anything, so I just stayed silent. He went on, "God sends down retarded babies because they're too perfect to be tried and tested by Satan here on Earth."

I wanted to tell him my son might not be retarded, but he kept talking.

"Sometimes I wonder why God didn't send me down retarded," he said.

I wondered if God had. After his voice sounded totally normal, I told him I had to go.

That kid, man! I wonder where he's hiding my friend—the cool one no one would rat on. The cool one that didn't think he should be handicapped and faultless.

Entry #18

We went and played at the wedding. The counselor's house is absolutely beautiful. It doesn't look like anything special until you get to the backyard and then it's like the secret garden came to life.

It was amazing and took me away from my problems for a moment. The bride looked gorgeous, and you should have seen the groom's face when she walked toward him. He must have

22

thought he was the luckiest guy in the world.

Entry #19

The grocery store was busy today. I live in a fairly small town and everyone shops at the local Walmart for everything. It's always packed, and Ruby and I were there forever. I got so tired of standing on my feet, I started feeling edgy. We'd made it to the check-out line, which was about forty feet long, when a superficial lady got in line behind us. She wore huge pieces of jewelry, which yelled, "Look at me, look at me." She made small talk, and seemed nice enough, but was obviously bored with life. I didn't feel like talking to anyone, even though I'm no good at shutting people down.

She went on and on, her huge golden earrings swaying maniacally. She asked how far along I am. I tried letting the conversation die, but she could revive a dead whale, that woman.

People always approach me because I look so friendly. I need to stop smiling, or something. I don't know why strangers always want to talk to me.

That lady fluffed her short, curly hair with a flawless hand and said how she could die, because her hair looked so bad. She could die because some guy messed up her manicure. Well, I wished she would leave, that lady who needed to talk to someone before her funeral. I told her I'm sure she wouldn't "just die," but she said she certainly would, because the manicurist had ruined her life.

That was when I lost it. I told her all about my boy, you know, the one I'm carrying who I want to live more than anything in the world; the one who might not make it because, for some reason, his body isn't perfect; my little boy who deserves to have a future because of his innocence; the one who I wanted to watch grow up to be the kind of man I could be proud of. You know, my boy. His life is hanging in the balance and that lady was having a bad day!

She turned whiter than me, and I swear I almost felt sorry—

almost. The problem is that it felt nice unloading on someone who wanted to talk so badly! Everyone looked at me like I'd lost it, but I'm glad I did something; she won't go to the funeral home anytime soon. Maybe she won't want to "just die" now.

I grabbed Ruby and left the cart in line, blocking the lady's way. I accidentally left my purse, though. I thought about abandoning it, because I was embarrassed, but changed my mind and went back. I plucked it from the cart and walked away as fast as my belly would go. I've adopted a waddle walk, but at least it gets me from one place to another. I don't care how much time we spent looking for those groceries. I'm tired of people with questioning eyes. I want to be home where my problems are my own, and they aren't around for others to paw through.

Entry #20

That girl actually called me, the one the counselors told me about, the one with a little girl who died. I met her for lunch and she's as cool as hell. She's older, about twenty-five or so, but pretty neat, and beautiful, too. She's the kind you'd imagine to be a perfect model, on a magazine cover, the kind who doesn't need to be touched-up and doesn't have kids with birth defects. I think I was supposed to meet her, through destiny or something. I'm not sure why, I just get that vibe about the whole thing.

She cracked me up. We talked on the phone before meeting for lunch, and then, when she saw me, her jaw dropped. She couldn't believe I'm not Hispanic. That made me giggle. I'm practically albino; what I wouldn't give for a tan.

I like it when people are truthful though, especially if they're honest about how they were wrong; it takes guts.

Entry #21

It's been about a month since I found out about the birth defects. Some days I try being strong, and on those days I feel a little better. I'm scared now though—I honestly am—but no one realizes it. I display my happy face for everyone; I can't stand seeing everyone sad. They pretend everything is all right if I do. But if I break down, they do, too. I keep having crazy labor pains.

The doc swears they're Braxton Hicks, but he's not the one feeling them. I'm not even seven months along. I can't have the baby yet, or he'll have an even harder time. I keep patting my belly, telling him to hang in there. He kicks when I sing. I'm falling more and more in love with the baby, but Cade is pulling away. I think he doesn't want to get hurt. He's spending a ton of time with Ruby though. I want to treasure every moment I have with my boy, but Cade isn't the one who's pregnant. It must be different for him.

I should put myself in his shoes. We've always been close, but I need him more now. He's still working out of town all the time. Maybe I should go with him sometime. That might help.

We're trying to come up with a name for the baby. Cade wanted to name him Dakkon, but now that we know he has problems, Cade wants to give him a different name. I can't figure out why; I mean, he's still the same kid and all. I hope we'll pick the right name. I want him to love it when he grows up.

Entry #22

I went to a Catholic church today. I used to go there when I was in high school. If I was sad or needed to feel close to God, I'd visit that cathedral. It is a beautiful place. It's really regal, inside and out. I didn't like going during church service or anything. I just went when the priest, or whatever he's called, was the only one there. I'd walk in solemnly, and act like I knew what it's like to be Catholic, but I'm a really bad Catholic, if you ask me. I've only been to a Catholic wedding, and I don't think that makes me a member. But I do like this one cathedral anyway.

I made Cade take me there. It was time we dedicated Ruby and the new baby to God. I just want them to be good people—

better than me.

Cade thought the place was pretty amazing, and said he'd been there before we left to Hawaii. Anyway, we brought Ruby up to the altar and I sat next to her. Big walls loomed around, and the painted pictures of saints looked toward a big organ on the second floor.

Cade and I prayed to God. Cade prayed first, and then I did. I'm not sure why, but I found myself praying something far different than intended. I prayed God would have His will in my life and grant me peace. It was weird, but the words rolled off my tongue. I sure hope God's will is what I want it to be.

Entry #23

We traveled out of town with Cade. It's cold here, but nice to be with him; Ruby's enjoying every minute. That kid loves to travel. You've never seen a kid who enjoys driving in a car quite so much.

We rolled down the windows and listened to oldies. I sang loud, and it almost drowned out all the crazy things I feel. Ruby loves copying music and noises. She's such a hoot, that kid. Today, when we sang "I Will Survive," I found myself bellowing the chorus.

Cade works for the construction company my dad owns, and he gets to see my dad more than I do; it's pretty wild, but they get along. They're working on this job together. My parents came out of town with us, and it's been fun. This place has a free continental breakfast, and I don't think there's anything better than free food, especially since I'm pregnant.

It feels good being away from home, and my family is taking my mind off things. My mom and I sure have great times together. Boy, that woman can make me laugh. We might go to a church tonight; it should be interesting.

Entry #24

I'm a bit nervous right now. I just found out a girl I dislike lives in this town. She's one of the only people I've ever had a hard time forgiving, and that's saying a lot, it really is. I'm having stomach pains more often and they're getting worse the more I think about it. I wish I could understand what's going on. I should calm down though, so I won't go into early labor.

Why is this happening? Why does my son have problems...and why does that girl have to live in this town?

When we were kids, we used to have sleepovers. She's about four years older than me, and she used to bully me around. When all of the lights were out, and everything was quiet, she'd make me kiss her and things. I hated it when she'd sleep over. I wished I was bigger—stronger—or something. But I wasn't strong, that was all. I wanted to tell my mom, because maybe my mom wouldn't let her stay over anymore, but "the bully" said if I told anyone, she'd tell them how yucky I was. Then she'd say I needed to give her my toys and crap, my damn toys, of all things. I gave her whatever she wanted; I just didn't want her telling my mom. I thought my mom wouldn't like me anymore. I wish that damn bully would have told someone, because my mom would have taught her a thing or two.

I've only told a few people about "the bully," but I never said she's a girl. That's the worst part for me. I hope they'll think it was a boy or something. Real dumb, I know, but it's just something I don't want anybody knowing, that's all.

I think I've actually helped a few people. It's amazing how many bullies are out there. I've met loads of people who know bullies just like the one I met. I've told them that whatever crap happened to them doesn't define who they are. You define who you are, not what some damn bully did. The bullies can let it define them, but I'll never let it define me.

So, I just found out from my mom that Miss Sick-o lives in this town, which is about a million miles from where we grew up. I can't figure why she has to live here—now! I'm as scared as hell I'll run into her. I never want to see her again. I'm stronger now, you bet I am, but it doesn't seem to matter. My insides shake when I think about it, and I'm actually scared. I heard she has a kid, and another on the way. It's strange thinking of her being a mom. I feel bad for her kid. I wonder if she still hurts kids like she hurt me, but I don't want to think about it anymore.

I went to the church service and looked around, hoping that girl wasn't there. I figured if anyone needed to be at church, it was her. I was half worried she would pop in (like a clown in a horror flick), but she never did. After a while I felt lost in the sermon and listened intently. It was a nice sermon about faith. When he finished preaching, I went up for prayer. They all put their sweaty, holy hands on my belly and prayed. I'm glad my mom was there, because she's really the only one I wanted touching my belly right then.

I don't like being touched by people, anyway, after "the bully." I only hug people I love; otherwise, it's just weird.

A fancy lady talked to me after the service. She told me all about faith. Apparently, she'd been listening to the sermon, too, because she regurgitated everything about it. She said if I have enough faith, I can move mountains. Damn mountains, can you believe it? Like I could do that. I think she meant God could, but like she told me, I'll know I have enough faith if my son is born healthy. I told my mom I'm trying to believe. My mom said she's having a hard time having faith and praying the baby will be healed. I wonder what she means.

Entry #25

It feels good to be back home. My bed is nice and warm, but I can't sleep. My ribs hurt because there's too much amniotic fluid. It's strange, since they took so much out for the amnio test. I guess the baby isn't recycling the fluid like he's supposed to, and the extra fluid is making me bigger and bigger. I don't completely understand, but I sure can feel it: a huge bubble about to pop.

It sounds like Zeke will be okay. Oh, and we decided on a name. We're naming him Zeke because Ezekiel means "strength of God."

I hope God will give him enough strength to pull through this. His middle name will be Jackson after Cade's mom (she loves that name).

I have to go to another ultrasound and echocardiogram to check his organs and heart. Maybe he'll be healed by then; I've prayed extra hard this week.

Entry #26

I visited a lady today. She has an eight-year-old girl who's mentally retarded. I wanted to meet her, to get advice on raising a handicapped child. I'm nervous because I want to be a good mom for Zeke, but don't know the first thing about raising a handicapped kid. I want to be prepared, just in case God doesn't have time to heal my boy.

This lady is so sweet. She's one of those people you meet and instantly like. Her house smells like cinnamon cookies and she has the sweetest smile. I bet she's like that all the time, as if her smile is painted there. I swear I'll try to be like her. She's such a good mom, and so nice. Can you believe she liked me too? She seemed as happy as hell I was there and said that proved I'm a good mom. She grabbed my elbow and pulled me and Ruby around. She showed us the whole damn house.

It was funny, and when she grabbed me, I really wasn't bothered. I actually had fun looking at everything. She's a real kindred spirit.

Her daughter can only move one of her hands. She has to live in a chair, and her mom says she mostly watches T.V. when she's not getting her diaper changed and all. Ruby really liked her, grinning at the lady's daughter and everything. I tell you, Ruby loves everyone. She's such a good girl.

We stood talking, and then I got this crazy impulse. I looked at the disabled girl and smiled at her really big. I told her how beautiful she is. Her face hung droopingly, and her eyes barely followed me, but I meant it. Then I got teary eyed and did the only thing that would make the tears go away. I kissed her lightly on the cheek and squeezed her hand. I told her she gave me hope and showed me how beautiful life is.

I looked up, and the kindred spirit lady was crying. I don't know why she cried, but it didn't bother me like it normally does when people bawl. Just then my tears refused to stop, and we peered at each other with a weird understanding. I only cried because she made me. You know, when you look at someone, and you're practically forced to cry? Well, that's why I did it, I swear.

Entry #27

I'm staying at my mom's house a lot. Well, it's not that I'm a pansy or anything. It's just that Cade is gone all of the time, and I get lonely. Plus, my mom has a piano, and I need it to pull my mind from things. Ruby loves bobbing to the music, and I figure it's good for both of us. That kid is so empathetic you wouldn't believe it. I keep playing "Amazing Grace," and a song I wrote for Zeke.

I hope this is all some dream, but I always cry at the songs' endings, because they don't take the pain away. I don't bawl or anything. I just cry lightly, so my mom won't hear. She's usually in the kitchen when I play the piano. Ruby stops dancing when I sob, and she cries, too. I keep playing while we cry, just so there's some background noise drowning out our sadness, but I still can't figure why Ruby is upset.

She knows something is wrong, just not what. I've tried telling her, but she's too little. Ruby is almost ten months old, and really smart for her age, but there are some things kids can't get. They're too perfect—at least some of them, like my Ruby. Try telling a kid about sickness and death—it's tough—they look at you blankly, and then go on playing with their binky or something. What really sucks butt is that I'm too damn young for this. Plus, nobody, no matter how old they are, should have to go through this. I need to enjoy my youth or some damn thing. I used to think I was invincible; I swear I did. I'd do the craziest things. I would cliff jump, and river raft without a raft. It was crappy when I got cut by rocks and stuff but addicting when I didn't. I never gave my safety a second thought, though.

Now, here I am, facing the toughest thing in life. We all have to die. I don't know why it didn't hit me sooner. It's a simple concept, and I'm not an idiot. I guess it did hit me, just never this hard. I can't figure why this is happening to my son.

I wish my boy could be healthy. God can heal him, but just in case He doesn't, I wrote Zeke a song. It's the one I keep playing, that and "Amazing Grace."

I'll sing his song when he's born, and if death steals him, then I'll sing it at his funeral. I named the song "Zeke, Strength of God," since that's what his name means.

It's pretty, and I wish you could hear it. It's powerful and moving, not like the regular happy things I write about love and God. I swear it shot straight from my soul. I heard it all in my head and wrote it down as fast as I could.

It's my way of coping, because I feel better after playing it for Zeke, and he really starts moving when he hears it. He's a strong little boy. Anyway, I guess the song is powerful, because I weaved my prayers into it, just in case God hasn't heard me yet. He'll hear this prayer for sure.

Here are the lyrics:

Zeke, strength of God
Come now, and strengthen him,
Love him, and help him through the battle.
My Baby, it's so hard, yet so beautiful.
God, please give me understanding.

No matter what may come,
I will always love you.
Struggle so deep for a gift so pure.
I can't imagine life without you.

Sorrow is around me,
but it will never drown me;
Our love will see me through.

Our love is timeless:
No beginning or end.
Our love will tie us;
I'll never lose you...
I'll never lose you...

Entry #28

The hospital where we'll have Zeke is really nice. It's right next to a children's hospital, so they can take Zeke over to the NICU if he needs to go. I'll have him at the women's center—the place where the "experts" work. They say we'll be in a special room with a funny little window. I guess they'll deliver the baby and send him through to another room. They'll help him breathe because he probably won't be able to breathe right after he's born.

So, he'll be in that special room, and if his body stabilizes, they'll take him to the children's hospital, which is connected to the women's center by a long hallway.

We toured the whole place. It was nice of them to show us around, in case God didn't hear my song.

Entry #29

Cade's cousin drove into town today. We visited him at my in-laws' house, and the whole time he glared at me with an incredibly weird face. He concentrated hard, and I wondered if he was constipated. It freaked my mother-in-law and her friend out, too.

I don't know why he stared at me. His "life-mate" and little girl were there but didn't notice what he was doing. They were too busy ignoring my presence. She's a cute lady, and looks great with her new, red hairstyle. She's about my age, and I've always wished we could be friends, but it didn't pan out that way. We ended up fighting over potatoes. She doesn't like me, if you want to know the truth, even though we've got a lot in common, and she was there when Cade and I first took our vows.

Anyway, I left the weird-feeling room because I didn't like getting stared at just then. I played with Ruby, and after a while, overheard some of Cade's conversation with his cousin in the other room. Cade told his cousin about Zeke, and his cousin went on and on about how I'm the reason Zeke has problems. He said my energy isn't balanced, and because I'm such a messed-up person, I'm even ruining Cade's kids.

I wanted to tell him he's a jerk! He has no place jumping into my problems, as if he has any idea what it's like going through this. He's still just a little boy, playing like he's an adult, and I'd tell him, if I didn't think it would hurt Cade.

Cade said there isn't a damn thing wrong with me, and that his cousin needs to stop saying such crappy things. Cade left the room and sat really close to Ruby and me. I told him I wanted to leave, so we packed our stuff in half a second, and left his parents' house and the cousin who knows everything about birth defects. It was a strange day, and I wish we hadn't gone to visit. I just wanted to see his life-mate and all.

I haven't been comfortable around Cade's cousin since last year, when he knelt down in front of me, and told me about a discussion he had with a phone psychic. He said he used to be King Arthur in a past life. At first, I thought he was kidding, but he was serious.

He went on, "The phone psychic said you were Guinevere,

and Cade was Merlin. I guess I found out you cheated on me with Merlin, and I killed both of you." He paused and cleared his throat. "I just wanted to tell you I'm sorry for killing you in a past life. Will you ever forgive me?" I drew a blank before composing myself. "Sure," I said. I looked over at Cade while I raised my eyebrows. Cade gave me "the eye," and I almost died of laughter when I saw his face. "King Arthur" is Cade's best friend, but I thought he might throttle him just then. The guy is weird. He seems like a nice guy, deep down; he has some odd ideas though. Cade says his cousin gets them from books, but I wonder if he gets them from phone psychics.

Entry #30

Cade and I bought Zeke a Scottish outfit. It's really cute, like the kind in magazines. It's so tiny, and I can't wait to see it on him. He'll look handsome and stylish. I wonder what he'll look like. Like Cade (I hope), because Cade is really handsome.

I'm a little nervous Zeke might hate me after he's born. Everything is fine while he's inside, but after he's born, life might be hard. This whole thing could be my fault, and I sure hope he'll forgive me if he can. I told my problems to an old lady at the store. She just asked if I was having a good day, and ten minutes later she knew my life story.

Old people always pry information from me, even when they don't try especially hard. I almost told her my whole confession list, but then I omitted one story about the sixth grade.

I sat next to a greasy kid. He was one of the nicest kids I ever met, but his attitude didn't make up for his greasiness, or that he was the tallest and dirtiest kid in class.

Anyway, I sat next to that kid, and one day I had gas, really bad. You know when you hold it because you don't want other people getting a whiff, or even worse, hearing it. Well, the thing was a 9-1-1 fart that needed out. So, I sent the stinker sailing and everyone in a forty-mile radius heard and smelled it.

Then, what did I do? I turned to the nice, greasy, fat kid next to me, and said, "Corey, eeewwweee!" Everyone laughed at him, even though both our faces were red; like I said, I'm a bad liar. I wanted to cry when I got home, because the greasy kid wasn't any worse than me. In fact, he was better, because he never would have done that. I know he wouldn't have.

He saw me one day in high school, and waved, just like the fart thing never happened years before. I waved back, but it didn't make up for anything, and I felt crappy all day. I should have told him I was sorry, but I was too prideful. I hope he believes he was the one who farted. You know how memories aren't completely clear sometimes? I wish that on him. I still feel bad about the 9-1-1 fart thing, but I didn't tell the lady at the store about it. I just told her about my son instead.

She sat and listened politely. She nodded, and then I crumpled and told her how it's my fault because I'm not going to church. I confessed my fear that if God doesn't heal my son, Zeke will hate me because he isn't perfect like every other kid I know.

She smiled a little sadly and told me not to fuss about unchangeable things. She said I should stay strong because my family needs me. She also told me my baby won't know anything different, since he won't know what it's like being perfectly healthy.

It hit me—maybe he won't hate me. I hope that nice old lady is right, and I'm glad I didn't end up telling her the fart story. Old people always think I'm weird when I tell them the fart story.

Entry #31

I went to an ultrasound and echocardiogram today. We got some good news. Zeke's liver went back down through the gap in his diaphragm, and the hole in his heart healed itself. Everything is looking better, except his brain. It looks worse than before, I guess.

I'm only thirty-one weeks along, and already dilating. They

35

put me on bed rest and everything. I have to take these sickening blue pills, which taste like plaster. Not that I've tasted plaster. But anyway, the pills make me sick, like I got off a crazy roller coaster. My feet don't want to stay where I put them and my body sways when I tell it to stay. It's weird, but I'm taking them anyway.

I was scared they might hurt Zeke, but the doctor said they won't. I'd rather go to Hell than hurt my boy. I have to take these pills because, if I have Zeke before December 8th, he'll have to go on a respirator and probably hemorrhage. They say when a baby's brain bleeds, they'll get brain damage. I have to make it five more weeks, that's all. I know I can do this.

Oh, and you've got to hear about the guy who did the echocardiogram. Cade and I thought he was great because he told us funny stories and jokes. I laughed so hard my belly shook, and he had to stop so he could see the baby's heart. When he said the hole in Zeke's heart is healed, I cried. Then I said I hope Zeke won't be retarded. That guy got so defensive you wouldn't believe it.

He said he doesn't like the word "retarded," and was very offended. I thought he was joking for a minute, but he wasn't. He looked at me seriously with blue eyes which could turn people to dust or something. He said he has a son who is "mentally handicapped," and that he hates hearing the word "retarded" coming from people who don't know what it's like having a son with disabilities. I rubbed my hand across my belly when he said that. Zeke (my boy who still has brain abnormalities) kicked my hand just then. After that I tried lightening the mood, but the technician was tired of being funny.

I'm so happy Zeke's heart is okay; I didn't mind how the technician acted. It sure feels good being home. I need to have faith that Zeke's brain will get better, because I really don't want him to be mentally handicapped.

But even if he is, I'll love him anyway.

Entry #32

It's a really hard day, and I'm miserable at home. I want to stop thinking about things, but everywhere I look, I remember what is going on. I look over there and realize that's where I got the first call from the doctor, or I go into Zeke's room (which is all decorated) but know he might never see it. I don't mean to be so cynical, but things are getting me down. Ruby cries for me to hold her, and I can't because my belly is the biggest thing you've ever seen. Those pills make me feel horrible, and what's worse is that now the baby is putting toxins into my body. Most of the time I try being strong, but not today—I can't be strong today.

Poor Ruby, she must think I'm nuts, but I have no real control over anything. Bad things happen all of the time, and they can't be avoided. I mean, honestly, people I love can die any minute, and I can't do a damn thing about it. I can't heal anyone, or make them better, if they need me to. I'm powerless, just hoping God will look out for all of us. It's hard putting faith in God when all this is going on.

To top everything off, my cousin called, telling me how lucky I am. I guess she had a miscarriage a few months ago. She caught "it," and everything. That was how she referred to her baby, as an "it." I guess she saw some fingers before her husband helped her bury "it." (The thought made me sick all over.)

She wanted to tell me how much worse her life is because she never got to meet her baby, but I'll get to meet mine. I know she meant well, but her whole "you're really lucky" approach didn't help at all. I was nice to her, even though I raged inside, and could have broken some antique China.

Crap is crap, there's no one-upping when serious stuff like this is involved. What am I supposed to learn from all of this, really? The truly hard lessons I've dealt with only affected me.

What am I supposed to learn from my innocent son going through this? I wish I could trade him places. In some weird way, I'd be the one condemned to an imperfect body and he'd be healthy. I hope God will heal him, but I'm losing faith, feeling

37

like some crazy balloon maker, refusing to accept reality. God, if you can hear me, please help us. Please help my son!

Entry #33

Cade got laid off today. I don't know what we'll do, but we still have each other, and I know we'll make it somehow. I can't believe all this is real. I keep wondering if someone just stuck me in a demented soap opera, even though I don't have fake boobs like soap actresses do. So, this must be real, really it must, like my boobs.

My grandpa said this is happening because God knew I was strong enough, and Zeke needed to experience life, but I don't feel very strong today.

Entry #34

I had a crazy dream last night.

I prayed to God, and our house started on fire. Ruby knelt beside the table. She laughed when the flames took her, and Cade walked around in the fire like it was no big deal. I stood there, and didn't run from the flames, either. I faced them as if I knew deep down I was strong enough to be there, too. They didn't burn my body. They weren't even hot.

I noticed for a moment it felt good not being pregnant, but then my thoughts returned to the fire. We stayed like that for a while: Ruby laughing, Cade walking, and me just standing there. The fire ate everything we had, until it left us in a musty desert. The only things left were these crazy-beautiful flowers blooming around our feet. They were pansies, aqua and purple all mixed up, and more fascinating than even the fire had been.

I looked at Cade, but he no longer saw me, and even

though I stood by him, we had lost each other.

Entry #35

Cade and Ruby are asleep, but I can't rest; I'm going into labor. I tried calming down by taking my medicine, but my body won't listen. Cade looks so handsome when he's asleep, he really does. His face doesn't sink with worry or fatigue, like it does when he's awake.

We've been growing apart over the last few weeks. I don't want to bother him with my troubles, and I'm trying to act happy—like we used to be—even though I know I'm coming off flat. I'm not a great liar, but I can tell he appreciates my efforts. There have been so many times when I crack a lame joke, and he just looks at me with a wry smile, before turning without a word. I think he has a broken heart. He wanted a healthy boy, too. I hate to wake him. But even though it's the middle of the night, we need to get to the hospital.

My labor pains are pretty consistent, and the doctor needs to stop them. We live over sixty miles from the hospital; thank God I married a man who can drive fast.

Part II
Found

Entry #1

I'm at the hospital right now. Sorry my handwriting is shaky, but I'm not feeling good. I can't open my left eye, and I look like I just fell from a plane, but don't let that fool ya, I'm a beauty inside; trust me on that one. They put me on all sorts of medications to stop the labor, since I'm only thirty-two weeks along. This magnesium sulfate stuff is really uncool. We've been in here for quite a while, and I'm getting so tired of this. I want to move around, but they won't let me get away from this bed, and earlier today God taught me a lesson about that.

I can see a little window in the room, the one they'll take the baby through if he can't breathe on his own. This is a nice, big room, but I'm still feeling really claustrophobic. I keep focusing one eye on that window. It's my lifeline now; it might save my son's life.

They gave me two steroid shots for Zeke's lung. It's to help it grow before he's born. The nurse gave me the shots in my butt cheeks. I got the first one over twelve hours ago, and they just barely gave me the second. She shot me in the other cheek this time, and at least I'm not lopsided. I hope none of my family saw my butt, because its whiteness would blind them, and I'd hate for them to lose their eyesight or something.

It's strange that I'm in labor. They didn't give me anything for the pain, but it's not too bad. My mind is just somewhere else. Don't get me wrong, it hurts like hell, and everything, but I don't care.

I almost hope I'll die if he does, I really do, but then I'd break Ruby's heart, and maybe Cade's, too. I think they need me. Anyway, I'm too damn scared and depressed to feel the pain, and my brain is numb. I need to stay pregnant for at least twelve more hours so the second steroid shot can seep into his system, but this sucks. I don't know if I can make it that long, not through writhing contractions, stupid medications, and the fact that I'm strapped in, and have a catheter.

I've never had a catheter, and it would be nice to maim the

nurse who gave it to me. She said it wouldn't be a big deal, but she was wrong, because I'm potty trained and everything. Seriously, would it hurt to let me go to the bathroom on my own? A few hours ago, back when God taught me the lesson I mentioned, I informed the nurse that I had to poo. I thought she'd let me move, but the damn woman brought me a pan. I told her I suddenly realized I didn't have to go. Then, she got all concerned, and wanted to give me an enema. My plan really backfired then. I didn't even have to poo. I just wanted to get up, for crying out loud. I didn't want to get pumped with suppositories and all.

God punished me because I thought of myself instead of my baby. I won't do it again, God, since pooin' in a pan sucks! Not to mention that it was damn uncomfortable.

Have you ever tried pooing in front of someone when you don't even know their name? At least she could have said something like, "Hey I'm Irene, and I'll help you poo in a pan!" It was the height of awkward. Not only did it smell, but there was no one else to blame it on because she knew it was me.

I had a catheter stuck up my pee hole, a suppository in my pooper, and the baby is pressing down so hard in my private area I almost broke down. There's nothing like feeling all plugged up. You should try it sometime; really, really you should. Whoever thought it would be cool to glorify labor on T.V. was a real winner. If most teens knew having a baby is like this, they would stay away from doing the nasty for a very, very long time—even until they're thirty—no kidding!

I'm already dilated to a seven, or something. I was at a five when we got here. I know I should stay put, but I'm itching to move. Cade is asleep in a chair across the room and a bunch of my family is sleeping in the hallway, but I can't sleep, not after the whole pooing thing. Plus, I don't know what will happen.

Will Zeke die soon? I want to stay pregnant as long as I can, because this might be my only time with him. But if I don't move from this stupid bed, I'll lose it. I really need to calm down. I'm so glad I brought you to the hospital with me. I'm trying to be strong; my family needs that, and Zeke does, too. It's good writing things down, and being weak, if only for a minute. These meds are totally affecting me, and I'm not making sense on paper. I hope I'll be tough enough to deal with what the future will bring. God, please help me and my boy! Most of all, please let Zeke know how much I love him.

Entry #2

He's here and he's beautiful! I was so scared about what to expect. I can't believe how beautiful he is! My baby boy! I didn't make it as long as I'd hoped. I only made it nine more hours after the second shot (instead of twelve), but he's here, and we're both alive. They let me hold him for two seconds before whisking him through the window, since he turned blue and all.

The nurse took a picture of him and brought it to me. He's in the women's center NICU. I guess his lung seems to be working pretty well. He's on a vent. If he continues progressing, and his lung doesn't burst, he'll go to the children's hospital. We need to take this a minute at a time. I want to see him again, but they need to get him completely stabilized before we can go in there.

A bunch of curtains surround him, and I can't see a damn thing! I'm really glad that nurse took a picture for me. It was awesome, and the woman needs a raise! He looks blue in the picture, but I'm glad to have something to study while I'm waiting.

I always knew he would come out fighting, but I didn't expect him to come out the way he did. I told one of the nurses (obviously a real "expert") that I needed to push. But she said, "Calm down. You don't need to push, because you aren't in enough pain, and people who don't have pain meds always freak out when they're ready to push."

I told her again, quite loudly, that I really needed to push. So, she checked me, and found I was dilated to a ten. She ran from the room and got the doctor; she's a real quick one, that nurse.

The doctor sauntered in and broke my water. I guess I had a lot, because it hit her in the face. I've got a good aim! She screamed all girly-like, and I pushed because I couldn't help it anymore. The doctor couldn't see very well and continued shaking about the amniotic fluid on her; you'd think she'd be used to it, or something, since she's an OB doc and all. Anyway, Zeke flew out right onto the delivery chair. The doctor barely caught him. I'm glad she stuck her hands out in time. He's a small little guy, and a lot more important than her sticky hair and stuff.

So, anyway, they're still trying to stabilize Zeke, and I'm just in here, waiting. My catheter is gone, and I can finally move around. It feels great to be off those meds, but I miss my boy.

My family and I have been talking in my room, but I decided to sit and write, instead. There's too much going on in my head. I gave everyone a piece of paper so they can write what they think about the day Zeke was born; I'm excited to read what they'll write.

Letters

Here are the letters written after Zeke was born on 11/18/2002. I put them in here in the order my family gave them to me.

Elisa,

When you were first born, I held you in my arms and said, "Today is the first day of the rest of your life." Well, today is the first day of Zeke's life and I feel it is a new beginning for the rest of all our lives as well.

So, we'll take every day as a blessing. Today we got a special blessing (little Zeke Jackson). I know that he will bless each one of us because no matter what happens in his life, he will influence all of ours. God doesn't do anything without a reason and even though we don't understand why things are the way they are, it's not our place to ask.

We need to have faith because we are truly blessed. I love you and Cade with all my heart and now I have little Ruby and Zeke too. My heart could just overflow with an abundance of joy. I love you.

–Dad

Elisa and Cade,

Thank you so much for allowing us to be part of such a special experience. Never in all of the births that I have attended have I seen a mother handle labor the way you did. You showed such dignity, love and concern for your unborn baby and such appreciation for those attending you. You are a wonder, but then that's because you are our Elisa and that's just who you are—we love you.

I was pleased that he looked so good and that the news now is still upbeat. You always kept your smile, never complained even once and just kept your patient attitude. I think that's what made this experience so special for us all.

He was beautiful and tiny. I was filled with gratitude because he looked so much better than I had prepared for. Thank you for a job well done!

We love you with all of our hearts and hope and pray you know how special you are to us.

Love always,
Grandma Stilson

Zeke,

Happy Birthday!
You are a beautiful little boy. You look much bigger than we thought you would be. You have such a wonderful mom and dad. Right now there are ten of us waiting to see you. Hopefully, all of our prayers were heard, and you will be with us for a long, long time. I can't wait for your big sister to kiss you. She gives such good ones.
I hope you'll be able to know how much you are loved.

Love,
Your Grandma Marie

When we first got the message from dad that Cade and Elisa were headed to the hospital there was a feeling of anticipation and anxiousness to know what was going on. We waited for another call to tell us it was time. Cade called and asked us to bring our guitars so that if Zeke didn't make it, he could play for him. The thought of that just made me cry.

We were waiting in the hallway, commenting on pictures when Cade came out in the hallway and told us Zeke was born. Mom came out with tears in her eyes. It was a special birth. Zeke seems to be stabilizing and there is a great sense of hope that he will make it. Everyone seems to be saying small prayers in their hearts for this tiny, special spirit. He was loved so much before his birth and will be loved so much now, if not more in time to come.

Our prayers are with you, Zeke!

We love you Cade and Elisa!

--Mark and Rendy

Elisa,

What a blessing you are to all who know you.

It's a great blessing to be your grandfather and to have you as our granddaughter. We love you dearly. As you gave birth to your son on this 18th day of November 2002, we all marvel at the sweet and loving spirit you have been blessed with. It brings tears of joy to be with you and have you share your sweet spirit with us. You have such a great love for others and such strong faith. You're always so positive and happy. You always look for the good and welfare of others. We want you to know of our great love for you and we pray you will always be this beautiful child of God. The Lord knew that this son was meant for you and that it would take a special daughter to send this special spirit to.

I love you dearly and I am so proud of you. May the Lord always love you, watch over you, and bless you and your family.

Love you,
Grandpa Stilson

Entry #3

I saw Zeke! They finally got him stabilized. He's so tiny, and perfect—to me. It's strange looking at him, and thinking things are so wrong inside his body. He has one of my ears, and one of Cade's. I told Cade he's our perfect mix. Cade laughed a bit when I said that. I loved seeing Zeke's little hands. They're extra small. One of his pinkies has a nub on it like it thought about growing an extra finger from its last knuckle, and then changed its mind. I love that finger though. It's got tons of personality, and I like personality.

Zeke only weighs four pounds, no kidding. At first, they had him on one-hundred percent oxygen, and worried it might puncture his one good lung. His oxygen is doing better now; it's down to sixty percent instead of one hundred. This is so scary. Have you ever felt like someone was pushing you closer and closer to the edge of a cliff, but you couldn't run away? I have, and I hate cliffs because there's nothing good about them when you don't have any climbing gear around. I don't want to lose my baby.

I'm sitting in one of those funny hospital beds, the kind with a button that makes it go up or down in about five-hundred different ways. I pulled my mind from things by hitting the buttons and rearranging the bed in funky positions, but then a nurse gawked at me from the hall. She even had a funny tilt to her arms, so I stopped and started writing instead, just so she won't be stuck like that permanently.

I wonder why things happen the way they do. I feel like a felon who should be arrested again. I can't quite explain it, but if you were here, you'd know what I mean. Zeke is so handsome; to me he is. The cleft lip doesn't look as bad as I thought it would. That kid can pull anything off—obviously. He must be one of those strong silent types who like to show their best qualities fairly quickly. He has a bi-lateral cleft which means his skin isn't connected on either side. There's a big flap hanging from his nose, and he doesn't look like he has an upper lip. It's weird, but he's still an adorable kid.

There are a bunch of tubes going into his mouth, anyway, so it's hard to see exactly what he looks like. I try remembering his face when they set him in my arms, but I can't remember that well. He was all gooey, and covered in fluid and blood, anyway. I hope someone took a picture without all of the tubing and bluish tint to his skin. At least he's more of a peachy shade now.

They have him so drugged it makes me sad because he can barely open his eyes. I was like that last night, and I wish he didn't have to go through this. It's crazy, but looking at him makes me realize this is worse than death; I want to trade him places. He doesn't deserve this, and I've lived a really good life.

I'm too young for this. I can't handle seeing my little guy suffer! God, please help me know what to do! I should enjoy Zeke, every moment of him being here. This is so hard.

They've taken x-rays to see how much his diaphragm is stressing. I guess it's a way of telling how close they are to puncturing a lung. While they moved Zeke for an x-ray, some of the tubing slipped in and out of his throat. He cried really hard, but no noise came out—just silent misery. The useless cry was worse than any wail I've ever heard. It's the worst oxymoron! I bawled, too, because it made me hurt for him.

They won't let me hold Zeke because he's not stable enough. So, I put my hand on his head, stroked his hair, and sang to him, seriously, even while we walked down the hall and everything. That was the only thing he'd stop crying for. He opened his eyes when he cried. He has such beautiful dark blue eyes. Oh, and he held my finger today! I love him so much, and that proves he can move some things when he wants to! There might not be as many problems with his cerebellum as they think.

I'm going to sneak out of this room. The nurses told me to stay put because I've done too much since Zeke was born. They think I'm nuts, already donning my regular clothes, and wanting to visit my boy. I guess most ladies stay in their pj's for years after they have a baby or something. I'm just not one of those people, and if these nurses have a problem with that, then they can kiss it. I'm going to see my son right now, whether they say it's okay or not!

They insist on pushing me around in an ugly wheelchair. The damn footrests don't work, and my legs are so long my feet get sucked under the wheels. I bet if I hurry, they won't even notice I'm gone; they'll just think I'm in the crapper or something. I'd give anything for a skateboard right now. It sounds like so much fun to sit on, and cruise down the hospital hallways, but if I did, I'd put my hospital gown on again, just for the right effect.

It feels really nice to be in regular clothes. Well, except for this diaper that I'm wearing. Isn't that great how I just had a baby and suddenly I'm the one wearing a diaper? I've got my maternity pants on over my diaper and my butt looks super sexy. I wish you could see the damn thing, it's bigger than Milwaukee.

Entry #4

Blake and Cammie visited the hospital today, you know, the couple that had a baby girl who passed away. I guess she was almost a day old when she passed, no kidding. Zeke is already over a day old, and I feel bad for them. They didn't get to keep their baby long, and I don't want them feeling bad that Zeke is still alive. They'd never say they felt bad, but I'm trying to think of their feelings, because they've been there, and "there" sucks!

When they came, I didn't know what to say, so I shot the bull to get their minds off of things. They kept bringing the conversation back to Zeke, and I swung it way far away from him again. I got really desperate one time, and even asked Cammie if she's ever had a suppository. Cade gave me "the eye" then.

He's always giving me "the eye" when he thinks I'm being a goofball. I wish he would have known I worked for the greater good this time. It's not that I'm unhappy this whole situation brought us together, but I don't want to make it depressing for anyone. That's about the last thing I need right now: to cry again.

Before anyone knew it, we all laughed about who-knows-what and felt much better. Cade even stopped giving me "the eye."

Right after we finished laughing, things got quiet. Cammie looked at me seriously, and said, "I hope your boy will make it. I'd feel so good, thinking one of us got to keep their baby." I didn't know what to say. She's one of the sweetest people I know, made of homespun candy or something. I avoided tears by talking about other crap. But this time it wasn't about suppositories, and I think she knew what I was doing. She didn't get serious again, though, because she knew what I needed, since she's been "there" before. I bet her baby girl was beautiful. Her parents are hella good people, and hella good people always pop out amazing kids, trust me, they do. It's what they're trained for.

Entry #5

They took Zeke to the children's hospital. That was the longest walk of my life. Every step stretched for millions of minutes. I was so scared for Zeke the whole time, and then there were tons of metal strips we bumped across every few feet. The tubing moved up and down in him, then the silent crying followed, along with my not so silent crying, and more bumps, and sighing from the nurses.

I'm glad he's there now. They seem like they know what they're doing, not like the "experts" at the other place. They've all been so nice and helpful. They gave us a cute little book called, "Welcome to the NICU." It's pink and blue—cute and everything—but I'm still a bit nervous. There are some emotions cute NICU books can't take away.

We can see Zeke pretty much any time, but it feels weird he can't come home yet. I don't like the thought of other people taking care of my baby. He can't drink milk, but I want to nurse him. They have several breast pumps here and they let me pump and save my milk for when he's ready. There's a fancy little freezer they put the milk in. I guess I'll get to use the top shelf.

My milk hasn't totally come in, but I've been pumping anyway. I want Zeke to drink good stuff as soon as he can.

The nurses insist on wheeling me around everywhere. I was able to sneak away that one time, but then my nurse found me. She was waiting outside the NICU. She had a wheelchair with her, and the footrests actually worked! I can be released tomorrow. It will be nice not to see a wheelchair every time I turn around. I didn't lose my legs—all I did was have a baby, for crying out loud.

Entry #6

Zeke is doing much better. I want the "experts," who apparently work at the children's hospital as well, to fix his diaphragm as soon as possible. His organs are still up in his chest, and I can tell he's struggling to breathe, even with the vent's help. They don't want to do the surgery yet, though. They want to do another chromosome test. They already did one when I was pregnant but want to be sure before continuing.

So, we're waiting for them to give him the test again, and then we'll have to wait for the results. Wait, wait, wait, and our little man is suffering the whole time. I'm glad he's on pain medicine, though. I guess that giving pain medicine to infants is a new thing in the NICU. A few years ago, the "experts" didn't think infants felt pain. "Experts" are so dumb. For being such educated people, some of them can be so damn stupid. Of course, babies feel pain; just because they can't talk, doesn't mean they don't have senses when they're born. Thank God Zeke wasn't born until now. I would have lost my mind.

Entry #7

They finally released me. It feels good to be free. Yahoo! Freedom rocks it like the 80's!

Remember how I told you Cade got laid off? Well, he can't find another job. He keeps looking and looking, when he's not at the hospital or helping me take care of Ruby, and all, but he can't seem to find work. He's a construction kind of guy, and I guess winter isn't the best time to find work anyway. I think God is looking out for us, though. I applied for Medicaid a few months ago but found out we made too much to qualify. The hospital told us we'd have to pay for all of Zeke's medical bills. We could start on a payment plan, but that's a lot of dough! Anyway, we make less now because of unemployment. Maybe we qualify now.

I've met a few different people in the NICU. There's this really nice lady who stays in the hospital so she can be close to her son. She's a good mom, you can tell. The children's hospital is requiring her to pay so much money a month she might lose her home. Her kid has been stuck in this place for almost a year now. She wants to have a huge first birthday party in the NICU. See what I mean? She's a good mom, making the best of things.

Well, I guess the hospital uses the donations to buy equipment, instead of always helping patients who need it, or something; at least, that's what she said. She sobbed when she told me the story, and then cried about her kid. That poor lady, she's worse off than I am, no kidding. She got me thinking, though. I wonder how we'll pay for all of this. But I won't cry because Zeke is more important than money anyway. I'd rather have him than a house.

I'll apply for Medicaid first thing in the morning, though. I can't believe how happy I am we're not making much. If we qualify, I'll feel bad taking money from the government, but we can't afford paying a million-dollar medical bill; we just can't, and I'd feel worse about that.

My sister and brother-in-law gave us six-hundred dollars to help with all the bills we've had so far. I can't believe they gave us so much. In fact, I didn't want to take it—so we'd look like we're handling everything okay—but we really need the money. This whole experience has humbled me something fierce. I used to try acting like everything was okay, but I can't now because it's so obviously not. I can't hide this situation or put a big band-aid over it; everyone knows it's not okay. I'm not okay. We need all the help we can get right now.

This is hard enough without thinking about all the extra crap. Plus, in a weird way, it feels good to be humbled—like I don't have to hide. I'd almost have a damn skip in my step if I just knew Zeke will be a happy old man.

Entry #8

We qualify for Medicaid. They'll cover all our bills and some pre-existing ones, as well. It's a good thing! I might actually sleep tonight, and we'll have a good Thanksgiving now. There's a lot to be thankful for.

We went home today, without Zeke. Cade drove the car, and I cried in the passenger seat, since Zeke's car seat is empty. It's like the thing had a beacon on it, and I couldn't survive without staring. I just can't shake the feeling that someone is missing, no matter where we go. If I'm in the NICU, Ruby can't be with me. No one under two is allowed in, and if I'm with Ruby, then Zeke isn't there. It's horrible coming home from the hospital without a baby.

Ruby was already upset, so when I cried, she did, too. I tried to stop because Cade's knuckles turned white from strangling the steering wheel, but that just made me cry harder. Finally, he couldn't take it anymore. He turned to both of us and yelled, "SHUT UP!" But I couldn't. He pushed the gas pedal down hard, and we made it home in record time. We live over an hour from the hospital, and that was the longest, saddest trip ever, despite Cade's speeding. I miss Zeke. I want to sleep so I can get up early and see Zeke again. They're giving him the chromosome test tomorrow! I hope everything will come back good.

Entry #9

The chromosome test finally came back, no kidding. The

results are the same as when I was pregnant. What a surprise, I just love surprises I already knew would come.

They went ahead with the surgery. The surgeon took him, and we've been waiting. The nurse said it can take up to two hours, but it seems longer to me. The surgeon is using a new type of mesh cloth to create an artificial diaphragm. I hope Zeke will be okay. He's such a strong little boy, but the doctor told me Zeke might not make it. He said little girls handle surgeries better than boys do. I pray to God Zeke will make it. I'll do anything if he'll just have a normal life! I'd even shave my head if it would help, and I love my hair.

I've been thinking a lot today. Life is hard, but so beautiful. Even in the hardest times, if we step back for a second, we'll realize God is with us the whole time. I thought about Zeke, and how hard this is, and asked myself if I still love God. I pondered long and hard, then finally decided yes, I still love God more than anything. Then I thought about if He had to take Zeke away during surgery, and I wondered if I would still love God.

I looked at the ceiling because I always do that when I talk to God. I said, "Yes, I'll always love you, God, no matter what."

An old man turned to me, and empathy wrote on his face. He's waiting for a little baby to get out of surgery, too. I bet he's the grandpa or something. He stared at me, and then at the ceiling, like he wanted to see who was there. After he did, a faint smile played across his face while he nodded at his cane and fingered some crazy rhythm on it. I knew he understood exactly what I'd thought and didn't condemn me like some people would. I like that old man. He's good people, and he has an amazing sense of rhythm, just like my mom. She's a drummer, and I like her so much I'm practically forced to love anyone with a sense of rhythm.

Anyway, I don't quite know why all of this happened, but I do know I'm learning. I love God, not for making my life great, but for making me in the first place. Plus, there is good in everything. I'm just realizing that sometimes you have to look for it.

I've been living my life focusing on the end, searching for a meaning in all this. Now I'm realizing I should be enjoying the journey, not constantly seeking answers. I was preoccupied with what happens after we die, but right now, I don't care. Isn't that crazy? My son might be dying, and I don't care what happens after we die. My brain can't go there today. I'm enjoying what is going on right now, and I'm enjoying my son for as long as I can. I'll think about death when it comes, and not a second before.

Entry #10

My father-in-law couldn't write a letter in the hospital after Zeke was born, so he wrote one while we waited for Zeke to get out of surgery. I love Cade's dad; he's one in a million. I still remember the first time I met him, and how I liked him from the get-go; that's just how he is. I remember he sat down with me, and asked, "There are three vast unknowns in this life. I'd like to know...what do you think they are?" I thought he was interviewing me, and if I answered incorrectly, he wouldn't let Cade date me.

I paused for a minute and then said, "Where are we going, where did we come from, and who am I?"

He slowly smiled at me, and I felt like I'd just passed the biggest test ever given.

So anyway, he wrote a letter about Zeke:

Dear Family–
I just wanted to keep everyone up to date. It's been a hectic week (and I spent part of it with the flu), so I haven't kept track of who's getting what information.

THE BIRTH
Zeke Jackson "ZJ" Morris was born on November 18th at 5:04 am. Weighing in at 4 lbs. and 17" he came in swinging, or at least the nurses swung him immediately through a little window into the

ICU part of the hospital. He does seem like he has the will to live. He's already beaten a lot of odds. ZJ didn't get to cry, and they didn't want him to because his good lung might rupture under the pressure from the diaphragmatic hernia.

ZJ's hernia allowed his stomach, liver, and intestines to move up into his chest and crowd his lungs and heart. So, he's been on a six-hundred mini-pumps-per-minute vent since birth. It makes his little heart flutter fast.

I was surprised at first when I saw him because he was bigger than I expected. I figured, being a preemie, that I could hold him in one hand, especially if he was only three to four pounds. They actually didn't expect him to be bigger than three pounds.

Elisa went in early Sunday morning, and they prolonged the birth as long as they could by giving her magnesium and some other stuff. They injected steroids so that the lungs would grow a little more before being born. This tactic worked for a little over twenty-four hours which may have helped.

After ZJ was born a lot of us (Marie, Cade, and Elisa mostly) spent a lot of time touching ZJ. These modern "open air" incubators are quite cool well, "warm." They have a radiator a few feet above the baby that keeps him warm. Sensors on the baby allow the incubator to maintain a constant temperature. So, ZJ doesn't need a lot of clothing on to keep him warm. That allows us to touch him freely. He sure is full of a lot of needles.

THE BAD NEWS

Around 6 months along, Elisa's doctor first brought up the possibility of birth defects. An early ultrasound showed a cleft lip and a hernia. That started a lot of stressful times for Cade and Elisa (and Grandparents).

As time went on the other tests were run. Things such as misplaced liver, possible missing kidneys, kidneys that weren't working, a heart with only 3 chambers, under or non-developed lungs, missing brain parts, etc.

THE SURPRISES

Before ZJ was born they determined that his heart was okay and had no missing chamber, his liver had mysteriously moved back down, a part of his brain they had thought was missing was there and he had at least one good lung which couldn't work properly because of the hernia (the other organs were squishing it so much that it couldn't expand).

Several days after Zeke was born they discovered that his partial lung had grown to a decent size. It's good that at least one lung grew because he wouldn't have survived if he didn't have part of one to work with. They also found that the rest of his brain (which they had thought was missing) wasn't missing. I think these doctors need eyeglasses. They sure seem to misinterpret a lot of things. Maybe from their perspective it's better to err on the side of bad news rather than missing something bad and being surprised. Who knows....

THE DREAD

Before the doctors could operate on ZJ's hernia, which has to be done so he can breathe on his own, they needed to know for sure that his chromosomes are okay. So, they ran that test again. They also tested Cade and Elisa for any chromosome abnormalities. Cade and Elisa's results came back fine, but since ZJ's test was from fluid and not directly from him they have ruled it out as inconclusive. So, they ran the test again. We waited all weekend for the results. If the results came back positive, then they wouldn't perform the operation, effectively ending ZJ's life. That possibility hung heavy on everyone.

Cade and Elisa have really dealt with all of this quite well, considering. Elisa, bless her heart, never leaves a stone unturned. From the start, she's used every available resource to understand and deal with all of the bad possibilities the doctors were throwing at her. They became friends with a couple who lost their baby this past year to similar circumstances. She investigated all of the financial resources and possibilities. Elisa's quite the little lady. Cade's lucky to have a wife that's so on the ball.

THE GOOD NEWS (FINALLY)

Monday Cade and Elisa were scheduled to meet with the doctors and some other people at 4pm to discuss the test results, because it was fully expected to have bad news. But, by mid-afternoon shortly after Marie arrived at Elisa's parents' house to baby-sit little Ruby, the doctors called Cade and Elisa to tell them that the chromosome test was completely negative. Marie said she'd never seen Cade and Elisa so happy. Christmas came early. So, they're doing the hernia operation right now. This will be a Thanksgiving we can enjoy, hopefully. We still need to keep our fingers crossed that ZJ will come through the hernia operation okay.

ZJ will probably spend his first four to five months in the hospital. As far as we can tell, at this time, all of his problems are superficial and can be fixed by operations to the point that no one will ever be able to tell he had them. Maybe we've seen a miracle or two here.

Love,
Van

Entry #11

The surgery went well. He's using extra support now but will get more self-sufficient as time goes on. His little tummy is all black and blue. I can't look long because he's in pain. Poor kid, he didn't do anything to deserve this. His skin won't stretch as far as it's supposed to, and a little bit ripped from the original incision.

The nurses don't want to cover the rip and said it will heal faster if it's in the air. I'm really worried about him getting an infection from the open wound. I hope these "experts" know what they're doing. It's hard trusting other people with my baby's life, but what else can I do? I feel so helpless. I've never been good at trusting people. I like to do things myself, just so I know they'll get done right.

So, I don't look at his belly. Instead, I stare at his little face. Cade says Zeke looks just like me, but I can't see it. He looks like my brother, to me. After Zeke was born, I got all excited, and called my brother, so I could tell him. My brother is so awesome. You'd like him, really you would. He's the sort of guy you can't help but like. He's got real charm; he's as funny as hell, and that's why I wanted to be just like him.

When I called him, and told him all about the baby, I could tell he was worried, but he acted like he wasn't, just so I wouldn't feel bad, or something. It's crazy though, he's one of the only people I could have told the whole situation to. I'm just honest with that guy because he goes against logic and loves me for me. Anyway, when I told him the baby looks like him, he sort of laughed, and said, "Oh, is that a good thing?"

I said, "You, dork! Of course, it's a good thing." My brother cracks me up.

I stared at Zeke today but tried to stop gaping at his distended belly. He opened his eyes again, no kidding! He's so beautiful. I wish I could spend every second with him, but I don't want to neglect Ruby. It's hard knowing what to do. I feel like a bad mother no matter what.

I saw my best friend today. She's nervous to visit Zeke, but I know she's thinking about him. She bought him a saint card, for me to put up while he's here. It's a pretty Catholic card, and I hope it will help him somehow. That was thoughtful of her.

My sister also saw Zeke today. She said he doesn't look very good, and he's suffering. I told her he just had a surgery, and he'll get better soon. She's seeing things differently than I am, though, and it upsets me. She's one of the smartest people I know, and I've always trusted what she says. I wonder if I'm too close to see things clearly with Zeke—I wonder. I know I shouldn't be upset, but I am. I even raised my voice when I talked, and in my family, that's practically yelling. She gave me a hug then, and said she knows this must be hard for me.

"It is," I said, and I hugged her tight. "It really is."

I want her to be happy he's made it this long, but I can tell it's sad for her. She can't stand seeing him in pain like this. I wonder if she was surprised when he was born, and really did have birth defects. I know a part of me was surprised. I remember how she said sometimes doctors are wrong, and I clung to that hope, but they were right this time. This is painful for everyone, but we've got to make the best of things, we have to, or I'll go insane.

Entry #12

Cade cradled me in his arms tonight. He's so strong, and it feels nice to be in his arms. I don't know what I'd do if I didn't have him. We didn't kiss or anything, just held each other for hours, and watched the stars through our window. Cade seems to be doing all right, but he doesn't talk to me like before. Maybe he needs time to think. After we held each other, he drifted to sleep. I couldn't, though, so I went and checked on Ruby. She has the longest eyelashes, and when her eyes are closed, she looks surreal. I told her today that, when God gave her to me, he got mixed up, and instead of a regular person, he gave me an angel. I think He did that so I could handle what we're going through now. She really is an angel, that kid.

Anyway, I still can't sleep, so I'm in the kitchen, writing for a while. I hope Cade is doing okay. You wouldn't believe how tired he looks; he even has black circles under his eyes. Before I gave birth to Zeke, Cade had a hard time breathing. He breathed into a brown paper sack. There I was, the one in labor, and Cade kept playing with that crazy brown bag, testing how many times he could blow the damn thing up. That guy makes me smile, even in the hardest times. When he held me tonight, I remembered how I fell in love with him.

The night I met Cade, he wore a big, black, biker jacket. His hair hung long past his shoulders, and he was as sexy as hell. He didn't say a lot, but he didn't have to. I just hoped I was destined to meet him. He leaned next to an old, beat-up car, and smoked into the wind. He didn't care he breathed in his own second-hand smoke. I don't know why, but I thought that was cool. It was twice as dangerous, and really edgy. It almost wasn't real at that moment because he looked like he jumped out of a James Dean movie. We talked for a while that night, and I guess when he went home, he wrote a song on his guitar, and the song was for me. He didn't tell me that until later.

I dropped by his apartment at five in the morning the next day, just for the hell of it. I guess Cade was sleeping on the couch when I stopped by. He'd stayed up all night, playing the guitar, and had fallen asleep right there in the front room.

When he answered the door, I looked at him, and thought how gorgeous he was in the morning. His eyes were big and bright, and he seemed excited to see me. I'd worn a purple tank top, and my hair was wild because I refused to do it, but I hoped it looked pretty, anyway. I could tell from the way he eyed me that he fell for me, and I couldn't help wondering why I didn't feel in control of the situation. I was always the one in control, when it came to guys.

I told him to grab his guitar, since he'd told me he played. I drove to a coffee shop, then headed straight for the mountains. We sped along a super windy road. I loved moving fast, and Cade almost spilled his coffee a couple of times.

I pulled off at a nice-looking place, and we hiked up the side of the mountain together. At one point we ran into a huge stream. Cade insisted he could find a way to cross, and I jumped in. That water was hella cold, but just my style. I didn't care how wet I got, or anything, because it sounded like fun, and I wasn't born with patience anyway. I made it to the other side fast, and told Cade to jump in, but he looked at me fondly, and stifled a grin. He walked up and down the bank, and said he'd be right back. After a few minutes he showed up next to me on my side of the bank. I was soaking wet in the cold, and he appeared as dry as the sun. I laughed about it and told him he was missing out. After all, there's nothing like cold water to wake you up in the morning.

"That's what the coffee was for," Cade said, and I smiled. I'd never met anyone like him in my life.

I packed my violin the whole time and itched to play it. I always get like that when I'm in the mountains. Nature and music go hand in hand, practically.

I went up first, and Cade followed me. We traversed a steep part once; I caught him staring at my butt, and I raised a brow. His face turned a little red, and I grinned big when I moved back up the mountain. I even swayed my hips while we went just in case he looked. After a while we made it to this nice, flat spot. I sat down without saying a word and played my violin. Cade's jaw dropped, and I thought I might have to screw the thing back in place or something. I pulled out all the stops for the guy. We played a couple of songs together. I was impressed with his skills, and that says a lot, because I've played with a ton of musicians.

He showed me a song he wrote. When the chords swam around us, I heard a crazy-beautiful melody in my head. I played it because I couldn't help being a conduit, or something. Then Cade sang with his solid voice, and chills flew up my spine as something awakened inside me. No one had ever made me feel like that. He sang the same melody I played—note for note. I stood because the music poured from me. At that moment I couldn't have told you where I was. I was the music, no kidding.

We continued like that for a while, playing the same choruses and melodies like we'd performed together since birth. When we finished, we just sat silently and looked at each other. It was one of the weirdest moments in my entire life, not that I've lived that long, but still. I had goose bumps running over my arms, and they weren't because I was soaking wet. That was when I knew I'd met the man I would spend the rest of my life with. The man with the golden voice, the patience I'd always lacked, and the most striking eyes I'd ever seen. He was my future. We got married three weeks later.

Entry #13

We're staying with my mom. It's too hard traveling to the hospital from our house. I don't want to impose, but I don't know what else to do. It's been a couple of weeks, and Zeke is doing much better. He has those terribly silent crying episodes about once every day, but other than that, he's progressing. I think he cries when he needs more medicine. I hate it when he cries and turns blue and purple. He always calms down when I put my hand on his head, though. He's a good baby, honestly. There are a few nurses at the hospital who just love him. One takes care of him every day, and another one takes care of him at night. I swear God is looking out for Zeke, since those nurses are golden, pure gold, I swear.

Entry #14

Happy Thanksgiving, no kidding. We are having a great one. It's been a few days since the surgery, and Zeke is doing awesome.

When they told us everything, I wish I'd known he'd do this well. I got my baby, and now I get to keep him. See what I mean? This really is a good Thanksgiving. The doctor told us that, after the surgery, kids with CDH (that means they're missing part of their diaphragm) usually do worse before they do better. But Zeke is already doing better. The doctors and nurses are amazed! His incision is five inches long, and he's only seventeen inches long. I hope he's not hurting too badly.

We had turkey dinner in the hospital cafeteria. They have the best mashed potatoes ever; about everything seems better today. The food tastes better. The world seems brighter. The NICU doesn't even smell like iodine today.

Entry #15

My brother and sister-in-law are having a baby girl. I wish they lived close so I could meet her right after she's born. I bet she'll be beautiful, and healthy, and fun, just like her parents. I swear they're some of the best people in the world, and I'm glad they won't go through this horrid suffering we're experiencing now. No one should have to go through this, no one. My mom is flying to Arizona so she can help with the baby after she's born. I almost wish I could stow away in her bag. Then I could remember what a healthy newborn looks like, a healthy, happy newborn, who I have a special love for because she'll be the same age as Zeke. They're going to be great pals. I just know it! They're so close in age; they'll practically be twins! I talked to one of Zeke's nurses, and she said Zeke is still in critical condition. He's doing so badly today; you wouldn't believe it. They said his body is trying to reject the artificial diaphragm, and since this is a new type of procedure, they don't know what might happen next. His nurse said Zeke will most likely make it, but there is a chance he'll pass away within the next few days, while my mom is gone.

It's horrible, but before I talked to my aunt, I was really mad at my mom. I don't see how she can leave me—and Zeke—when we need her so much. I get worried thinking about her going, because it's just my luck that Zeke will die when she leaves, the moment she steps on the plane, or the moment it lifts off. I'm as scared as hell about it, and then I'll think he would have made it, if she'd stayed. I don't know what's wrong with me. I guess I'm not thinking straight and don't know how to be logical.

I was so upset I called my aunt. She talked to my mom the other day. I guess my mom is going bonkers. She needs to get away from this and have a moment to breathe. I know where she's coming from, I guess. It would be nice to get away, if I was the grandma, but I'm not, and there's no way in hell I can leave my son.

My aunt really put things in perspective for me. She said I should put my mom's shoes on, but this is so damn hard because I'm in serious pain. I don't want to see anyone else's perspective. I want them to see where I'm coming from, and that I need her here to help me. I should stop being so selfish, though. This ball of confusion we live on isn't about me, and right now my mom needs to get away, and my brother and his family need her.

Entry #16

Even though Zeke is doing well, I don't know if I am. I really need Cade right now, but he doesn't understand. He's on cloud nine, or something, and I don't know why I'm so damn depressed. I guess I feel bad my mom is gone. She went to Arizona because my sister-in-law is having the baby. I know why my mom needed to leave, but it's still hard. There are tons of other people around, but I still feel alone. I'm going nuts having to split my time between the kids—it's unnatural.

Maybe this whole thing is my fault, and Zeke is going through this because of me. I can't figure out what I did wrong. I didn't even drink coffee when I was pregnant, for crying out loud. I just need Cade to hold me, and tell me he loves me, but he said he doesn't want to anymore. He told me the way I'm acting is driving him nuts, and he has enough to deal with. I wish I could help him, but he won't even talk to me about it. I know he's the right person for me, but maybe I'm not the right one for him? Maybe I'm more trouble than I'm worth? Plus, I can tell he wants to be someplace else.

Zeke's nurse, Susan, told us we're such good parents. She said there was a baby born last year, and the parents couldn't handle it, so they left him at the NICU and moved to Colorado. She said the baby's problems weren't even that bad, and he left the NICU in less than a week. The state put him up for adoption, and everything. I bet he got better parents than the originals God gave him before—I hope.

Anyway, I wish I could make Cade happy again. If I was nicer, prettier, something! He told me that I used to be such a different person. I guess I was, but I didn't have a son in the NICU back then. We both had to grow up fast. We're doing everything right, but it doesn't feel very good right now. This would be hard for anyone, but especially us. We had so many dreams that slipped by because we have a family now. A day doesn't pass by that I don't dream about playing my violin and seeing the crowds smiling at me while I play, too many memories.

My destiny ran from me and swooned another lucky person. I never say this stuff aloud because once I told Cade, and he broke down. He told me that the night I got pregnant with Ruby, he did it on purpose—when I was drunk—and he was drunk, too. All my energy just left when he told me. He said he worried I would break up with him. I can't believe he did that, and now he doesn't even want me. It feels wrong, writing this down, but it doesn't seem too bad, just this once.

Cade started working again. When we returned from Hawaii last year, he got a job working for my dad's company. My dad taught him everything he knows about drilling holes. Anyway, Cade's working for him again part time. We still qualify for Medicaid, and I'm glad Cade is pulling in some money. It's hard surviving on unemployment. It barely covers the house payment, and we're not even living there right now.

Maybe I should do something fun. I wish I could go skydiving. All my baby weight is already gone, and I want to enjoy life. I'm young, and there's so much life ahead. Isn't it funny I'm writing this while I'm waiting to see my son? This hospital is really getting me down, I tell you what. I feel trapped.

When I was seventeen, I ran away from home because I felt trapped. I was young, and there's no justifying it. But when I was home it seemed like my mom wasn't; she was either working or wanting to spend time with my nieces. But we fought when I did see her, and I wanted to be free from the whole dilemma. Well, I'm free now and there's no place to run or even hide.

I almost wish I could die—almost—but Ruby needs me, and so does Zeke. I tried talking to Cade, and he said this is all his fault. That didn't help me at all. We can travel and play music when Ruby and Zeke are all grown up, if Cade even wants to go with me. Why did God put such strong desires in my heart if I wasn't destined to do something with them? I guess I'm down on myself. I must sound so young and stupid, but I swear I'm not stupid, not really.

Everyone tells me how strong I am, but I'm not. I'm still performing for an audience, but without my violin. I'm putting on the greatest show of my life, though. I seem like I'm doing great, but inside I'm dead, like a smelly corpse or something.

Anyone who contemplates death as easily as I do, isn't strong. I wonder if Cade ever feels like this, but he won't talk to me about things. That's why I'm here, talking to you.

Entry #17

Ruby turned one today. We went out of town with Cade. He's working in Jackson, Wyoming, and I think he needed us to visit him. We'll only be gone for a night, and I needed a break from things. This is the farthest I've ever been from Zeke, and I feel it. We're staying in a cute log cabin. It has a fireplace, and my parents are here, too. Ruby had a fun birthday, so far, and squealed when she opened a movie called "Ice Age." She's seen pictures of it in the store, and wanted it for her entire life, I swear! She's watching it while I wait for my mom to come visit with us. She's in her cabin but will be over with some more presents for Ru.

I feel bad I left Zeke overnight, but this is Ruby's special day, and she needs to have a good birthday. I neglected her so much by going to the hospital. She hugs me hard when she sees me, and she doesn't want to let go. When I leave the room, she freaks out. It's nice spending special time with her so she knows I love her.

I need to stop worrying about Zeke. I've already called the hospital a few times, to check on him, and they said he's doing fine. I'll get to see him tomorrow morning and will be happy when we're close to each other again.

Entry #18

My sister visited the hospital today. She wanted to meet us there so she could say "hi" to Zeke. They only allow parents or grandparents to see the baby alone, but we can bring one visitor at a time if we want to. The NICU is a funny place. You have to push a button to be allowed into a long, sterile-smelling hallway. There are a ton of seats lining one side and they're usually filled with all sorts of people wearing sad faces. There are a few doors on the other side of the hall. I've spent tons of hours staring at those doors and I have every detail memorized. One of the doors leads to a surgeon's office. Another door leads to a bathroom, which has come in handy, and the last door leads to this colorful room where a bunch of toddlers always hang out. Ruby loves that room. She likes watching the T.V. and playing with the toys. It's not a bad room, but I feel bad for first time parents who wait out in the hallway and hear the healthy kids playing. I'm glad I have a kid who can play in there. If Zeke was my first, I don't know how I would survive.

There's an old off-white phone hanging from the wall in the hallway. You can pick it up and talk to a nurse. Then some more doors open if they deem you worthy. You go through those and enter the wash-up room. You're supposed to clean under your fingernails, and everything, as if the worst diseases known to man live under your nails. I could have nightmares about the crazy diseases they think are under my nails. They want you to scrub all the way up to your damn elbows. I scrub so hard my skin is wearing thin, and I wish God gave me an extra layer.

Anyway, after washing up, you can enter the baby area. Zeke's in the scary part of the NICU. The babies there need a lot of help and might not make it. There are a few babies with defects, but most were born early. I've met some of the parents. They're good people, and I hope their babies will make it out of this place. So, it's really a locked-down type of area, and my sister met us there so she could get in and see Zeke.

Cade watched Ruby in the playroom, and my sister and I went into lock-down. I pulled up a stool and sat next to Zeke. They've got him in a warming bed that's high up. The stool is the perfect height, and I'm always glad when I can snag it because sometimes the nurses sit on them, shooting the bull, while all the moms stand. Zeke's nurses aren't like that, though. They don't sit and gossip, not when babies could be dying. I like his nurses.

My problems always seem stupid and small when I go visit

Zeke, which is about twice a day. He's such a cute kid.

My sister asked the nurse all sorts of questions. She's good at knowing exactly what to ask.

While they talked, I sang to Zeke. Whenever I sing, he calms right down. I don't know why he likes my voice so much, but he does. I made him this crazy collage that's above his head. It has pictures of our family so he can see us. I know it sounds silly, because he's only opened his eyes a few times, and he can't see the thing, but it makes me feel better like I'm with him when I'm not.

Anyway, Susan, who is Zeke's nurse, asked if my sister could watch Ruby so Cade and I could talk to the nurse practitioner about Zeke. We went and didn't get the best news. They can only stick a thermometer a quarter inch up Zeke's butt hole. Either there's a blockage or his intestines aren't connected to his hole. If they aren't connected, he might need a bag, and it's not for trick-or-treating. They'll cut Zeke open again and pull his intestine out so he can poo. We finally thought Zeke was doing better, and now they might cut him open again.

I'm sad, and Cade is, too. I tried talking to him, but he said there's nothing to talk about because we'll just do what we have to. I want to talk to my family, but I'm tired of all their opinions. Cade stayed with Zeke while I told my sister. She got really upset and said we should let Zeke go because he has no quality of life. She doesn't know that, and it's easy to talk about letting a baby go when it's not your baby.

I don't want him to suffer, either, and I want him to live a normal life someday, but sometimes you have to fight hard for what you want. No one said this would be easy. We took the hard road; we did, not my family! I know this is difficult for them, too, but none of them understand what it's like holding someone's life in your hands like this. I swear, no one else knows. Even the people in that stinking hallway don't because their babies will be fine. Most of the kids who come in here don't have problems like Zeke does. I'm happy for them, but I sure don't want anyone telling me what to do, as if they know how sucky this is!

Entry #19

Zeke is exactly one month old today, and he pooped for the first time in his life! I told the nurse it was the best day of my life. She looked at me really funny. I was all sorts of happy, and she couldn't believe it. Anyway, Susan (his nurse) smiled, shook her head, and looked down at Zeke like he has the craziest mother known to man.

Susan is funny. She's just that way because, whenever I see Zeke, I act like I'm as happy as hell. I know life sucks for him, and I want him to have good times, too.

I don't think Susan is used to people like me because most of the NICU moms act like someone just stole their souls. I swear they think it's against the law to stop talking in monotones, and they only know how to answer in single syllables. It shouldn't be called the NICU, it should be called Robot City.

Remember how we talked to the nurse practitioner, and she was very concerned about my boy's rectum? Well, there was just a blockage. Susan pushed the thermometer up his butt, and it went through a flap of skin that had grown there. Now the poop is flying! And he looks so good since he let it rip.

Anyway, he pooped, and it was that black goopy stuff they send out to the world first. Susan was about to change him when she looked at me and asked if I'd like to change him, instead. I was nervous, as if I'd never changed a kid before, but really, I'd never changed a boy. So, you can see why I freaked out. The nurses never offered to let me change him, and I didn't want to ask, in case I wasn't allowed or something.

There are so many things I can't do with my baby; it makes me sick. I can't hold him or give him a bath; sometimes I can't even touch him if he's not doing good. I did get to give him a foot massage once, and that was awesome! So, when she asked if I wanted to change that diaper, I raced next to his butt in less than a second. Susan just shook her head at me. That lady must think I'm nuts, but I'm growing on her, I swear.

I changed his diaper, and it wasn't as scary as I thought. It might even be easier changing a boy's diaper than a girl's.

Cade looked at Zeke's pee pee and said, "Boy that kid's well endowed." I wanted to smack him for being inappropriate in front of Susan, but there was poo on my hand, and I thought he'd give me "the eye" if I got poo on him. So, instead, I looked at Susan, and told her again how this really was the best day of my life. She smiled at Zeke and touched his cheek. She said it was probably the best day of his, too.

Entry #20

Zeke has a huge infection. Part of his incision is still open. The medical staff refused to cover it, and now they think Zeke is getting infected from it. I don't know why they won't cover it up. They went on and on about how it needed to be in the open air, and how he's on antibiotics, and everything. I don't understand these "experts," but what do I know—right? I'm just the mother.

Janet, one of his other nurses, was there today. She gave me a huge hug and told me everything will be okay. She's a sweet lady who was with him the day he had his surgery. I know she didn't mean everything with Zeke will be okay, but that the whole situation will turn out for the best. It's hard knowing what she really meant because I wish she'd tell me Zeke will live a long, happy life, but she's a nurse, not a psychic, and I wish she were both.

I guess all of us, at one point or another, wish we could know what the future holds. My future seems scary and unsure, because my kids are my future, and one of them might not make it. All I can focus on is the present, and right now I'm breast pumping.

Zeke has only drunk a little bit of the milk I've pumped for him, but I'm pumping more and more, anyway. I'm hooked to a breast milk machine at the hospital. It really does make you feel like a cow. These two little cups hook onto your boobs, and like two blood-sucking insects, they deflate your boobs in about five minutes flat. Technology is crazy.

Well, I do know what one part of my future holds. In about three more minutes I'll have two A-minus size boobs that used to be a nice, milky size 32C. I've got to hold onto the present right now, not just because Zeke is alive, but because A-minus boobs suck!

Entry #21

When Cade and I drove from the hospital, he was in a crappy mood. I don't know why, but whenever he's angry, I think it's as funny as hell to tease him. I poke him, and give him wet willies, and then make up ridiculously funny stories about him. He absolutely hates it, but it's hilarious—to me—and you should see it. So, this one time I grabbed him by the inner thumb and squeezed the tender area in his hand.

He said, "Knock it off, Elisa! Watch the road," and then gave me "the eye."

"I'm trying to cheer you up!" I said, wanting to get my mind off the day and how badly Zeke is doing.

"Quit looking at me and watch THE ROAD!" he yelled.

"You're always telling me what to do! Can you just let me be the boss of me for two seconds?"

"Yeah, if I thought you could handle the responsibility!" he countered.

I looked in the back seat, and Ruby stared at us. Her eyes grew big as they shot back and forth between me and her daddy. "You're upsetting Ruby!" I accused him.

"JUST KEEP YOUR EYES ON THE ROAD!"

"I AM KEEPING MY EYES ON THE ROAD!" I yelled, and we both looked forward in time to watch me rear-end a van.

We smacked the windshield pretty hard, and then (after I hit the windshield) the air bag shot out and pushed me back into my seat. Some weird, filmy stuff filled the air before someone else ran into us. I dug through the air bag so I could get to Ruby and Cade but couldn't do it fast enough. I tried to open the driver's door, but it was jammed. I kicked and kicked until it opened. "RUBY? CADE.... RUBY?"

I opened the back door, and Ruby quivered, quiet and scared. It wasn't until I grabbed her and held her in my arms that she cried. Cade rushed over and put his arms around us. We watched as the person who hit us drove away.

"Oh, my gosh," I said as I looked ahead. "We got in a four-car pileup, if you count the guy who left." A tire rolled from the scene, and I hugged Ruby hard. "Are you guys okay?" I asked when Ruby finally stopped crying.

"Yeah, we'll make it," Cade said, and I noticed he had a huge goose egg on his forehead.

I told them I'd be right back, then made sure the other drivers were okay. I don't know why, but I shot the bull with them. They were all pretty shook up, and I guess I wanted to make them feel better. Some paramedics arrived, and I heard one ask Cade if I had gone into shock.

Cade said, "No, she's always hyper like that," and walked away.

I found out the other people came from the hospital, too. We each had sad and unique stories, and it was nice knowing I wasn't the only idiot driver on the road. I had a big bump on my knee, and the paramedics checked it out, but said it would be fine. They wanted to take us to the hospital and check for concussions, especially since we'd hit our heads, but we said "no."

My mom picked us up since our completely paid off car is now totaled. When I called her, she sounded super upset on the phone. She couldn't believe we'd just gotten in an accident. I laughed it off, though. I'm just glad the only thing that's totaled is the car, and not one of us, instead.

Entry #22

My sister got a letter in the mail today. I heard all about it from my mom. I guess the lady said Zeke is sick from the sins of my father. He had a construction company that went under, and some of the investors thought he hoarded money before the company went out of business. My dad is one of the nicest people you'd ever meet. He's generous and self-sacrificing and would never hoard money. Sometimes businesses go under, and that's all there is to it.

He was able to start his business again and that's who Cade is working for now. Anyway, his first drilling business went under awhile back, and some people tried suing him, but there was nothing to sue him for. He was innocent. Well, the letter my sister got said my dad is a sinner, and God is punishing my dad's family through Zeke.

I wish I knew who wrote that. My dad is going through enough! He doesn't need to hear that malarkey!

People keep inventing crazy reasons for why Zeke has problems. It's amazing how much people think they know. Why can't they just realize, sometimes crap happens. Life isn't always pretty, and it certainly isn't always fun, but we have to make the best of things and enjoy the ride while we're on it. We won't always be here, and definitely won't have every single answer. It's how we react to things; that's what shows who we are. I won't let those stupid people get me down. Instead, God will show them compassion towards others because that is something they lack.

Entry #23

I went to church and prayed for Zeke. There's this really great church downtown. You'd like it, really you would. The people there are actually genuine, and there's a nice feel to the place. I went in there and sang with Ruby, when suddenly I caught a glimpse of my ex-boyfriend. Well, we can call him "the ex." I guess I'll call him that since he's the only other guy I've ever loved like that, other than Cade.

It was really hard seeing him because he looked depressed, and for a minute, I felt myself remembering how happy I used to make him. We'd sit, talking for hours, and I felt like those times would never change, but they did, and I'm glad, because I have Cade now.

Anyway, "the ex" saw me and left the church as fast as he could. I couldn't believe he left just because of me. It's not like God left the building when I walked in. Plus, wasn't the guy there to commune with God?

"The ex" came back after the service was over. He even talked to me, which was a shocker since he'd run away minutes before. I looked hard into his eyes and was pretty happy when I didn't feel anything like I used to. He told me how I'd broken his heart when I took a ring he gave me, and ran away with Cade, instead. I didn't really like hearing all about it because it made me sad, but I sat and listened anyway. I even said I was sorry because I was selfish and should have been straight with him before, instead of sneaking away.

The whole time, Ruby ran in between the pews, and I got a royal kick out of that kid. I almost forgot about "the ex" until something he said brought me back to the conversation. I guess he'd been all romantic, well as romantic as you can get with someone of the opposite sex, and she'd broken his heart. He seemed really torn up about it, and I felt bad that someone else had stomped on his heart, too. I wished I could patch the thing up real nice, but knew it wasn't my place anymore. So, I left the church really quick, and said a prayer for "the ex."

I hope he'll be okay. He was such a nice guy, but I always thought he'd be a real sucker for drugs. I guess I knew, somewhere deep down, and that's why I left him. I couldn't stand watching him spiral down. I hope he'll be okay, but I sure am glad I ended up with Cade. He's a strong guy, and I don't think he'd ever let drugs have a hold over him like "the ex" might, someday, you know with drugs.

Entry #24

I held Zeke today! He had all of his tubes in, but I still held him. Susan set me up in a rocking chair, and then handed him to me. I had to be careful not to rock too hard because I could pull some of the tubing out. So, I rocked slowly, and sang his song to him. He fussed before, but as he rested in my arms, he quieted down. Today was the first time I've gotten to hold him since the day he was born. I swear that kid melted into my arms. It's like he was meant to be there. I held him for a long time, and then Cade got a turn. We took Polaroid pictures of each other, and I put them in Zeke's baby book. His little book is so cute. My aunt bought it for him, but it only goes up to three months. Isn't that weird? What kind of baby book only goes up to three months? I'll have to add more pages when he gets bigger; I want to record everything for at least the first year.

I'm so happy he's doing good enough we can hold him now. Susan said I can start taking classes to get ready to take him home. He's breathing better, and I think he'll be off the vent soon. It will be such a good Christmas; I just know it.

I love teasing Susan. She's such a serious lady, you wouldn't believe it. Well, she's not serious as much as she's somber. It must be hard working in the NICU. I always say silly things just to get a rise out of her. Today, while Cade held Zeke, I looked at Susan, and asked, "Do you get a lot of them?"

"A lot of what?" she asked.

"Repeat offenders?"

She pulled a funny face. "Repeat offenders?"

"Yeah," I said, "You know, people who have multiple children with birth defects?"

She rolled her eyes "You make it sound like it's a crime."

I laughed. "Well, you ladies do make it seem like lock-down in here."

"I've never heard it put like that. You sure are something," she said dryly. I laughed again and turned to Zeke and Cade.

I saw her from the corner of my eye. She had the biggest look of pity on her face but would never pull that if she thought I could see her. She's always acting so tough, but I know she cares a lot about us, maybe even too much.

Her look really got to me, though, because I couldn't figure why she would pity me now. I asked her if there was something we should know, and she said that two things concerned her. Zeke's brain still has a chance of bleeding inside, since he's been on the vent for over a month; that bleeding can cause retardation. She also said she's worried he's already retarded because of what the doctors thought about his cerebellum.

I teased her by fake punching her in the arm; I guess I didn't know what else to do. Cade gave me "the eye" then, but I was just joking around. I wish he'd stop giving me "the eye" when I'm not doing anything wrong. So, I smoothed Susan's sleeve out, you know, where I'd fake punched her, and told her not to worry, and everything will work out, but she didn't seem as certain as I am about things. She just shook her head and gave a pathetically sad smile. She thinks she's seen people just like us before, people full of hope.

I went to the cafeteria and bought mashed potatoes and gravy. They're under a buck, and really filling, so I eat them for at least one meal a day. It's not much, but we don't have a ton of money right now, and they're tasty enough. Ruby even likes them.

When I finally made it through all of the doors to the NICU, Susan prepared to do some blood tests on Zeke. Every shift they do tests to see how his levels are. She told us she'll have the next week off for Christmas since she's been at the NICU so long. I guess all of the hardcore nurses like her get the week of Christmas off. I really hope she'll have a good one, and I feel bad that I fake punched her in the arm, even though she knew I was kidding. Plus, she smiled at me when we left, and I know she didn't mean for me to see it, but I did. She can act tough as much as she wants, but I know she likes us, especially Zeke. She really cares about little Zeke Jackson.

Entry #25

Zeke has pneumonia. I went to see him as soon as I found out. After I went through all of the doors, and washed up, I was surprised to see Susan there. She was supposed to be off for Christmas, but was in the NICU, taking care of my boy, instead. She was with another nurse and their backs faced me. They didn't notice I'd come into the room, and they talked in hushed tones. Susan seemed really upset, and I didn't want to interrupt her. So, I stayed back a few feet and caught a glimpse of my son between the two women working on him. He freaked out. His arms flailed, and his skin blotched with purples and blues. It wasn't just his face turning colors this time. The rip in his skin is still there, even though it's been a month since he had the surgery, and it's still not covered up. My heart hurt for him as I watched him struggling to breathe, but he freaked out so much he couldn't breathe if they wanted him to. Susan motioned for the other nurse to hurry. They put some type of medicine into his IV, and he stopped moving within seconds. His color slowly calmed, even though he still looked oddly bluish-orange. Now the only movement I saw was the little rise and fall of his chest from the vent.

The nurses had still not seen me, so involved in the moment. Susan wiped her forehead, and said quietly, "I can't believe the new girl put milk in his lung instead of his stomach! Of all incompetent things!"

I gasped. "So, that's why he has pneumonia!" Heat laced my voice. It's hard to make me angry, but that did it. No one hurts my baby! Susan paled when she turned and saw me.

"I didn't mean for you to hear it this way," she said. "I'm so sorry, Elisa." She looked over at Zeke. "And he was doing so well."

"Will he be okay?" I asked, fighting back the tears.

"I'm not sure. We've had to up his support, and he's still

struggling. I can't guarantee anything except that the nurse who put the milk into his lung has been let go."

"Poor Zeke!" I said, as I rushed to him and put my hand gently on his forehead.

"I know," she whispered. "He's such a fighter. We gave him medicine to calm him down. He was having another one of his episodes. He's already had a few of them today. The medicine should help him now, though."

"Susan." I paused. "Why are you working today? I thought you were supposed to be off."

"I needed the hours."

"Really? But you said you get a paid Christmas vacation," I said.

She looked away.

"Did you call to check on Zeke while you were on vacation, or something?"

"Yeah, I guess I did." She looked at all of his monitors and adjusted them since he had calmed down. "I really did need more hours though."

Sure she did.

"When I'm home, all I think about right now is work, anyway." She gazed at Zeke fondly, and I realized how much she loves him.

I waited until she had completely looked away from us, and I put my finger in Zeke's little hand. A tear slid down my cheek, and I silently thanked God for giving Zeke such a good nurse.

Susan did some paperwork, and then asked how I was. I exercised my very brightest smile and said, "It's going wonderfully! Zeke is still here. How has your day gone, woman?"

She just shook her head. "I'll leave you two alone for a bit. I'll be right over here if he needs anything."

I still don't understand why the other nurse put milk into his lung, but I'm trying to calm down and make sense of things. It will drive me crazy—like an animal balloon maker—if I don't stop thinking about it.

Everything happens for a reason, right? Everything?

Entry #26

"Mom, please pray that Zeke will get better," I paused, "and make it."

"No," she said, "I don't want to pray that."

"What?" I was irate. "Why won't you pray for him?"

"I'll pray for him," she looked down at her hands, "but I'm not going to pray that he'll make it. I just don't feel that in my heart."

"So, you think he's going to die, and you won't raise a hand to stop it?" Tears jumped in the way of my vision.

"I'm going to pray for God to have His will," she said solemnly.

"Oh," my voice flattened. "I need to go." I turned from her then.

"Elisa...don't go," my mom begged, but I was already on my way, and I wasn't about to stop.

Entry #27

Cade got a letter from his cousin, "King Arthur." I asked Cade if I could read it, but he said it would just hurt my feelings. It's probably full of more useless opinions from yet another person who has no idea what it's like going through this. I don't want to read it, especially if it says more crap about why Zeke was born with defects. People always want answers, don't they, and want to feel like they are the ones who have them. I wonder what God thinks of people when He looks down and sees our foolish reasoning. He laughs at us; I bet He does.

I've had some time to seriously reevaluate my life. I'm sick and tired of feeling sorry for myself. I'm not going to sit around and regret my choices. If I can't be happy now, then I never will be. I'm going to enjoy every second of my life, and not look back, I swear. There isn't time to regret this life I'm living. I'm just too damn busy. What is important, right now, is that my children know how much I love them, and Cade knows I'll be there for him—no matter what. I need to be strong and I'm going to be!

Entry #28

My mom didn't write a letter the day Zeke was born. She wrote it today, instead, and I wanted to put it in here. This is what she wrote:

12/19/2002
Dear Elisa,

It has been over a month now and Zeke, my little beauty, is at the children's hospital. Cade came home from Jackson, Wyoming last night and you went to see Zeke together. I feel bad because he was doing so well, but a new nurse just put milk into his lung. I pray he is okay.

Elisa, through all of this time and even before he was born, I must say, you have had such a strength to carry it all and such a love...so deep. I know that God has given you this strong desire and love for little Zeke. He is blessed to have such a mommy as you and Cade has been right there with you. My heart is blessed watching you two.

When Zeke was born, I cried because he was so beautiful...a gift from God. Elisa, know that God has a plan and a purpose in

85

all of this. He is the maker and creator of the universe. He chose you and Cade to take a stand...and yes! Stand Strong! God will be glorified.

I am so proud of you. All of the doctors and nurses can only say how amazing you are. When you were in labor with Zeke and in the delivery room you didn't think of yourself, you put your baby first. He knew that and he loves you too!

You are such a wonderful mommy to little Ruby 2. She is as beautiful as the Kiss of Springtime. She is truly blessed to have such wonderful parents. I know that God is doing great things in and through you. He is God almighty, will never leave you or forsake you.

He gave His only Son for you because He loves you that much. I will always love you too.

Love,
Mom (Ruby I)

Entry #29

It's the day after Christmas. I feel really bad because yesterday was the first day that I didn't go to see Zeke at the hospital. We brought him presents today, and everything, but I still feel crappy about it. I got him this cute little stuffed bug, and Susan hung it over him for me. Anyway, I guess I felt like it was important to be with Ruby all of Christmas. That's not a very great excuse, though. Zeke deserved for us to be with him, too.

I wish Ruby could see him. Then I wouldn't feel like I constantly have to split my time between them. I also feel bad that my mom and mother-in-law have to watch Ruby so much. They watch her every time I go visit Zeke. They enjoy it, though. It's always so great spending time with that kid. She's the only one who can get my mind off things.

She's been doing this funny thing lately; I call it the buttscoot. She pushes herself backwards on the tiles in my parents' house. She sits on her butt and scoots just like a dog, I swear. It's the funniest thing ever because it's in fast forward, or some weird thing.

She's so funny. She learned how to walk before Zeke was born, but walking isn't hip anymore. Life is all about the buttscoot right now.

That reminds me of something I used to do. When I was in junior high, I used to love watching exercise videos in fast forward.

It looked so funny when they'd jump, jump, sit, jump, stretch, jump. All exercise movies are pretty great in fast forward, but Richard Simmons' ones are the best. Hell, he's even funny when he's not in fast forward. I wonder what it would look like when you're rewinding it! That sounds awesome. I've got to try it the next chance I get.

Entry #30

Zeke has a huge infection now. He isn't doing well at all. He hasn't opened his eyes in weeks, and they have him heavily drugged. He just lays there like a rock, or something. If they stop giving him the medicine, then he has what Susan calls an "episode."

He freaks out so bad that he stops breathing and is in serious pain. He's gotten so swollen you wouldn't believe it. My precious baby is hurting, but I need to stay strong. I keep wondering if I'll wake up, and he'll be gone, you know, dead. I don't want him to die when I'm not there to make it easier somehow. I hate thinking about this. He still might get better, but he's doing so crappy!

I talked to his main doctor today and asked him if he thinks that we should let Zeke go. He said we haven't given him enough time. He also said it's only been a month and a half since the surgery, and that Zeke has done amazingly well, considering. Zeke doesn't look like he's doing amazingly well to me, though, and I told the doctor so. He said I should be patient and give Zeke time. I wanted to give Zeke a chance, and that's what they're doing, but the kid is suffering and I'm not sure if he's getting better or not.

When I saw Zeke, I pulled myself together. I didn't want him to feel how sad I am. He needs happy, positive people around if he's going to get better. I believe that with all of my heart. So, I tell him how good he's doing, when I shoot the bull with him, just to make him feel better.

Susan took care of him when I got there. She's almost always there. I joked around, and said, "Woman! How in the hell are you, you good looking thing?"

She gave me "the eye" then. Maybe she's been taking lessons from Cade. I think she suppressed a smile, but after a moment her serious demeanor came back fully.

"Elisa," she said, "you need to wake up and realize what's going on around you." She cleared her throat. "Your son is very sick, and you don't seem to be accepting reality." Her eyes caught mine, and she peered at me steadily. "Why are you so happy all the time?"

"I'm just happy he's still here," I whispered. "As long as he's still alive," I paused, suddenly sad in the moment, "there's hope."

She looked at me differently then and sighed as if she was sorry for making me sad. "You're one of the strongest people I've ever met," she said, and then filled the syringe she held in her hand, "and I've met a lot of people in here."

"A lot of repeat offenders?" I asked with a laugh in my voice because I wanted to choke out my tears. Susan laughed so hard that part of the fluid from the syringe shot out.

"Oh, you're a card!" She looked at the partially empty syringe in her hand. "You know that, don't you!" It wasn't a question.

Entry #31

Another baby with a hole in her diaphragm came to the NICU a couple of days ago. She was really bad off. They didn't know she had complications until she was a few weeks old. I guess the mother came into her daughter's room the other day and found her hardly breathing. They rushed her into the hospital, and had the surgery done. I guess her great-great-uncle had a hole in his diaphragm, but they didn't know what the problem was until they did the autopsy.

Anyway, the little girl is doing so well she can already go home. I hugged her mother and told her I wish them the very best. Tears flooded my face as I watched her take her baby from this place. It must feel nice being able to take their baby home. The mom said how hard it had been going through this. She really felt bad for herself, and I found it ironic she didn't think of me, because my baby is the one who is still here. She'd barely even asked about Zeke now that I think about it. She was so absorbed in her own problems. I prayed for her little girl today. I hope she'll live a long, healthy life, and that she'll be a bit more empathetic than her mother is.

Entry #32

It's a miracle! Zeke is doing so well, and I got to hold him again today. We might even get to take him home in a month or so. He's almost completely off the damn vent! The doctor had me take some classes about home care. They taught me how to place tubing to give Zeke milk, how to do CPR, how to give him oxygen, etc. It was actually a fun class, except that I popped the baby's head off when I did CPR on it. Thank God that wasn't a real kid. I can see why they use dummies, for sure!

I couldn't believe I was actually in the class. The other parents told me about it, but I've never been able to go until now. I'm so excited. This has been a long haul, but Zeke actually might come home and see the cute little room I decorated just for him. Oh, I bet he'll be happy with us. We love him so much. Ruby can't wait to meet him. She still hasn't been allowed in lock-down since she's so little.

Entry #33

I feel really old right now. Cade's grandma died a couple of days ago. His mom seems to be having a hard time. I wish I knew what to do for her, but I'm lost. I keep calling, just to make sure she's okay. She's one of my best friends, and I'm worried for her.

A bunch of her family is in town now. I waited for my mother-in-law to finish visiting Zeke with one of her sisters, since only two people can see him at a time. I was sad that I had to wait to see Zeke again.

So, while I waited, I met a couple who have a baby in here. They are both seventeen, and neither one of them has a job. They're completely incompetent, and I wonder if they're on drugs. They're staying at a Ronald McDonald house the hospital offers as free housing for families of patients. They seem so hillbilly you wouldn't believe it. They talk in crazy, drawling tones, and while I visited with them, I actually struggled understanding all their words. They say "warsh" instead of "wash" and "buggy" instead of "shopping cart," that kind of thing. It was wild, and I talked to them for so long I kind of started talking like them until I realized what I did, and wanted to punch my own mouth out.

Anyway, their baby was born at twenty weeks. The baby is on a vent, and he severely hemorrhaged. The doctor told them they absolutely need to let their baby go because he'll be a vegetable for the rest of his life. The parents wouldn't have it, though, and said their kid doesn't know no diff-ernt. They'll keep him alive as long as that there medicine and machine'll hold him.

Well, the whole thing made me ill. When my mother-in-law finished visiting Zeke, I gave her a hug, hoping she'll know how bad I feel about her mom. Then I quietly sang to Zeke.

Susan was there and looked at me funny because I was serious. She said, "Dare I ask what happened to the cheerful girl I used to know?"

I told her about the couple I just met. She nodded, understanding why I was upset. She said, "There are worse things than death."

"Don't you ever get tired of working here?" I asked. "You see so many sad things, and you still want to work in this place?"

"It's not...too bad," she said. "We help a lot of babies here. Plus, I get to meet some really different people." She smiled then, and said, "Like you."

"Different, huh?" I asked.

"Oh yes," she said, "very different," and she laughed at her own joke. That was the first time I've heard her do that; you know, make a funny.

Entry #34

Zeke got another infection. He's doing worse than he was when he had pneumonia. They put him on so much medication I'm worried for him. His poor body is really swollen now. I've never seen a little baby look like this. I'm helpless and don't know what to do.

So, I merely stay by his bed and sing. I keep the tears from my voice because I want him to feel better and crying upsets me lately. If I hear someone crying, I want to slap them. It makes me want to cry, and I simply don't have time for any more tears. Plus, it might be fun to slap someone who is weak and crying, just for the hell of it. You know, if I wouldn't get in trouble, and it wouldn't freak them out too much, just help them stop crying over something dumb.

After I saw Zeke today, I couldn't take it anymore. I needed a change, so I chopped off my long, blond hair. It's all spiky now, and I dyed it a deep black burgundy. Cade saw it and his jaw dropped. He didn't even recognize me at first. I don't think he likes it very much, but I feel better for the moment. Everyone else seems to like it, though. I wish I could be someone else, just for two minutes. Would that hurt God to let me have a break, for two minutes?

Entry #35

I got a call tonight, not the kind I hoped to get. I couldn't sleep after talking to the nurse. This is too damn depressing and confusing. I'm staying at my mom's house, and I sit on the floor in the computer room and wish the floor could swallow me. Then, if I knew where a freezing machine was, scientists could freeze me, and I could wake up in twenty years when these decisions won't be here anymore—someone else can take the blame.

A new nurse took care of Zeke last night. She said all of the other nurses, and even some of his doctors, are too close to see the situation clearly, and that I should know—we need to let Zeke pass on. She said he's suffering, and he probably won't even make it past this week. I acted strong on the phone, like I always knew everything she'd just said. I didn't want her knowing how much she'd busted me up inside.

At that moment I felt like I'd been the one born with a freakish diaphragm, and that my organs were all up in my throat. I hung up the phone before calling Cade. It's about two in the morning, but he picked up the phone really fast, anyway. He got a new job and is working in Montana. It's probably killing him being away from his boy, but this is life, and right now life sucks.

I told Cade everything, and he said he'd call me back in a minute, after he talked to his new boss. While I waited for Cade to call back, my mom woke up and gave me some water. She's always pushing water on me, it's hilarious—any other time. You walk into the house, and she already has a glass of water waiting for you. She gets it all cold and nice, but I detest water. I'm a soda kind of gal because I didn't get to drink it much growing up, and now I can't get enough.

Anyway, my mom handed me a nice, cold glass of water, and I'd like to drink it just to make her happy, but I can't. You know, when you wake up in the middle of the night, and water tastes like the cat your dad threw out last summer? Well, this water tasted about ten times worse, and I found myself thinking it tasted like death. Death surrounds me right now, and I can't shake him. My mom sat at the table and read her Bible, while I stayed quietly on the floor in the computer room. I wonder what she's been reading.

Cade called me back faster than I thought he would. He said he was already on the road, and all. That guy sure knows how to hurry when it counts. He should be home in a while. It's a long drive from Montana to Utah. Anyway, he told me he talked to his boss, and that his boss ended up crying in the hotel's hallway. He had a daughter who died a long time ago, and he still feels really bad about it. Cade said they actually hugged each other, and it was the height of awkwardness, hugging someone he barely knew, but significant since we might lose our baby soon, too. I told Cade to drive safely, and he promised he would.

So, I'm still here on the computer room floor, thinking about how one decision will change our lives, and Zeke's, indefinitely. I should call the hospital and make an appointment with a few of Zeke's doctors. I need to know if they agree with the new nurse that Zeke has tonight. I hope they won't! I don't know if I can handle this. I need Cade home now. I don't want to face this alone.

Entry #36

My parents arrived at the hospital early in the morning, and Zeke's nurse, Lisa, let them hold him for a long time. My mom said it was wonderful holding him like that. I'm glad she got to, and I'm sure he loved every minute of it.

93

Cade drove into town just before noon, and I waited at the hospital for him. We had a meeting with a few of the doctors. We asked if we should let Zeke go; this time they said, "Yes. He's just not getting any better."

"And he's gotten infection after infection," another added. "This is a very appropriate time to think about letting him go. He'll probably be better off if you do," the one with the gray hair said mildly.

"Honestly? You really think he might be better off if we let him go?" I pleaded, practically repeating what he'd just said.

"I really do," he said. "There are worse things than death." I wanted to turn away then. If I got a dollar every time I heard that stupid phrase in the NICU, I could pay everyone's medical bills.

"What do you mean...might?" Cade asked.

"Well, there's a small chance he could pull through this. If he does, he could live a normal life, but there's a far greater chance that he'll live a very hard one filled with surgeries. He'll probably need a tracheotomy and be permanently reliant on machines." His gray hair dulled in my blurring vision.

"There's also a big chance he won't make it through the week," the young doctor said. "If you don't let him go now, you'll risk not being here when he does pass."

There was a long silence as what he said sunk in. That was one of my deepest fears. I wanted to be with Zeke if he had to pass away.

"Elisa?" Cade asked, as I looked at him. He appeared much older than his twenty-two years. "What should we do?" he whispered, hoping the doctors wouldn't hear him.

I stood straight and pursed my lips in determination. "I think we should let him go. This whole time he hasn't been fighting for him; he's been fighting for us. He knew we wanted him to live." I choked on the last words, and a sob left my throat. The doctors turned slightly away, from respect or weariness. They must deal with this same situation far too often. I thought of the seventeen-year-olds I met weeks ago: the ones who wouldn't let their

94

hemorrhaged-baby go. "We've given him his chance," I reassured, "but now it would be selfish to keep him alive."

Tears filled Cade's green eyes. Then the strong, intelligent man I married crumpled before me. Huge sobs racked his body as he knelt next to the table in the little room we were in. I fell next to him and molded my body against his as if protecting him from a terrifying storm. I stroked his curly black hair and told him not to cry. "It'll be okay," I said vainly. "Hush, Honey, it'll be okay." I cried then, deep cries, because the simple truth was that it wasn't okay, and no one knew if it ever would be again. The doctors slowly filed from the room. They left us with nothing except our misery.

Entry #37

I can't tell you what color the sky was the day Zeke died. I can't even tell you if it was cold or warm the moment he passed. The truth is simply it lasted forever, and I can't remember much. Today is my birthday. It's been three days since we let Zeke go. His viewing is tonight. This is the worst birthday ever. I am no longer a teenager, as of today, but I have aged so much more. I feel like someone punched the wind out of me, and they took my spirit for life as well. Sadness is my shadow and sorrow my companion. I've told them to leave, but they won't because they know how powerless I am. I couldn't even save my own son.

Even though I can't seem to remember much, I'll tell you what I remember about the day Zeke died. The things I do remember are important. I was numb most of the day.

Cade and I talked, and then told the doctors we wanted to let Zeke go. We called everyone in our families, and they rushed to say goodbye to our baby. Some of our aunts and uncles even came and held him. They drove a few hours to be with us, and that meant the world to me.

I called my brother on the phone and told him I had to let my baby go. He didn't understand how things could spiral down so quickly. You see, I'd been trying to make it seem like everything would be okay when I told him about Zeke. He got choked up on the phone and said he couldn't make it from Arizona in time to meet Zeke—his only nephew. That broke my heart, but I understood. He said he would leave as soon as possible and would attend the funeral. When I called my sister, she was really nice. She said she was proud of me for being so strong. But I'm not really strong. I guess I was born to be an actress or something.

We dressed Zeke in a darling little blue outfit, and Susan put two tiny rings on his fingers. It was the first time he'd been allowed to wear clothes. Everyone got to hold Zeke, even a lady we barely knew. I guess one of our family members called her. She came like a bug attracted to a light. She held Zeke for what seemed like forever, and the whole time Zeke grew more bluish and purplish. I know she really didn't hold him all that long, but it seemed like eternity because I wanted to rock him. I still can't figure why we let her come, but we weren't thinking too clearly just then. Finally, Susan tapped her in the shoulder and said it was time to give someone else a chance to say "goodbye."

I talked to one of Cade's brothers then. "Will you please hold Zeke and tell him goodbye?"

"I don't want to."

"But he's your nephew. Please?" I couldn't understand why he wouldn't hold my son.

"All right, but the only reason I'm doing this is for you," he said, sat down in the rocking chair, and held Zeke lovingly. As he rocked him, his manly attitude fell, and tears flowed down his cheeks. His lanky legs rocked back and forth, and I realized how hard this was for him. He really loved Zeke, too, even though he hardly knew him.

After a few hours, my chance came again. That was the fourth time I'd ever held Zeke if you count the time right after he was born. I held him lovingly in my arms, as if I'd never let him go. Susan adjusted his tubing so it would be more comfortable for him.

"Susan," I implored, "do we still have to let him go? Can I change my mind?"

"No, Hon," she said in a monotone voice; she'd been crying. "It's too late for that. See his coloring?" I nodded that I did. "He's already starting to go," she finished flatly, as more of a strange hue crept over his tiny body.

I stared blandly at the little bundle in my arms. I studied, ingraining every detail into my memory, so I could summon it whenever I wanted to. I'd only held him for about ten minutes, but suddenly couldn't take it anymore. I hugged him one last time before telling Susan I was done. It was Cade's turn and he held him for much longer than I did. He cradled Zeke in the rocking chair and told him how he wished things were different. I remember putting my arms around them, my husband, and my only son.

Zeke's other nurse, Janet, tapped me on the shoulder. I turned around and she gave me a huge hug. She'd come on her day off, just to say "goodbye." That lady is one in a million. Every time she took care of Zeke, she matched his sheets and blankets, and styled his hair in a mohawk. That lady is awesomeness personified.

"We have something for you," Janet said as she looked at Susan. They passed me a small little box full of cotton balls. I opened it. I tried to be careful, but some of the balls fell on the floor, anyway. "Don't worry about it," Janet said, and bent down to pick them up.

I pulled out a tiny porcelain hand from the container. It was so small and perfect. It looked like a real little hand. I peered at each finger and recognized Zeke's pinkie with the nub on it. "It's absolutely beautiful!" I said.

"We thought you'd like it," Susan said. "Did you notice the pinkie?"

"Of course, I did! This means so much to me. Thank you...both of you." I cried and hugged them hard.

Janet left shortly after, and I pulled out the little hand so I could look at it again. I briskly walked to the corner of the room, behind the rocking chair, and through the wall of crying family encircling it. I wanted to be alone, but one of my relatives followed me all the way to the corner. She decided it would be a good time to convert me to Mormonism. She told me I needed to think about my future in eternity, and about how I could be with Zeke again. I remember the last few moments Zeke had in that room—the one where he had always been, and I remember the awkwardness that followed as my relative told me what I should believe.

Susan heard part of the speech and acted like she'd intervene if I wanted her to. I gave her a smile and a slight wave before turning to the "preacher" next to me. I looked at her, and with a grace and assuredness I'd never known before, I said, "I know you mean well, but this is neither the time nor the place. I need to go be with my son now." I left her sulking in the corner.

Cade smiled up at me with tear-stained eyes as he saw me appear around the back of the rocking chair. "I think it's time," he said, and I nodded in agreement.

My mother-in-law pulled me aside. She gave my hand a bear squeeze, and said, "Elisa, you're so strong. You've been so strong for...everyone." I smiled weakly and told her how much I love her, and how happy I was she was there.

Cade's oldest brother hugged him, and I overhead what he said to Cade. "You've done everything right, Cade. You gave Zeke every chance, and if I could have picked my parents, I would've picked you and Elisa."

Cade buried his head into his brother's chest at that moment, and they hugged. "Thanks...Scott," he said, crying.

Susan led us to a room where they'd take Zeke off the support and let us hold him until he passed. It looked like a glorified hotel room, and I shuddered, thinking about all the other babies who'd spent their last moments in that very room.

I stepped from the room, and Ruby bounded toward me, down the hall. She was so excited because she'd finally been let into the NICU. Plus, today was the first day she would meet her baby brother. I thought for a second about how it would be the first and last she'd meet him, and I stifled a cry.

We sat down in the room. Ruby sat between Cade and me. Susan told us what to expect, while my mother-in-law took a picture of what should have been our happy little family. I couldn't summon a smile as I locked gazes with the flashing camera.

I asked Susan if she could give Zeke some medicine to lessen the pain, but she said they don't kill babies at the NICU, they just let them go. I don't remember at what point they took Zeke off the support; I just know that he was suddenly off it. Susan handed Zeke to us, and Cade and I cradled him on either side. One of his silent crying episodes started, and Ruby got nervous. She tried gently touching him, but her tiny one-year-old hand was much rougher than she'd intended, and Zeke turned even bluer as he struggled for breath. I could hardly look at him, thinking it was about to get much worse. I looked around, frantically searching for my mom, and when I found her, I asked if she could take Ruby out into the hall while we let Zeke go. She hugged me before taking Ruby, who waved "bye bye" as she left. Everyone slowly said "goodbye" to Zeke until Susan, Cade and I were the only ones left in the room.

I tilted toward Susan again, while stroking Zeke's tiny head like I'd done so often—for almost three months. "How long will it take him to pass?"

"It can take anywhere from thirty minutes to an hour." She stiffened and looked away from Zeke.

"Why can't we give him any medicine? I don't want to kill him. I just want to make his passing easier."

"It's the hospital's policy, Elisa. There's nothing more I can do. Just let it be enough that you're here with him now." His little hand wrapped so tightly around my finger, it turned white from the pressure. He was very aware right then. "Do you want to be alone?" Susan said, but it wasn't really a question. She walked from the room, and the door creaked shut.

I've never been a person who could handle the sound of crying, but at that moment I wished, with all of my soul, some noise would rise from Zeke. Nothing was worse than that silent death-cry. His body stiffened and slacked, stiffened and slacked, while his coloring increased deeper. I was shocked, watching him suffer for what seemed like an eternity. Some part of me, way deep down, must have thought God would wait to save Zeke until that exact moment. I kept expecting him to suddenly breathe on his own without any machines or any type of support, but it never happened.

Instead, the episode worsened, until I wanted to run from that room, grab a nurse—any nurse—and tell her to save my son, but we couldn't go back, and I felt sick of being selfish and wanting him to live, just because I needed him so desperately. Toward the greater end of that half hour his crying spell weakened. The lack of oxygen finally numbed his brain, and he didn't feel the pain of suffocation anymore.

His crying subdued itself, and although I wanted to look away, I couldn't pull my eyes from the tiny person whom Cade and I grasped so tightly. He stopped crying at one point; Cade and I looked at each other. "Is he—," Cade asked, but before he continued, Zeke cried again. He did that several more times, stopping and starting. The length of the silences in between got longer and longer, until one of them lasted...forever.

I kissed Zeke gently on the forehead, then said, "Goodbye." For the first time since Zeke's crying had become subdued, Cade and I cried. I passed our son's body completely to Cade before running headlong into the bathroom adjoining the death room. I slammed the door as hard as my small frame could, and willed life to be over for me as well. I screamed then. I cried out to God—the cry that I'd been holding in since the whole damn ordeal began. I screamed into the silent, black bathroom, "GOD! WHY? I CAN'T TAKE THIS ANYMORE!"

I covered my face with my hands, and was about ready to

scream out again, when someone hugged me in the darkness. He hugged me from behind, the type of hug you'd give to your oldest, dearest friend. He stood much taller than me, and his skin felt warm and strong. He felt...healthy! He bent his head low, so that his head almost rested on my shoulder, and said, "Everything will be okay." I cinched my eyes and sobbed. He held me for only a moment more, and then was gone. He left me standing alone. I quickly turned on the bathroom's light, but no one was there; I was alone. I ran from the bathroom and told Cade what had happened. I said, "I think it was Zeke, Cade. He hugged me in the darkness, and he felt so healthy!"

Cade still cradled Zeke, not willing to abandon him as I had just done. Cade's red, splotchy face turned toward me, and he stopped crying. "Why didn't he come to me?" he asked.

"I don't know," I heard myself saying. "Maybe I needed it...more."

I don't remember exactly what happened after that. I was in a haze of disbelief and sadness. All I do remember is that, somehow, all of our family filed back into the room, and people wanted to take pictures of Zeke—of his body.

Everyone cried and held him for hours, but Cade wouldn't go near him after everyone entered the room. He said his spirit wasn't in there anymore and wouldn't hold him. I remember holding him for a long time, though. I hugged him like I'd always wanted to, his small frame molding to me as it stiffened in death. I took the little rings off his fingers. I kept one and gave the other to Cade. I kissed the ring to my lips, and then cried for the time we'd lost with Zeke and the time we'd had. He'd suffered almost every moment.

So, now it's my birthday. A bunch of my relatives are in town for the viewing and the funeral. We're supposed to eat out before the viewing. I hope everything will go well. I hope Zeke will be proud of his funeral. I've always heard that dead people go to their own funerals. He'll be there. I'll rest in that hope.

I've asked everyone to bring something for Zeke. Since he

won't ever have a birthday, or anything, I thought it would be nice to have people bring him things so I can remember what he might have enjoyed, had he lived. I'm crying as I write this, and it's getting hard to see. My writing looks horrible, but I couldn't care less, everything is horrible right now. I can't believe he's gone!

We met with a lady at the funeral home yesterday. She's a laugh and a half. Have you ever met someone who can make anyone feel at ease, regardless of the circumstance? Well, that's not her, but it's me. There we sat, discussing what type of casket to put my son in, and she started telling me how much she likes me. She shot all types of the bull, and before I knew it, I had her laughing up a storm. She told me all about how Halloween is her favorite holiday. Cade gave me "the eye." He didn't think it was appropriate to make people laugh in the "death home," but I didn't care.

So, this incredibly comfortable-feeling "death home" employee continued telling me how Halloween is her favorite because they put potluck food in the rental coffins. Then they have a party amidst the coffins. I laughed courteously, but the idea was worse than "Silence of the Lambs." Cade didn't give me "the eye" then. Instead, he gave her "the eye," which made me less squeamish as I laughed for real.

Cade and I decided to have Zeke cremated. I can't stand the thought of them closing that lid on my son. I can't think about his little body being stuck in that box forever—underground. Especially if it was filled with potluck food. It's not that I don't like potluck food, just not in conjunction with a "death home." That's all.

So, he'll be cremated for sure now. My aunt thinks that's a horrible idea. She's Catholic, and said it's against the Bible to be cremated, but I don't care what anyone says. My son will not be stuck in that potluck box forever, he just won't. I love my aunt. She's one of my favorites. You wouldn't believe how much money she and her husband gave us to help with all the bills.

She's been a real doll through this whole thing, too. I'm glad I have her in my life, but Zeke was my son.

Entry #38

The viewing went really well. It was nice to finally play music for Zeke, you know, now that he's out of my belly and all. It was weird seeing him lying in the coffin. He didn't seem dead, just drugged, like he was for the last month or so, since he got pneumonia. We dressed him in that cute Scottish suit we bought him so many months ago. He looked really great in it. It came with a darling hat and everything, but the hat doesn't look Scottish, not really. It looks more like a sailing hat, and I thought it fit the occasion, seeing as how he's just set off on the greatest journey of all—while I'm still on the path to nowhere.

Family and friends (that I didn't even know we had) came to the viewing. They were full of well wishes and of kindness. Everyone brought something for Zeke, just as I'd requested. They put all of his gifts on a table next to him, and I smiled at all the wonderful things he got. My brother was there, and he gave Zeke a real film clip from the first Star Wars. My Uncle Wayne and Aunt Judy gave him a handmade fishing pole, and I smiled, thinking how Zeke would love fishing, just like I do.

My best friend came and sobbed really hard when she saw Zeke. She said she won't be able to come to the funeral because she can't bear it. She's such a strong person, and it was weird for me, seeing her so shook up about my boy. She hugged me hard and told me she's sorry for my loss and didn't know how we made it through. I didn't want to tell her, but I think the worst is still coming. I was okay as long as he was alive, but I don't know how I'll survive now that he left and took all of that hope with him.

Susan attended the viewing. I heard she's never been to one of the viewings or funerals for one of her patients before. She said none of the nurses really ever come to these things. Cade and I each gave her a hug, and told her and her husband, "Thank you."

Ruby noticed us hugging her and got curious. She danced up to Susan. Ruby had a little red dress on, and enchanted Susan's heart for a moment.... I know she did. Susan got to hear us play a few songs.

We've played for so many other viewings that we decided to play for Zeke's. After Susan heard us, she went on and on about how talented we are. That was nice of her. She gave us a beautiful card, and inside was fifty dollars. I blinked back tears when I opened it after the viewing. I still feel blessed that Zeke had Susan for a nurse.

We had the potluck "death home" do an open casket for Zeke, just until it was time to bury him. I wanted everyone to see how handsome our son is, because not very many people were able to come and see him at the hospital. We'll bury his casket with his treasures inside, and then sprinkle his ashes up in the mountains and over his grave. My aunt and mom still think we should bury him in his casket, but I can't think about that. For now, it almost seems like he's still with us, just really drugged, and in serious lack of oxygen.

Entry #39

Zeke's funeral was today. I had some special time with him before the service. I found myself singing to him like I used to. I tried putting my finger in his hand, but his hand was stiff and cold, and I couldn't fit my finger in. So, I just kissed him on the forehead and noticed how different he looked now that his spirit has passed. Finally, the potluck lady told us it was time for the funeral. We had his body placed in the front of the funeral room.

My aunt talked to me right before the funeral. She told me about her husband who died in a mining accident. It was really nice talking with her, and I think God planned it that way. She calmed me down just before the funeral, and I'm so thankful she talked to me.

When the funeral started, my grandpa gave the opening

speech. It was really good. He kept calling Zeke a choice son. I love how that guy talks. He calls me "sister" instead of Elisa, even though I'm his granddaughter and not his sister, or anything. It really got me how he kept calling Zeke a choice son. I liked it though. My grandpa is gold, pure gold. He thanked God for letting us know Zeke, and said, "This choice son was a fighter. He was strong, and willing to face the trials life laid before him. The day will come when we will return to your presence, Heavenly Father, and will reunite with your choice son, Zeke." He wrapped up his prayer soon after that, but those other words kept playing in my head, and I missed the last of his prayer. I didn't want to think about anyone else being reunited with God. I can't take it if more people start dying off now.

After my grandpa finished talking, my father-in-law sang a song called, "In the Garden." I wanted him to sing that song because, when my mom was two years old, her dad died, and one of the only things she remembers about the funeral is that song. I wonder if my mom's dad met Zeke yet. They're having a real laugh about the fact that the same song was sung at both their funerals.

My father-in-law did an awesome job. He could have been a famous musician, but wanted a family, instead, that's all. He has a rich voice, which carries and makes you half-way want to sing, and half-way want to dance, at the same time. Plus, he's really good on the guitar, and everyone always begs him to play when we have family get-togethers.

The song ended, and my mother-in-law spoke. She said, "My mother died on January seventh. On the third, when she still knew who I was, I asked her if little Zeke had to go and...she nodded. I asked her if she would watch over him for me." My mother-in-law stopped and wiped under her eyes before continuing. "She said, 'Yes,' and a tear rolled down her cheek. She loved babies, and one more wouldn't have been a burden to her at all." My mother-in-law looked over at my mom and smiled. "Zeke brought our families together. It's amazing how a little boy, who couldn't even speak, could bring so much love." She told about the many times when she'd go to the hospital and run into my mom. Then they would visit Zeke together. I remembered how my mom said she called Marie after we found out he had problems. They talked, cried, and laughed on the phone for hours. Zeke really did bring those two together.

It was Van's turn to speak, and he brought a prop with him. With little Ruby in his arms, he began talking from the podium. "Zeke wants you to take really good care of Ruby. This is what life is about, taking care of family. This kind of precious life is what makes it worth it." He let Ruby go back to her grandma, faced Zeke, and continued absently, "He always quieted right down when I hummed to him. He had music in him, just like Ruby does." My father-in-law stepped down slowly, and my mom took his place. She adjusted her fancy outfit, and stood straight, as she tilted the microphone.

"I'm so happy I had the opportunity to know my grandson." Her eyes scanned the crowd. "I'm richer for it and will never be the same." She read a tiny paper in her hands, and said, "Your reward in Heaven will be great, Zeke. You have run the good race and finished. You will always be in my heart, and no one will ever take your place." She looked at Cade and me, before whispering, "I love you!"

Cade and I sang a song to Zeke. It's a song Cade wrote for my mom but seemed profoundly appropriate for Zeke's funeral. We sang:

"When I lift up my hands to you, oh Lord,
You fill me with your light and joy.

Hear me out, oh Lord, Attend to my cry.
You are my El Shaddai.

I've found my most precious jewel.
Sustaining me, you satisfy my soul.

When we lift up our hands to you, oh Lord,
You fill us with your indescribable love.

Constant guide, advise us in our trials.
Through your love set us free.

Set us free,
Set him free!"

Cade sang the first part alone; I didn't harmonize until the second chorus. I played a violin solo, which flew through the middle of the song, and then sang quietly at the end, "Set him free." I left the stage, and Cade stepped up to the microphone. I've written down his entire speech so I could put it in here. It was really powerful.

"When I first found out I was having a boy," Cade cleared his throat, "I was in St. George. Elisa called me on the phone and told me how excited she was to have a boy, because that was what she'd always wanted. The next day was so great. Then, I got another phone call. They'd found some complications—something to do with his heart, but they didn't know. So, I came back, and we went to the University of Utah with Elisa's mom and dad.

"When they first told us his problems, it was hard to accept...it wasn't real. They did the chromosome test, and it came back okay. Rather than terminating the pregnancy, we decided to give him a chance. Every day Elisa would sing to him. We loved him as much as we could because we didn't know if he'd make it after he was born.

"Well, the day finally came that he was born. They said he'd probably pass in the first twenty-four hours, but he was still here, even after the surgery, weeks later. He seemed to be doing better, and then struggled for a bit. He had trials his whole life. At that point I remember wondering, 'Why does something like this happen?' I thought, 'He tried making an evolutionary leap for man, and just tripped, and didn't quite make it.' It was just yesterday that it dawned on me: he didn't trip, and he didn't fail; he changed every person he came across. And that was more of an evolutionary step for man than he ever could have made in any other way.

"He's the biggest hero of my life. I've never known someone who tried so hard to hang on. It seems to be the only reason he hung on wasn't for him...it was for us. He loved us so much...and his life had a meaning. I love him so much! I love you, Zeke."

I took my place at the piano and sang the song I wrote so many months before, the song to give Zeke strength, if he lived, and the song to play at his funeral, if he died. I played it with soul and emotion. When I fell into the last words, "Sorrow is around me, but it will never drown me. Our love will see me through," so many emotions swelled; my voice boomed high and strong. I felt my vibrant youth, and at the same time, my intense humanity. I sang to Zeke, and God and I know everyone in that room felt the power of those words, and the truth which they contained...his love will see me through.

After I finished singing, I walked over to the podium and spoke. My notes sat right in front of me, but rather than looking at them, I spoke from my heart. "You know, when you're going to have a baby?" I asked the audience, imploring them to see my side of this case. "Even from the time you're a little girl, you imagine how your baby will be, and all the things you'll do with them. You'll read books to them and love them with all your heart. I always wanted to teach my kids how to play music. It was really hard when we found out everything, because I couldn't do all the stuff I wanted to do with him. All those dreams crashed to the ground. I thought I lost my future, and kept asking, 'Where is my future going from here?'

"I had so many dreams for Zeke, but he accomplished far more than I ever wished he could have. In his two and a half months I think he did more in people's lives than I've done in my twenty years. He just had such a special feeling around him. I love him with all my heart. He blessed me so much while I went through this experience. I've grown up, and I don't know why he picked us to come to, but I feel like the luckiest person in the world because he was here," I motioned to Zeke, "for the last two and a half months. They've been the best months of my life.

"I remember before.... I had expectations. And then, after he was born," silence lingered as everyone waited for me to continue, "man! It was a happy day if he pooped." Laughter fell, and the mood softened a bit. "I learned to appreciate the small things, not just the huge ones. Every little moment in life matters, because it's just short...like that sentence from 'Dust in the Wind,' 'I close my eyes and the moment is gone.' It is so fast, and I want to appreciate every minute. Every minute is so beautiful—even the hard times, and the good times—every moment is so amazing!"

I looked at his little body, and then the ceiling. "Zeke, I want you to know I love you, and I'm so happy you came and were part of my life!"

My dad sauntered to the podium as I took my seat. He sniffled a few times, trying to clear his nose. He wore this awesome western outfit that looked like he'd stepped out for a gun fight. His black jacket hung past his knees, and he had cinched his real western tie with a silver clasp at his neck. Man, that guy has class. He always dresses to the hilt and is such a handsome man. "Dear Heavenly Father," he began. "Thank you for the many blessings you've given us." In that moment he changed the prayer, and instead of speaking to God, he spoke to Zeke, "It must have been such a sacrifice to come down here and know how short your stay would be. You must have known things weren't going to be easy for you, but I want you to know...your life wasn't in vain. You taught me so much. You taught us how to appreciate life and each other."

Then my father spoke to God again. "That reminds me of a song," he said, and I smiled, because my dad is full of so much personality that I can hardly believe it. I opened my eyes, even though I shouldn't have, because it was supposed to be a holy moment, but I figured since he talked to God about lyrics it'd be okay, just once. Everyone else had their eyes closed, and I noticed a couple of Zeke's nurses had come to the funeral, and Blake and Cammie were there, too. That meant so much to me. I smiled at my dad because I love him so much. I looked at the crowd again. I caught the potluck lady's eyes and hurried to close mine. I still can't believe she looked around, but then I thought about how I was such a hypocrite for thinking that, and how I should pray for forgiveness, in case God takes me to Heaven next.

I listened to my dad again and heard him paraphrasing words from "You'll Never Walk Alone."

"When you walk through a storm, hold your head up high, and don't be afraid of the dark. At the end of a storm is a golden sky," he cleared his throat. "So, walk on, walk on with hope in your heart and you'll never walk alone," he paused, "because we live in the hope that you are in Heaven with Jesus, and you'll never walk alone. I look forward to the days when we'll be with you. You'll never be forgotten."

The potluck lady stood then and said the service had ended. I said goodbye to Zeke, and then to his little body. The funeral attendants said it was time to take Zeke's body to be cremated. Cade and I took the casket and filled it with most of the gifts people had given to him. There were a few pictures of relatives, and several letters in the pile, which were all addressed to Zeke. Instead of keeping them, and reading them, I put them gingerly into the casket, and we closed the lid forever.

My mom bent and looked at the casket. I smiled at the tissue in her hand. If you ever need a glass of water, or a tissue, she's the one to ask. She's always prepared when it comes to those two things, and they both come in pretty handy when kids are around.

"Elisa," she said, "I'm so glad you're having him cremated. I understand now."

"You understand?" I asked.

"I can't stand thinking about them closing the lid on Zeke!"

"I know it!" I said and hugged her tight. "I love you, Mom." I smiled at her. "You look so nice, and your speech was really good."

"You liked it?" she asked.

"I loved it, and I think Zeke would have loved it, too."

When I walked away from the "death home," a couple of my mom's Pentecostal friends waited there. They both motioned for me to come over, and then one of them said, "It's too bad you lost your son. Just think, if you had more faith, he would still be alive." Cade grabbed me by the elbow and pulled me away to the car. I didn't even think to ask him why, but when I was in the car, I saw the redness of his face, and the anger just under its surface. I didn't say a word.

We drove in a long line to the cemetery. It was really cold outside when we got there, and Ruby had to be taken back into one of the cars. Cade and I helped shovel some of the dirt over Zeke's grave, and I found it interesting that the man helping us at the grave was born with a cleft lip. It had been fixed and everything, but I could still see the plain scar on his face. I didn't say anything, thinking how glad I am he's still alive, and that he grew to be a nice man who helps sad people at the cemetery.

I looked at Zeke's grave before leaving. We bought a nice stone for him. At the viewing a bunch of people gave us money. We got more money for our son dying, than we got for our wedding. It was sad in a way, but I was glad people helped us out, because all of the money still didn't cover the funeral costs, so both sets of our parents helped us with the additional expenses.

We have the sweetest, most supportive parents in the world. I love my in-laws. I swear they're so awesome, even if I wasn't totally head over heels for Cade, I still should have married him, just to be related to them.

Anyway, the stone we picked out is beautiful. It says:

111

The Golden Sky

Our Hero

We Will Love You Forever!

Part III
Lost

Entry #1

We moved to Colorado for a few months. Remember how Cade got a new job? Well, the company that worked in Montana is centrally located in Colorado. We moved there, even though my dad told me not to. He said I'm running away from my problems, but I said if I had to look at Zeke's baby room one more time, I would have a fit. He wants me to get over it, but it's not that easy.

I didn't tell him the real reason, though. I keep seeing a little boy in our house. He's not real, but sometimes I see him from the corner of my eye, and when I try to look at him, he disappears. My mother-in-law said maybe it's Zeke's ghost, but I can't stand thinking about that. The kid I've seen is perfect and healthy, everything I wanted Zeke to be. He's got cute blond hair, and I want to squeeze him. I think I'm losing it, and that's the real reason we went to Colorado, because I don't want to live in a nut house.

We listed our house for sale and got ready to skip town. Just before we left, the counselors (who saw us when I was pregnant with Zeke) stopped by the house. They brought a cute bear with a poem attached to it. I said thank you, and they're some of the best people I know. They saw our vehicle packed as full as it can get, and the "For Sale" sign in our yard. The taller one said, "But if you move, no one will know your history. It would be better if you stay here, where people know what you've been through."

"I make friends pretty quick," I said. "And this isn't something I want a ton of people knowing, anyway." But, when we were in Colorado, I realized they were right. I would be in a department store, and would end up bawling, right there in the aisle. I'd tell some poor schmuck how I had a kid who passed away, and then they'd practically have to hear my sob story. I swear, half of the time they didn't want to be there, but they'd stay anyway. They'd be a nice shoulder to cry on, and then they'd leave, and I'd never talk to them again. Yeah, that gift I had for making friends, it left me in Colorado, because no one wants to be around a sob story, that's why.

It was a long drive to Colorado, and I don't know why, but I held Zeke's ashes in my lap for most of the drive. I just wanted to feel like he was with us, even though he wasn't. And, the whole time we drove, I wished I would've held Zeke longer, before they took him off the vent for the last time. I replayed his life over and over in my head, and still wonder if we did the right thing, or if I robbed my son of his only chance: the one I had when I was his age, the chance to live, and not have my mom pull the plug and end my life. It's a crazy thing, feeling like a murderer. I hate it, but the feeling won't go away, and I don't think it will until we get his autopsy back and find out if we made a mistake.

Anyway, Cade's first job in Colorado was in this small gambling town. We stayed in the world's crappiest hotel. There was a hole in the wall by the heater. It got so damn cold at night. There was as much cold air coming from that hole as hot air from the heater; they mingled, becoming this rancid lukewarm stuff that stank of mold or something. My mother-in-law has family nearby, so she came to visit us. She saw the holey hotel, and nearly flipped out. She couldn't believe we'd stay in such a yucky place. I told her it wasn't all that bad, but I lied through my teeth. I had to sleep next to Ruby, just to keep her warm at night, and it wasn't very fun, because the kid kicks when she sleeps.

While we were in the gambling town, this guy Cade worked with asked if he could borrow a quarter from Cade. The guy popped it into one of the machines and won two-thousand dollars. That drove Cade wild because it was his quarter in the first place.

Cade took twenty dollars in quarters and practically threw them all away. He didn't come back from the casino with anything but empty pockets, and an end to his gambling addiction. I was proud he quit there because I've heard of people who didn't, and I thank God he's not one of them. I guess his co-worker is different from Cade, though. He's a real giver. He took that two-thousand and gave it back to the casino. It only took him a couple of weeks, but that guy isn't a cheerful giver.

We were in Colorado for about three months before Cade got fired. We ended up staying at his aunt and uncle's house, with his mom, for the last month. I think she didn't want us to stay in those crappy hotels anymore.

I love Cade's aunt and uncle. They showed Ruby the time of her life. They let her feed the cows—the ones they'll eat soon—and they also took us snowmobiling. Cade and I used the snowmobiles to herd the cattle. His uncle let me wear an awesomely orange face mask—the coolest thing ever—nothing is better than orange, honestly.

So, Cade needs a new job, and we had to come back home to that baby room I hate staring at all day. I guess Cade pissed off one of the mechanics, who just happens to be a big shot in the company. The owner—the same man who hugged Cade in Montana and cried with him—fired him without any notice. It was a good time, let me tell you.

The mechanic screwed up on the semi brakes because he never replaced the ones that burned up. When Cade drove down through the gambling town, he realized the brakes were completely gone. He couldn't slow down with his jake-brake and crashed the semi into a big pile of snow right next to the mountain. Cade's story didn't go over well with the mechanic, especially since it was his fault for not replacing the brakes in the first place. I think he fired Cade just to cover his blunder.

Now we're back in Utah, where everyone knows our history, and pitying eyes stare all around. The disappearing boy returned the second I got home. I wish he'd go away because I've never liked magic tricks. The day we arrived, our neighbors got together and gave us a neat Precious Moments figurine. It's of a little boy holding a heart. It's nice and everything, but it still makes me sad. The heart is crystal, and when the sun shines through it, the light reflects on the boy's chest. It's neat; I just think whoever made it was clever, that's all.

Can you believe Cade doesn't have a job again? They didn't want to give him unemployment, but he went and fought it. I guess the unemployment place thought Cade was right, because he's getting money now. It isn't very much, and we're struggling to make ends meet. I'm so sick of eating Top Ramen, and my wallet thinks mac and cheese is spendy. All I can say is, I'm glad Ruby likes cheap food, because that's all she's been eating lately. We could ask our parents for help, but they've already helped us so much, and they're going through a lot, as it is. I don't want them knowing how hard things are for us right now.

Entry #2

I keep seeing that little boy around the house, you know, the "disappearing act." Not all of the time, just every once in a while. Man, I must be going nuts. I don't know why, but I see him on the stairs, like he's trying to walk toward Zeke's room, but never makes it because I always look at him right before he's there, and then he disappears. It's making me sad, though, seeing that kid. That's how I pictured Zeke to look, and I wanted him to make it so bad. I guess I can't accept it! Zeke is gone, and now I'm seeing him in the house. My brain is going crazy and there's nothing I can do about it.

I know the "disappearing act" isn't real, and this isn't a wildly spiritual experience. I just can't handle things, that's all, and my damn imagination is trying to help me cope. But I hate my imagination right now. It's painful seeing the kid, and thinking how Zeke could have been, if the world wasn't imperfect and full of pain.

I told my mom about the little boy, and she said it's a demon. She doesn't believe in ghosts, and she said I should go in for prayer. I really didn't want to because I thought they'd think I was nuts. I went in, though, and the pastor of the church was nice. He said it's perfectly normal, what I'm going through, because I've lost something close to my heart. I guess I'm trying to fill the spot somehow.

117

I prayed with him then, even though I don't like praying since Zeke died. After we finished, the pastor asked, "Is there a reason you keep seeing him walking to Zeke's room?" I thought about it and told him how I'd wanted Zeke to come home and see the horribly cute baby room.

He said, "I think the image never makes it to the room since Zeke never did." I heard crying around the corner, and I figured the secretary had been listening. Before we left, she shot into the room, and gave me a hug. "You poor thing," she said, sobbing. She even gave me one-hundred dollars to go towards our medical bills. I tried giving it back to her, but she wouldn't take it. Isn't it amazing how nice people can be!

I felt better after we left the church. I'm glad I listened to my mom and went in for prayer. After we left, we drove over to the hospital, sat in the parking lot, and cried for a while. It was a yucky, sad moment, but I needed to do it. When I got home, I didn't see the "disappearing act" anymore.

Part of me is learning to let go, and it's sad because I don't want to lose my memory of Zeke, but I need to move on with my life. I have little Ruby to take care of, and my little boy doesn't need me like he used to—he doesn't need me at all, if you want to know the truth.

Entry #3

Cade's been hunting for a job, but I guess he wasn't a natural born hunter. He can't find a good job, and my dad can't hire him right now, since things are slow for his company. I know Cade's trying, and everything, but I wish he'd try harder. He's depressed, though, and I don't know how to help him. I'm trying to be happy, so he'll get motivated, but I think I'm driving him up a wall. He thinks I'm nagging him. I'm not, though, not really. I'm just offering a bunch of constructive criticism. He keeps looking through the want ads and saying, "They won't pay more than unemployment, and they won't, and they wouldn't...."

Well, I'm going to look for a job in the morning. I know I'll find something. I'm a damn good worker, and someone would be crazy not to hire me. I'm worth my keep.

I could work at a photography place. I'll go to one and see if they'll hire me. I bet they will. It will be fun to take pictures again. I'm crazy about pictures, especially of kids. Some kids can be snotty sometimes, and I don't like snotty kids, but it's still a paycheck, and that's what I'm after. I'll go apply tomorrow, and won't take "no" for an answer, because I can tell they'll be better off with me working there, and I'll let them know first thing.

Entry #4

I'm working at the photography place. It was a great job, for the first day. The lady who hired me paraded me around all of my coworkers. She'd say, "Now this girl, she's made to be a photographer. See how happy she is, and how her happiness rubs off on our clients." She was right, for part of the day, until a customer from Hell decided to come in.

This lady strutted into the store, and practically ordered me to take pictures of her baby boy. I didn't really mind, though, since it was my job. She sat her boy down and told him to smile, even though he's too little to talk. He wouldn't smile, but I was overjoyed, anyway, since his eyes were open. I clicked away.

We are only allowed to take six pictures, and then the shoot is over. So, I took five awesome pictures, and informed the lady there was only one picture left. She pulled the craziest pucker face you've ever seen, and said, "But he isn't smiling in any of those pictures."

"But those pictures were very precious," I pointed out.

She rolled her eyes and turned back to her son. "Okay," she said, "we'll just have to make this last picture count." We tried to get him to smile for over a half hour, and the whole time I was timed. I did everything for the baby boy. I put the duck on my head. I acted like it bit me. I even tried to put the thing in my mouth, but that baby didn't smile, not once. By the end of my charades the mother freaked out at her son, her handsome—

healthy—son. She screamed at him, "SMILE, DANIEL! I SAID, SMILE! SMILE, DAMN IT!" She had turned into a suburban mom-ster and I couldn't take it anymore.

I ran from the room, behind a backdrop, and cried. My boss found me, and instead of acting mean, she said, "I heard the whole thing. I haven't had a mother act like that in a few years. Are you okay?" I shook my head. "Oh, calm down, Honey. You need to get used to this. We have to deal with this sort of thing every once in a while. You'll learn how to handle it."

"You don't understand," I sobbed.

"Trust me. I do, Honey. She was horrible and rude to you and her baby."

"No, you don't understand!" I turned to her as I raised my voice. "My little boy died three months ago. I loved him, and—I wanted him to live." I paused for effect. "It makes me sick, seeing people treat their kids the way that lady did."

"Oh, Hon." Tears filled her eyes. "I'm so sorry. I didn't know."

"I can't figure why God would let her keep her son," I motioned to the other room, beyond the backdrop I hid behind, "and why He took mine. I would never, ever, treat a child, let alone a baby, like that."

"I don't know," she whispered, more to herself than to me.

"I can't do this." I fell flat of emotion. "I'm so sorry. I hope I haven't wasted your time, but I can't do this right now."

I walked from behind the backdrop, and the suburban mom-ster stood waiting. Makeup ran freely down her face, and she mouthed, "I'm so sorry," as I passed her, but I didn't have time for her just then. I grabbed my purse and keys before walking from the building, like it was on fire. I never want to go to that photo place again, ever.

Entry #5

I called the lady who had a little girl that died. I told Cammie I can't handle things, and I'm losing it. We cried on the phone together. I said, "This is so much harder than when he was alive!"

"I know, Elisa," she said. "No one knows how hard it is after. It's amazing how everyone forgets and moves on so quickly. It's almost been a year since Josie died."

"I'm so sorry!" I wanted to say more but stopped because lately I hate when people try relating to me, or go on about their own problems, when I need to vent about Zeke. "I wish I could've been with her longer. She wasn't alive very long."

"I can't imagine how hard," I said, even though I had a bit of an idea.

"One of my relatives called me the other day, and I told her about you."

"I'm sure that was a fun story to tell," I laughed sarcastically.

"You wouldn't believe what she said."

"What?"

"She said," Cammie paused and took a breath, "you had it so much worse than me."

"What?"

"She said you got more attached to your baby. You had to pull the plug, and that was worse."

"Why do people always have to compare? What you went through was horrific. You hardly got to spend time with your baby." Anger weaved into my words.

"I can't believe some of the things people say."

"I can't either. I wish people would stop comparing and trying to make things better. I think they mean well, but it makes things worse, and when Zeke died, I didn't think things could get worse."

"I know what you mean," she said, and her voice shook like a leaf in the wind.

Entry #6

We stayed the night at Cade's parents' house. They live a couple of hours from us, and when we visit, we usually end up staying the night. I love visiting with his mom, and she's an amazingly good cook. Oh! Her food tasted so good! It was like heaven to me. I smiled at Ruby after asking her what she wanted to eat. She said, "Oatmeal!" That kid cracks me up. You'd think she'd be sick of oatmeal by now. She missed out on some damn good noodle casserole, too!

Cade wanted to come over so he could play computer games with his older brothers. They both still live at home, and Cade has fun playing with them. They stay up all night and have a really good time. I talked to one of Cade's brother's last night and found out he's in a band. I told him he should ask Cade to be in the band, too. Maybe Cade would be happy and feel more like getting a job.

When I visited with my mother-in-law, we talked about the "disappearing act." I told her I haven't seen him in my house since I went to church. She smiled, and said she's seen ghosts before, too. I nodded to be nice but didn't agree. I know that boy was a figment of my imagination. I know it with ever fiber I have. My mind was coping.

Anyway, she said a couple of months ago her mother visited her in the middle of the night. "She sat down on the foot of my bed, and you know what she said?" my mother-in-law asked.

"What?" I took the bait.

She said, "'Everything will be okay,' and then she was gone."

I cried after the words registered, and I told Marie all about what happened right after Zeke died, and how he said those exact same words, and of anything else that's ever happened to me, I know that moment was real. We cried together and gave each other a hug.

"They're right, you know," she said. "Everything will be okay."

Entry #7

I got another job, if you want to call it a job. I'm modeling, because there aren't a ton of chicks with spiked, black cherry hair. A lady told me it's a great way to make money. So, I gave it a shot, and they paid for my pictures, and everything. I asked if they could take pictures of Ruby, but they said I'd have to pay for those. I guess I'll think about it.

I've already gotten a couple of jobs, and they didn't pay too badly, but it sucks, because it cost me a lot in gas, getting to the auditions, and I had to pay for copies of my head shots, and stuff. Anyway, I modeled for a little magazine, and they put a picture of me on their wall. In the picture I'm leaning against a brick background, and have a fitted, daisy dress on. It's an okay picture, and I'm not sure why they like it. I have a ton of makeup on, and look really fake, but at least I got some money.

My second gig was today. All of the models met the camera crew in a new development area. Developers plan on putting a bunch of houses there soon, even though it has its own ecosystem. I stood from my car and was shocked to see a mega swamp. It wasn't the happy place you'd imagine for a photo shoot. No, it was grimy and dirty. I thought how much fun it would be to play in the mud, if I wasn't there to model. I rolled my eyes at the thought of posing. I've never been much of a girly girl.

Pussy willows hung out around the mud, and the main photographer practically loved pussy willows, or something. After everyone got out of their cars, a girl did our makeup. Then, the main photographer sent us to a little port-a-potty the construction crew must have used. That was where we changed. I couldn't believe I'd landed a modeling job, and how unglamorous it felt.

There were eleven other girls there, enough to make an even dozen, and out of all of the other girls, only one of them was nice to me. The other ten reminded me of Piranha, and they were the most gorgeous Piranha I've ever seen. They walked with their butts perked, and their boobs out, at the same time. I watched them in amazement, because I can only stick out one set of curves at a time, but those girls can multitask like you wouldn't believe.

I was the first girl to change, because the other girls were so puked-out about changing in a port-a-potty, but port-a-potties don't bother me. I've been around them before. I pulled on my swimsuit, and felt weird, walking out in front of those gorgeous models. The nice girl grabbed me by the shoulder and pulled me away from the Piranha. She said, "I think you can use these more than me." She handed me two huge water bra pads. I took them and they smushed under my grip.

"Thanks," I said with a smile, even though I wondered if I should be offended. I turned away from everyone and stuck them in my bikini top. "Wow," I said, because my chest didn't look like it belonged to a little boy anymore. "I've got boobs!"

She asked me if I've ever used padding before, and I told her, "No."

"Where did you get these from, France or something?" I asked.

"Actually," she blushed, "I got them from Walmart."

I tried stifling an embarrassed laugh, and told her, "Thanks." She went to the end of the port-a-potty line. The other girls hadn't saved her place, and made her go to the back, since she'd stepped out to help me.

A camera guy saw me emerge toward the swamp and pointed for me to enter a clearing in the pussy willows. I stood in the middle, and he had me do all sorts of funny poses.

He said, "Look at me like you love me," and I gave him a crusty, but I guess you don't have to be very bright to be a photographer, because he didn't take my hint. Instead, he said, "Oh, that's sexy," but it wasn't, and I wanted to punch him. As I stood posing, I thought how guys always want women to be what they're not. They want a woman to hate them before they love them, and stay away when they want to be close. Some men drive me crazy. I'm glad I'm married to my sweetheart, and I don't have to worry about jerky guys anymore.

When I finished, the flirt gave me a check. I put my clothes on over my swimsuit because I was so cold, I practically shook. I'd only gotten a little bit of mud on my clothes and was proud of myself as I stood by the nice girl at the end of the line.

I wasn't chained there or anything, but I stayed, since I felt bad she was at the end of the line because of me. I handed my fake boobs to her, and then shot the bull for a while.

She's twenty-seven and said she's super lucky to have landed this job, because a lot of people turn her down when they find out how old she is. I told her I couldn't believe she's twenty-seven. She looks like she's eighteen, and her boobs haven't fallen off yet. Plus, she's about a century away from menopause. She laughed, and even snorted, when I said that. It was funny hearing a pretty girl snort. I don't know why, but it hit me weird, and I noticed it must have hit the other girls strange, too, because they stopped talking and stared at her.

We talked for a bit, and she told me she has two kids, and then asked if I have any kids. I was silent for a minute, and she looked at me all strange while I struggled with what to say. I didn't want to bring Zeke up, but knew I'd betray him if I didn't say I had a son, a dead son, who can never come back. I picked up little pieces of the Piranha's conversation while I was silent. One girl wasn't happy with her hair, another girl hated her butt, and another girl "could just die," because she hates outhouses. I felt bad listening like that, but those girls annoyed the hell out of me, as I stood thinking about Zeke, for about the millionth time.

I looked at the nice girl, and had apology written in my eyes. I said, "Yeah, I have a couple of kids. A beautiful baby girl, and a baby boy who went to Heaven."

"Your son died?" she asked, full of pity, as the Piranha's superficial conversations died.

I thought about how my sister told me Zeke's playing soccer with Jesus, and tried thinking about that, so I wouldn't cry and show all those girls what a mess I am.

"Oh my gosh!" one of the Piranha said. She was super tall, and I felt like a midget, a really sad midget. "I totally know what you're going through," she said, and I raised my eyebrows at her statement. "I actually had a miscarriage the other day, and it was pretty bad."

"Wow...that..." I struggled, not knowing what to say to the bimbo who knew nothing of my pain. "That sucks," I finished, and left with tears in my eyes because the bimbo had no idea what I'd been through with Zeke, and because I hate it when people tell me they know how I'm feeling. No one really knows or understands, exactly, no one but Cade. I wish I could talk to him about things, but he's too damn busy forgetting.

As I walked away, I heard the tall Piranha—the one who wanted to relate to me and my dead son—I heard her say, "How rude was that? What's her problem?" But no one answered her, so she continued, "Maybe she's just upset about her shirt. It's so ugly!"

I thought about poking her in the eye, just for the hell of it, but then decided that wouldn't be nice, and went to my car instead.

So, to make a long story short, I modeled for a swimsuit calendar. I'm actually embarrassed about it and won't even tell Cade. He has enough going on right now, anyway. I bet he won't ask what I did today because he couldn't care less. I'm not sure what month I'll be, but I hope it's February, because February is the coolest thing ever. I'd absolutely hate it if I got January, because that's when Zeke died, and it would make me sad. I wouldn't want to have my mug on his death month, and all. I just wouldn't like that.

My mom watched Ruby while I modeled. I didn't tell her I modeled in my swimsuit. I was too embarrassed, I guess. She didn't ask me, anyway, and I don't think it's always a crime to leave out information, especially if you think the person would be better off not knowing.

I picked Ruby up, and we cashed my modeling check. I drove right to the store, and we got sausage, and ground beef, and all sorts of yummy things. I made a stately dinner. It was really good, and a bit wasteful, because I shouldn't have eaten so much in one sitting. If I wouldn't have eaten so much, we could have saved it, as a side, for a few more days. Ruby even turned down the "oatmeal option" because she wanted some more sausage. You wouldn't believe how much we both ate.

It was awesomeness personified, but Cade didn't come tonight, and I feel bad. He was supposed to come home and eat dinner with us, but he stayed at band practice, instead. They practice about two hours away from our house, and he's been spending a ton of money on gas to get there. I guess I feel bad he didn't come home because I told him what we were eating, and he said he'd be home.

But he stopped by his mom's, ate there, and stayed the night. He's in the same band that his brother's in, the same one I suggested he should join. He's their singer, or something, and has been at band practice a lot lately. He ends up staying so late he just stays the night at his parents' house and gets to eat their good food. I'm sure he isn't even forced to take the "oatmeal option," not like Ruby and I are. I miss him a lot, but hope he's feeling better, and will get a job soon, so we can all eat like he eats every night, at his mom's house.

Entry #8

They got the pictures back for the calendar. The main camera guy asked if he could take me to dinner and show me the photos. I said, "No thanks," in the nicest tone I could, and then hung up. I'm curious to see the pictures, but don't want to if it means dinner with him. I don't need to see them that badly.

I've tried out for a few more modeling gigs but haven't gotten another one yet. I went to a singing audition the other day. Can you believe there were over two-hundred people there? I had to get a babysitter, and by the time it was finally my turn, I'd been there for over two hours. I just don't know if this is working. I want to do something where I can still be with Ruby, but this is a hit-and-miss business, and I need to pull in a steady paycheck, if

Cade won't get a regular job soon.

Today, when Cade was actually home, we snuggled on the couch and watched Ruby play. I asked if he's looking for another job.

"Of course," he said. "I've just been busy with the band."

"I know," I told him, "but we're really struggling." I nuzzled my head into his arm because he felt warm and cozy; it was nice he was home.

"We're doing okay," he told me. "We have each other."

"Yeah," I smiled, "but we're barely making ends meet. I can't stand living this way when we can be doing something...different. I've decided to look for a steady job. But I need you to be home, so you can watch Ruby. Okay?"

"You don't need to get a job!" he said and stood. "The band will get more gigs soon, and then we'll have a ton of money."

"Cade, be realistic! After you all split the money from your last gig, you made twenty dollars!"

"That was the last gig. We'll start making more, I promise."

"We made more money playing together." It was the truth, and he needed to hear it.

"Just give the band some time, Elisa. We might end up being famous someday. Have you heard the crap they play on the radio? Our band is way better than that!"

"You're better than some, but to get picked up, and go on tours: it's just not a family life, Hon. And the odds of it happening are really slim."

"If I become famous, neither of us will have to work again. We can travel around the world and do whatever we want." As he talked, I looked over at our empty kitchen pantry.

"Wow," I said in mock awe. "How fun..."

"Why can't you be supportive?"

"Because," I took a breath, "we barely have enough money to make the house payment, and you refuse to get a job!"

"I'm not refusing—"

"Well," I interrupted, "you sure as hell aren't trying very hard, are you? I heard you talking on the phone the other day." I talked in a low voice like Cade, "I'd like to take the job, but I need to be off by at least three every day. I can't work weekends, and I might need to take some weekdays off if my band needs to practice and—"

"The band," he hurled the words at me, "is going to be famous someday, Elisa. Just be supportive!"

"Even if it does go somewhere, someday, that's not a life I want for our family."

"It's what I've always wanted!"

"What is?" I asked.

"To be a famous musician."

"Well, then, you should have thought about that before you knocked me up!" I yelled so loud, Ruby stopped what she was doing, and she looked at me, like a deer in the headlights.

I picked her up, and hugged her tightly, as the front door slammed.

"Daa daa?" Ruby pointed and asked.

"Yes, DAA DAA," I punched the words out.

"Daa daa?" Ruby had practically turned into her own echo, or something.

"He's gone to practice again." I picked up the newspaper. "It's time for Mama to get a job, Honey. Daddy doesn't want me to, but I don't give a damn anymore."

Entry #9

I got an interview at a cute little diner. Yesterday my mom took me shopping for an outfit. I've lost a ton of weight since Zeke died, and hardly any of my clothes fit, but it's all right; now I know what it's like, living without a shadow. We picked out a cream dress and jacket set. It looks really good on me when I wear my padded bra, and I sure hope it'll help me get the job. My mom insisted on buying it, and that was great of her, because every dime we have counts right now.

My mom watched Ruby today so I could go to the interview. She made us some Swedish meatballs, and I'm excited to eat them. My mom is such a doll. I guess that's why I named my first kid after her, because I want Ruby II to be like her. My mom had a really crappy childhood. I wish I could have been her mom because I would have loved and taken care of her, just like her mom should have, but her mom was an idiot. I don't even call that lady "Grandma;" I call her Rose—instead of something else—just to be nice.

Rose was really good at being selfish, though; at least she was good at something. She left my mom and her siblings, and I'm not sure why. My mom was just a toddler when Rose left for a man. It just amazes me that my mom grew up to be so wonderful, no kidding.

She's one of the most amazing people you'll ever meet. You'd like her, if you met her because she's gold, pure and sweet. Every time I ask someone what they think about my mom, they say she's the kindest person they've ever met, and they're not joking, because she's really considerate, and always around with cold water or a tissue, when someone needs one. That's why I named my kid Ruby, since I love my mom, and I always want to be there, and give Ruby II exactly what my mom didn't have growing up—love.

I interviewed and am pretty sure I got the job. I don't think I got it because of my previous experience, even though I was super professional during the interview. It's, honestly, because I could tell the creepy owner was attracted to me. He practically undressed me with his eyes, and I hated every minute of the interview. I drove home and couldn't believe how someone that handsome could be so yucky. When I imagine sleazy guys, they're ugly and pimply. Well, this guy wasn't, and I can't get over how gross he made me feel while we sat there, talking about my hours of availability.

I'll take the job if I get it, though. I really need that job. I know I'll make a bunch of money working there, and it's close to my house. I asked if they could give me the graveyard so I can be with Ruby during the day. Then Cade can stay with her at night. That way he can still be in his precious band, while Ruby and I avoid the "oatmeal option," and afford diapers.

Entry #10

I got the job, and it's hella fun. Our moms watch Ruby for me, so I can work. Cade's been practicing with the band and hasn't really taken care of our baby girl. Ruby's getting close to Marie, and accidentally called me grandma the other day. It broke my heart in one-hundred pieces. I don't want my kid replacing me, but I feel good, knowing she's taken care of, and I'm doing the right thing.

I enjoy being a waitress because I love the customers. I can't believe I'm having fun, and making money, too. Last night I made over two-hundred dollars, and some of the waitresses seem ticked about it, but if they only knew how badly I need this money, maybe they wouldn't be so mad. I think God is blessing me, and I don't know why He's showing me His favor. I'm not doing anything differently from when I hoped Zeke would live.

I work the graveyard, and Marie comes all the way to our house and stays with Ruby. It's funny; she's been staying here while her boy is back at her house. I don't know why Cade thinks "trading places" is so awesome, but apparently, he does. I like working the graveyard. I meet all the happy drunks, just after the bars close. Then, I see them again when they get coffee, and sober up in the morning. It's just a damn good thing I like them, that's all.

Last night was fun. Old Slim struggled, because he'd had a few too many, and stumbled all around the place. He knocked over a pitcher of water on a dirty fellow who thought he'd wet himself. I was thankful "wet pants" didn't get mad.

I went to the drink station and grabbed the coffee, since a few people needed to be topped off. Wet pants followed me like a lost puppy dog. He made crude jokes and laughed at them. Then, suddenly, he turned sad, and talked about a little girl he'd lost custody of. He said his wife had left because she said he drank too much.

"Me? Drink too much?" He pointed a crooked hand at his own chest. "Never!" he bellowed. "And she took my little girl away, and now I never get to see her!"

I smiled at him and patted his shoulder with my free hand. "You'll see your girl again. When she grows up and realizes how much you love her."

"You know," he paused and put his hand to his chin, "she's about your age. How old are you?"

"I'm twenty," I said, topping off someone's coffee before asking if they needed anything else.

"She's barely eighteen," he said. "I can't believe you're almost the same age as my daughter. I feel so old." He looked down at his grimy, wrinkled hands.

I laughed then, because I feel leagues older than eighteen, but I didn't say anything. "I bet she's a beautiful girl. And she's probably got a lot of charm."

"I hope she's just like you!" Wet Pants said. "No, really, I do! I hope she's just like you." A crocodile tear painted a mud trail on his cheek, and I frowned, thinking how lucky he is that she isn't just like me, because if she was, he'd have a grandson in a grave.

I turned away as fast as I could. I even lost a tiny bit of coffee as I spun and walked behind the counter.

"How can you talk to them like that?" one of the waitresses asked me.

"Like what?" I was confused and thought about Zeke again.

"Like you really care about them," she whined. "I've tried your little game, and I don't know how you do this, night after night. I wish I could pull it off, because then I'd make as much as you do."

"I do care about them!" I said. "You care?" she snorted. "Maybe about the money."

"It wouldn't matter if I made a dime," I said. "I love these people. They're good people!"

"You love them?" Jody asked me sarcastically. "You love that homeless guy you just talked to?" She put one hand on her hip, and the other hip popped up like toast jumping from a toaster.

"Yeah, I do." I thought about explaining further, but then shook my head.

"Why? Why should you care about him?" She still didn't get it.

But, since she'd practically given me her written consent to continue, I said, "Because he's the same as me and you."

She gasped and put her fake-nailed hand on her chest. "He's not the same as me."

"Sure, he is. God made us all, didn't He?" I looked at her and thought of Zeke for a moment. I thought about God spending special time on each one of his imperfect details. "Bimbo Barbie" still didn't get my point.

I felt annoyed and said something she might actually understand. "At the end of the day we all have to piss and poo in the same pisser!" I walked away.

"Eww!" she was horrified, and I loved it. That was the best time I'd had all night, making that prissy girl shudder.

Entry #11

Cade and I went hiking today. We found a pretty stream, which has a huge mountain for a neighbor. On top of the mountain sits a cliff that's practically made to give the stream shade. We hiked there to sprinkle Zeke's ashes off the cliff. I thought how he'd love floating down all freestyle from that cliff, just flying in the wind. It wasn't a hard hike, and we stood on the cliff before we knew it. We both lay on our stomachs and were quiet for a long time. I heard some birds singing, and the sun felt good on my back and legs. I looked over at my shadow and noticed it had mingled with Cade's. I felt really close to him, glad he was the person next to me and not someone else.

I took a handful of Zeke's ashes and felt a crazy impulse

133

envelope me. I was sad, and happy—and lonely—all at the same time. I felt my world collapse, even though there was still so much room to breathe on top of that mountain. I held my palm out flat in front of me, and his ashes sat there in an orderly little pile; it seemed like they'd always waited for that moment.

I closed my eyes and blew. If someone didn't know, they would have thought I blew an eyelash, and made a wish. I didn't blow an eyelash, though; I sent my son away forever, because I knew this was something he would have wanted. I opened my eyes and watched as his remains spiraled down. Some of them fell silently into the stream, and others got caught by the wind. They danced for a minute before separating and drifting from my blurred vision forever.

Then, Cade held the little maroon sack that held the rest of Zeke's ashes, and he turned it upside down. We watched as a bunch of the ashes descended, seeking the peace of gravity. Cade didn't dump all of the ashes, though, and said he wanted to keep some of them to bury at Zeke's grave. He thought both our moms would appreciate that.

I told Cade Zeke would love this place, and then I cried. But the beauty around took my breath away, and it's hard to cry if you can't breathe. So, I stopped, and laid my head down on the stone surface. I pretended to be a part of the mountain: strong and unyielding to anything but God and time.

The trip down the mountain seemed a lot longer. I guess it's because we wandered off the trail, and while we walked, I saw a cougar. That's the only time I've ever seen a cougar in the wild, and it really scared me. I just saw its eyes, at first, and couldn't believe how good it blended in. It was only about twenty feet away when I saw it, and instead of attacking, it just stayed majestically. Cade saw it, too. We looked at each other for a minute, and both got nervous; we didn't have anything to defend ourselves with.

But, when we tried looking back at the cougar, we couldn't see the face anymore, and decided the beast must have left. That freaked me out, because it didn't even make a sound; at least I couldn't hear it. We practically ran down the mountain after that, and at one point, a rabbit jumped out in front of me. Cade laughed really hard when I screamed, but I thought it was a cougar, and I didn't think it was funny. I could have died if it was the cougar.

We finally made it to the car. I looked back toward the mountain and its beautiful cliff. I hope Zeke's glad we picked this place for him. It's a special place to us because it's where we got married, the first time, before I was old enough for it to be completely legal. We thought it fit because Zeke was born on our anniversary.

At least he can watch the animals if he gets bored. I wonder if that cougar meant something, but more than anything, it makes me mad we had such a beautiful moment sending Zeke away forever, and then that cougar showed up and scared the snot out of me. I've always wanted to see something like that in the wilderness, just not now, that's all.

I hope part of Zeke will always be with us, always watching us like that cougar probably did, the whole time we were on the mountain. But I can't help feeling a piece of me is gone now. I want to turn around and run back. I've left something very important behind, but I know I can never get it back. Even if I hunt for eternity—gather all those ashes and carry them with me forever—the pain won't stop. It seems like nothing will make the pain stop, and I wonder if anything ever will.

Entry #12

I had a hard weekend. Cade only came home one night, and we fought the entire time. I was a nag, and know it's my fault, but I won't apologize, not completely. I asked him if he could do the laundry, since I've been working so hard.

Cade's not the best at doing laundry, but I figured it wouldn't hurt him to help out. He put some red clothes in with the white ones, and now all of Ruby's clothes are pink. It's a damn good thing she's a girl.

I switched the laundry, and while I did, I found a used diaper in the load. It was just a pee pee, but still disgusting.

I brought it to Cade, and when I asked him who in the hell taught him how to do laundry, I noticed he was on the phone with his cousin, "King Arthur." When he got off the phone, he was in the worst mood, ever. He preached about how women shouldn't be nags.

"Is that what 'King Arthur' told you?" I asked, and Cade cringed when I said "King Arthur."

"Yeah, it is, but I agree with him."

"And you think I'm a nag?"

"I don't just think you're a nag," he said, and a smirk played across his face as he stretched out on our bed.

"Why don't you tell 'King Arthur' to stay out of our problems? He has enough of his own. Does he still think I'm Guinevere? Or is he on his quest, looking for her?"

"Oh, he found her. He realized she's not you," Cade bit into the words. "He said she's the girl he's been living with all this time."

"What a relief." I put my hand to my chest, and mocked Cade with my eyes. "I must say, I love the people you surround yourself with." I spied the laundry basket while I talked to him. "Since you think I'm such a nag, I better play the part. Who taught you how to do the laundry?"

"I don't know, but I'm the one who taught you." He rolled over and acted like he wanted to sleep.

"Well, I must have been a natural, or something, 'cause you're not very good at it. Cade? Are you listening to me?" He looked at me. "All of Ruby's clothes are pink because you put my red sweater with her white clothes. If you can't do the laundry right, don't do it at all!"

"I'm sorry, Elisa. I'm trying to help, but it's never good enough for you. You always think I'm doing something wrong. I bet you even think Zeke was my fault." He pierced me with his look.

"I would never think that!" I said.

"Yeah, you do, and I know your family does." He was serious.

"They do not, but your family thinks that about me." I paused. "I even think it about me, sometimes."

"What do you mean?" He sat up then. "How could Zeke...be your fault?"

"I don't know," I said. "Maybe I shouldn't have cleaned so much. All of those cleaning supplies might have done something to him."

"You hardly ever cleaned when you were pregnant. What are you talking about?"

"What? You don't think I cleaned?" I asked.

"Here we go; I didn't mean it like that!" Cade tried hugging me. "Elisa, I just want to make everything better."

"Yeah, you did, Cade, by saying I never clean!" I pushed him off. "You don't think I'm worth my keep, like I'm just some lump on a log, or something."

"I don't think you're a lump on a log."

"Yeah, you do," I reeled. "And what's funny about that is I'm the one with the job!"

"Do your own laundry from now on," he said, jumped back into our bed, and pulled the pillow tightly over his head.

He's sleeping right now. Ruby is playing with her toys by me, and I've been thinking about Zeke. I realized something while talking to Cade. I blame myself for Zeke's defects, and I blame myself for his death. In one reckless decision I let my son die, and now he can never come back. It's like he's stuck somewhere in a hole, and God won't let him out. My tears can't draw him from the grave, and God certainly won't return him to me. He didn't even let him be born healthy in the first place. I feel at a loss for everything and think my entire foundation might crumble. Is it worth trying to fix what's broken?

I couldn't believe Cade wanted to hug me today. He hardly

ever does that anymore. He thinks I've got the Bubonic Plague, or something. I've looked at him, my eyes full of love, but he doesn't return my gaze. Then, today, he suddenly wanted a hug, and expected me to come running, when he usually pretends I don't exist. Maybe I should apologize, but then he'd have the upper hand. I don't want to give in, not when he's hurt me so badly. I remember when Ruby used to make him laugh, and now she has a hard time making him smile. The Cade I married isn't here anymore. He left, somehow, and I feel like a lonely, jaded kid. I'm unwanted by my own husband.

At least Ruby loves me. She clings hard when she knows it's time for me to go to work. She loves her grandmas but is so attached to me lately; she doesn't want me to leave the room. I don't mind, though, because after Zeke died, I share her opinion. Life is uncertain, and I want to be with her all of the time, too. I'm scared God will take us from each other. I think Cade is already lost to me, and I can't stand losing Ruby, too. We can go at any time, and don't know when. Sooner or later death will come and take what it owns. And death owns life. I hold Ruby close each night, praying God will let us keep each other for a long time. That's all of my little family I have now: she and God.

Entry #13

I wish I could throw my heart away because it's hurting so badly. My dad has colon cancer again! I love my dad, and I can't stand this! What if he dies, just like Zeke did? I need my dad more than Zeke does, I really do! Why in the hell is all this happening? I wanted to be an adult so badly, back when I ran away to Hawaii and all. Now is it okay if I just want to be a kid again, a carefree kid who doesn't even know death exists? I was dumb and happy—before all this.

A few years ago, when I was a kid, I imagined what adult life would be like, but this is not what I pictured. It was all happy, rainbow crap, and there were birds, lots of birds, always singing joyful songs, not the stinking songs of death, for crying out loud!

Looking back, I remember this one time, when I was about five. I went into an old camping trailer, because there was some really great cherry taffy in the closet. I thought if I hurried, I could sneak some, and no one would ever find out.

Well, I found the taffy in the closet, and then the closet door shut really hard behind me. I couldn't get out of the thing, and it felt like I was in there forever. The only consolation was the taffy, and a game of pick up sticks I found, but it was too dark to play the game. I bawled myself out before sticking a big glob of cherry taffy into my mouth. I'd be happy until the crap vanished, and then I'd remember why I had cried in the first place.

It was a sucky feeling, being stuck in that closet, even though my favorite candy was there. That's what I feel like now: trapped, and there's no place to go. At least Ruby's my cherry taffy! I want someone to save me from this sadness, but I won't pray to God. I still love Him, and everything, but there's no point in praying. He'll do whatever He should, regardless of what I pray. And maybe it's selfish, trying to sway the Almighty. Why should He listen to me, anyway? I'm just like an ant, or something, compared to Him.

Entry #14

Cade actually came home tonight. It was super late when he walked in, and I was dead asleep, or at least I acted like it. "Elisa." He shook me. "Elisa, we need to talk."

"What, do you want?" I pretended like I just woke up, but in a really mad way.

"You never have time for me, anymore. All you do is sleep your life away." He kicked off his dirty boots and flopped down next to me.

"I'm tired, Cade! I have a job! You're the one who doesn't have time for me. You're hardly ever home. I've been working my butt off, while you're having the time of your life," I rattled on, reminding myself of a crummy, old typewriter.

"Is that what you call it? Ever since we've started fighting, the music sucks. I can't get my head into it. I can't do this unless we're getting along," he said.

"Why is that my problem? You're never here, Cade. And now you want to get along so your precious band can succeed?"

"That's not what I meant," he said, "and you know it."

"I don't know if I do." I rolled over to face him. "What do you mean?"

"I just want to be happy, like we used to be." He looked sad.

"I don't know if we'll ever get that back, Cade." His features were so handsome in the dim light.

"I know," he said. "I don't think things will ever be the same, not since Zeke died."

"I just wish you'd talk to me about Zeke," I said.

"I won't go there, Elisa...not tonight." He broke on the last words.

"Okay," I said, and turned my back to him.

Entry #15

Today I thought about my past and remembered how I ran away with Cade. It's a funny story, really. It wasn't then, but it's hella funny now. It all started with me dating this famous prophetess' son. I was excited to date that guy because I thought he was a good Christian. He preached in Utah when he met me, and for some weird reason, he picked me out of the crowd. I think it's because he heard me playing the violin. Well, anyway, he liked me, and drove from Colorado to Utah, just to see me again.

I really liked the guy, at first, until I found out he drank and smoked pot when he wasn't behind the podium at church. I hate hypocrisy, and drugs of any kind. The whole thing made me sick. I still had a butt-load of respect for his prophetess mother, though, until she announced that God showed her that I would cheat on her son.

Afterward, I realized sometimes hypocrisy is genetic. I broke up with the dirt bag and questioned the whole church thing. I still have a hard time listening to preachers of any religion. I wonder if hypocrisy runs in their families, too. I should focus on God, not his conduits.

Shortly after that, I met Cade. I married him, and it wasn't legal because my parents wouldn't sign the papers; but as soon as I turned eighteen it would be legal. It's funny, because "King Arthur" has his minister's license. He's the one who performed the ceremony, before he thought he was "King Arthur." But he didn't want Cade marrying me, and that's when I knew I didn't like that guy.

Anyway, the leaders at the church I attended decided I was possessed, because I was with an unbeliever, and wasn't legally married. They did an exorcism on me. It was really wild. You should definitely have one done some time. It's guaranteed to be something you won't forget...ever!

The lead exorcist made me sit in a dinky, pea-green kid's chair. I don't know why I wasn't worthy of an adult one, but I wasn't.

I closed my eyes and prayed because, being the schmuck I was, I actually wondered if I was possessed, because those all-knowing nuts told me so. Looking back, I know I was just possessed with stupidity! The lead exorcist said, "Open your eyes, demon!" over and over, until he practically shook me, and yelled, "OPEN YOUR EYES!"

"They're open, they're open," I finally yelled, quite scared. My eyes captured him, and in an ominous drawl, he said, "What's your name?"

"Ummm.... Elisa?" I said.

"No! Not you! The demon!"

"Oh," I whispered, "Sorry."

"What is your name, demon?" He grabbed me by the shoulders, and leaned on me, because the chair I sat in was so low to the ground. "I'm going to need everyone's help with this one." Everyone put their hands on me and prayed. I remember thinking how strange it was that each hand was a different temperature. I focused on that for a while, just trying to escape from the moment.

"What's your name?" His grip got harder, and my left shoulder actually hurt. "What is your name?" I started disliking the person with the iron grip and thought how the most evil presence in the room was his breath. I felt bad, and then judgmental! I felt...self-righteous!

"Self-righteousness," I said.

"Oh bate' joomba!" someone yelled, and don't even ask how I remember that phrase. I heard it so many times that night, it's almost engraved on my forehead.

"Hallelujah, Jehovah!" the bad breath exorcist said. "I know there are more in there. Tell us your names!" he continued.

"Tell us! Tell us! Tell us!" the people in the room nearly chanted, but not really. I got freaked out at this point, though, and said, "I don't feel anything evil inside me, guys. I don't feel..." I mentally scanned my innards, and said, "anything evil. I want to leave!" I tried standing, but they forced me down into the chair. I wondered if I was in a kid's chair because they knew it would be easier to keep me down. I grew angry.

"Name yourselves, demons!"

I was back in the chair again, and I cried.

"Hatred!" I yelled, "Contempt!" because anger brewed inside me, really it did!

"Bate' joomba. Praise the Lord!" I heard, and I wanted to smack that guy in the mouth.

"Violence!" I yelled, trying to stand again. "Rebellion.... Suicide." I would say anything to leave that damn claustrophobic room with the pea-green chair glued to my butt.

"Devils, come out! We rebuke you...all of you," bad breath said, but still wasn't done. "Name yourselves!" he commanded again, and I found myself wondering how many devils he thought I had. "Wait, I feel the spirit of lust on her!" he yelled, and I shivered visibly; things had gotten out of hand. "They're taking control of her body; we're getting close," he said.

I tried getting up again, but it was useless. I yelled then, "FEAR, JEALOUSY, ANGER!" Their grips got harder as I went on and on, hoping I could finally say the secret password to freedom. I screamed the names of different emotions listed in the Bible, and even ones from movies I'd seen, but the right name didn't come. I almost wanted to scream out "Rumpelstiltskin" at one point, but I knew that wasn't it, either, and the thought made me laugh, and cry, at the same time. "Jesus, help me!" I cried desperately—finally. I wasn't asking for deliverance from demons, but from the hands of men. Jesus didn't answer, though. So, I cried before bellowing, "LEVIATHAN!" because it was a particularly scary word in the Bible. It got quiet then.

"Ohhh," everyone said.

And that time I actually got an "Oh bate' bate' joomba!" from the bilingual to the side of me.

It all stopped shortly after that, because apparently the demons had flown out the window, or something. The exorcists left the room so they could call the pastor, and I stayed, crying in that pea-green chair. I remember turning around and kneeling down next to that chair.

"God, what's going on?" I asked, and knew I'd never be the little Bible girl I'd been in high school. Cade and I left a couple weeks after that. The only people who really knew what happened at the exorcism were "bad breath," the bate' joomba prophet, and the others who'd stood around that pea-green chair. I didn't want anyone else knowing, anyway. I guess I was worried, if I told them, they might think I was possessed, too, and I don't ever want to go back to the pea-green chair again.

It's crazy, though, because I was having a hard time back then, and instead of helping me back into the wagon, those judgmental people practically threw me off. My "best friend" (at the time) even told everyone and their dog that I'd committed premarital sex and had a million demons. That next Sunday I heard people whispering, when they didn't think I could hear, "Do you think she was ever saved? Or was it just an emotional roller coaster?" That's the great thing, though: is that someday they'll be judged by their own measuring stick, when they die, they might come up short. I wonder who will be sitting in the pea-green chair then. Come to think of it, I wonder if that's what we'll all sit in when God gives us our report card—at the pearly entrance to Heaven.

Over the last couple of years, I've tried to lie, by saying I have answers, but the truth is, I don't. I tried trusting in men and their foolish reasoning, but they exorcised me. Now I find myself believing only one thing is true about men: they, as well as myself, have no answers. Men are either dwelling in the past with regrets and memories of better days, or they are dwelling on the beauty of things to come. We should truly enjoy today, but I reluctantly join the masses, and hope for a better tomorrow.

Entry #16

I worked last night. After the dinner rush, the owner's sister asked a loaded question, "What do you think of my brother?"

I thought of the only good thing I could say, and blurted it out, "He's a very handsome man."

"I hoped you'd say that." She smiled as she wiped off the counter. "Really? Why?" I asked, before taking a drink of my chocolate coke.

"Oh, just because he thinks you're the cutest waitress here, and said, if his wife wasn't pregnant, he'd do almost anything to have you."

I nearly gagged, but tried keeping the reflux down, because it would be a waste, losing my job just then. I thought for a minute how I'd contained my emotions so well the whole time Zeke was alive, and how I lost the gift because he died.

"Oh, how...nice," I said, and we were quiet for a minute. "I'm going..." I looked around for something, anything, "to vacuum now." I hate vacuuming and couldn't believe that was the only thing I could do. It's my own version of Hell because I'd hate vacuuming for eternity. Plus, I bet there are some nasty things to vacuum in Hell, and that would make it about five hundred times worse.

"But the floor is already vacuumed. There's nothing else to do. Why don't you sit and talk with me?"

"It's just that I noticed a spot over there! A spot...that needs to be vacuumed." I wanted to leave the conversation fast, and I'd take drastic measures to do it.

"Okay," she said. "You sure are a hard worker. I can see why my brother's so smitten."

I vacuumed for what seemed like forever! I finally quit when a nice British man walked in. I felt thankful having a customer, because he'd saved me from that lady, and constant vacuuming. I showed my appreciation in my waitressing, and we kept laughing about how both of us thought the other had an accent.

Just before walking from the diner, he said, "You've made a lonely old businessman very happy, and given me the best service I've ever had."

I smiled, and for some silly reason, I gave him a curtsy. He laughed at that, and I leaned down to whisper in his ear confidentially. "You saved my night, the second you came into the diner." I know he thought I was kidding, but I wasn't.

After turning around and busing his table, I found a twenty-dollar tip, and a note on the napkin. I couldn't believe I'd made such a big tip because I'm not a stripper, or anything, and I felt pretty good about myself! I fondly picked up the little napkin. He'd written the note beautifully, just how you'd expect someone with a British accent to write. It said:

The greatest storm often yields
the loveliest horizon.
Keep smiling, it's contagious.

145

Then there was a cute smiley face following the cursive. I didn't know old men liked to draw smiley faces! It warmed my heart. I'll keep that note forever and use the twenty dollars to get Ruby's picture taken at the modeling place. The money will go towards something I'll always remember.

Entry #17

Ruby is in the bathtub right now. She's eating oatmeal, and I'm blowing bubbles to her. That kid is living the good life as long as she gets the "oatmeal option." She loves it when we do this because the bubbles don't pop on her wet hands, and she can hold them while she sings to them—like they're her babies, or something. That kid is one in a million.

Anyway, Ruby kept waking up last night. She's been vomiting a lot at night, and I can't figure out what the problem is. Every time I helped her last night, I woke up from the same dream. It was the worst dream, and I can't get it out of my head.

In my dream, I look in our front closet, like I'm getting shoes, or something, but instead of shoes and coats, Zeke is in there, all preserved like Snow White, or some damn thing. I remember how handsome he was, and then, all of a sudden, he starts moving. I'm not freaked out, just excited. He's alive, and he's okay, and he's perfect under that glass. God must have finally heard my prayers and let him be healthy, because he's breathing without the vent and everything!

I bring him, still in the preserver box, to the kitchen. I worry something bad will happen if I open the lid and scoop him from the box. So, I just leave him in it, even though it's super heavy. When I get to the kitchen, Susan is there, along with all my family. Everyone tells me how I should let him go. They say he'll have a bad life, and it will be my fault for making him live.

"He'll blame you forever!" one of them shouts, and I

don't know which one, because they're a thriving mass of voices. "He'll blame me forever, if I let him go!" I yell back. "He'll always feel like I gave up on him...like I killed him. You don't know! I've been down that road, and it's wrong. God gave Zeke back now, and I'll never listen to any of you again!"

The mass yells at me some more, and I look everywhere for Cade, but he isn't there. There's no one that understands or will ever understand. I look for Ruby, but figure she's with Cade because she isn't there, either. I lug Zeke and his box into the car and drive away. I go buy formula, diapers—everything to take care of my baby. But, the whole time, everyone in the store stares at me and my baby, who just happens to lie in his preserver, in the shopping cart, and I can't see anything weird about it. And people continue to stare like we're outcasts and I look at them totally confused.

"Can't you see?" I ask politely. "I just want to take care of him. I'm excited for him to grow up." But their leers respond where their words won't venture.

We finally get our baby needs, and go to the top of the mountains, like hunted animals who know they've run their course, and are about to die. I get into the back seat, and find that the glass of the preserver is hazy, and I can't see in.

I open it, but he's gone. I'm left there all alone, with a bunch of diapers, and formula, and a broken heart.

I wake up and feel like I killed my son. We still haven't gotten the autopsy back, and I wonder how many damn tests they'll do before giving us the final results. It's been months, and I can't take this much longer. Would our son have led a good life if we gave him more of a chance? I don't know how to deal with this. It's funny, though, because, when I think of the dream, I wish I would have opened the preserver right when I first saw it. Then, I wouldn't have dragged myself and Zeke through all of that useless effort, just to open the preserver and realize he's gone.

Sometimes I'm really mad at modern technology. If they hadn't known Zeke had problems, he would have been born in a normal hospital room, without that stupid little window, and he would have died an understandable death. I feel bad for all the pain I put him through but feel worse for taking part in his death. And I don't know how to deal with all of this regret!

Entry #18

My dad needs to have a surgery. I hope everything will go well. I talked to my mom today, and she tried acting happy, but I can tell she's nervous. My dad will have part of his liver removed, and that sounds pretty serious to me. It never sounds good when you need to lose part of your liver, if you know what I mean.

He's such a tough guy, the toughest person I know. I remember he went right back to work the day he got fixed and didn't walk funny or anything! All of the guys at work were a little jealous, because some of them had proved what boobs they are when they had it done.

Entry #19

My two "good morning yahoos" bought coffee this morning. I told them, "Good morning," and waved.

"Good morning, Darlin'," Sam's happy voice said.

"What's so good about it?" Earl snarled, because he hates everything.

"That's what I love about you, Earl. You're always so happy. I just look forward to seeing you all morning, and you know it." I gave Sam a knowing smile because Sam and I are the same. We're slap-happy all of the time, for no reason; I wonder if God gave me a serious defect, and maybe that's it. You're the only one I allow myself to be sad around; to everyone else I'm pretty much the happiest person alive.

Earl blushed. "You're the worst liar I ever met." Earl is always grumpy, but I love him for it.

I told him he wouldn't know a lie if it bit him in the butt, and then gave him and Sam each some coffee, and I took their orders. "Did you two know that I call you my 'good morning yahoos'?"

"Hmph," Earl grunted. "When my little girl asks how work was, I tell her all about you two, and how you come in for coffee and breakfast."

"She's a perdy lil' thing, Earl. Elisa showed me a picture of her once. That little girl's a keeper." Sam took a sip of his coffee.

"It sounds like she's too much like her mother," Earl grumbled in an angry tone.

"You make anything sound bad," Sam pointed out, and we laughed.

"You just have the one kid," Earl said sternly.

"Well, I had a boy, too, but he's gone now."

"Get taken away from ya, or somethin'?" Earl asked.

"I guess you could say that." I didn't want to get into this again, but at least these two wouldn't be able to say they'd had a miscarriage and knew what I was going through. Plus, I didn't want Earl thinking I'd been an unfit mother, or something. "God took him a few months ago," I finally said.

"Well, isn't that life?" Earl blurted, and I was surprised at how upset he seemed just then.

Sam hit him in the head with a newspaper, and Earl took it from him. "I'll teach you to hit me!" Earl lost it. He was more upset than usual, and I couldn't figure out why.

Sam asked me what had happened, and since no one else was there, I pulled up a chair, and told them the whole story. At the end I noticed Earl holding the paper close to his face, and I didn't understand how he could even read the thing, it was that close to his face, really. Sam saw me watching Earl, and said, "Don't mind him. He's an angry old coot!"

"Am not," Earl said, but he'd forgotten his condescending tone, and sounded like he'd been crying.

"I'm sorry to tell you all my problems, guys. I don't know why I tell everyone about this."

"You're grieving, Pumpkin, and it's okay to be sad. It's okay to grieve," Sam said.

I looked over at Earl's newspaper, and said, "No, it's not; my husband is over it, and I should be, too." I gave Sam my big, fake, actress smile, and briskly walked away, because I'm tired of being sad. God didn't make me to love wallowing in my own sorrows.

After a minute, I looked back, and saw old man Earl still sitting behind his paper, shaking like a boob. I didn't want to cry like he did, and wouldn't let myself, because I was strong just then. I noticed the trail of steam coming from the coffee and wished I could float away into nothingness—away from the pain and sadness I bring myself and everyone around. I just couldn't believe old man Earl cried, and it makes me wonder what his story is.

Entry #20

When Cade came home, he must have been a dirty mess. Ruby and I got there, and we heard the shower running. I wasn't surprised to see a trail of muddy footprints leading from the door to our bathroom. Cade hardly ever takes off his shoes, even though I ask him repeatedly because I hate spending my entire life cleaning and re-cleaning our carpet. I put on a movie for Ruby and cleaned the floor again.

As I scrubbed, I smelled something weird in a piece of the mud I picked up. It smelled just like pot. I shook my head because I thought I had lost my mind. Why would a piece of mud smell like pot? I grabbed the mud and dug through it. In the middle sat a huge piece of weed! It looked like it had been smoked and then stomped out.

I ran upstairs and banged on the shower door. "What the hell, Cade?" Thump, thump, thump. "What the hell!"

The shower turned off. "What's up?" he yelled from the bathroom.

"We need to talk," I hurled the words at the door.

Before I knew it Cade stood in our bedroom. He had a white towel wrapped around his waist, and tan construction arms bulged. I forgot for a minute what I'd been angry about and realized how much I'd missed him. "What are you so pissy about?" He interrupted my thoughts and I remembered why I was upset.

I got into his face, bypassing my loneliness from the second before. "You, jerk! Have you been smoking pot?"

"No," he paused to readjust his towel, "I haven't."

"That's a bunch of bull." I pointed at him. "You stupid...Pot licker!" I fumed. "That's one of the dumbest things you could have done, and I thought you were so strong."

"You're nothing but a nag!" he yelled at me. But I didn't cower; I wasn't afraid and wouldn't give him any satisfaction. "I can't stand looking at you. Every time I see your face I think of Zeke. He looked too much like you, and I can't stand it."

"Fine! Get out of here if it's that bad! I don't need you— you...liar!" I held up the little pot I'd found in the mud. "I found this in your muddy footprint! You know how much I hate this crap. You know that, Cade. How long have you been smoking?"

"Since I joined the band. I was going to quit, but I'll never quit now. Never! I'll smoke for the rest of my life."

"You wouldn't!"

"I will!" he yelled. "I'm leaving!" He stomped from the room, but forgot he only wore a towel, and how cold it was outside. I snatched his outfit from the bed and threw it at his back.

"Here are your clothes, SWEETHEART!" I yelled.

Now Cade's gone, and I'm as lonely as hell. All I want him to do is come back, but I don't know where to go from here. I have no idea how to get him back to the person he used to be. Honestly, I don't know if I should try. Maybe we're better off without each other, especially if he's addicted to drugs. I keep thinking how I remind him of Zeke, and it makes me think of that "disappearing act" I saw in the house. Seeing his face was pure torture—thinking how Zeke could have been if he'd been healthy. Now I'm Cade's "disappearing act," but I don't ever disappear. I torture him by being here, by being alive, and it makes me feel ill. I wish there was something I could do to help, but maybe the best thing to do is stay away.

Entry #21

My aunt called today and said I'm her hero because of how I handled everything with Zeke. I've never been someone's hero before; I should go buy a damn cape or something. I guess I just don't understand why she would think of me like that. I'm not handling things great, not really, and I'm surprised people miss that fact. The only person who notices I'm not doing well is my grandma, and she keeps calling me, just to talk. I don't know what to say half the time, but I'm glad she cares.

So, my aunt is really sweet, but doesn't know what's going on inside me. If she knew how sad and upset I am, I wouldn't be her hero. Maybe she'd be embarrassed she's related to me because I'm a lot weaker than I seem to be on the outside.

Entry #22

I had lunch at Walmart today; there were a bunch of handicapped people there. I think they were on an outing, or something. Anyway, this one guy, who was about ten times my age, came over and said, "Mom? Hey, are you my mom?" And then he laughed and snorted, laughed and snorted really hard. I don't know why, but it struck me sad, and did I mention that I have a hard time seeing handicapped people now, anyway? For some goofball reason they remind me of what could have been if

I hadn't killed Zeke.

So, this guy followed me around the eating area, and asked if I'm his mother. And I wanted to tell him, "No, I would have been negative two-hundred when I had you." But I didn't say anything and thought how this could have been me and Zeke in the distant future, and how it will never happen now.

I wasn't strong in that moment, not like everyone used to say at the hospital, and I cried. Then Ruby, who ate fries in a highchair, freaked out amid the madness. I boobed badly because I couldn't take it. I know I looked horrible because a couple of junior high kids walked by me and the mentally handicapped guy, and they said, "Hey man, look at the retard couple." They pointed at us as I struggled to pull Ruby from the highchair so we could leave.

The handicapped guy's babysitter finally caught on and told the motherless guy to leave me alone. I ran from the Walmart because I was sad, and because those junior high kids had seriously dented my self-esteem. Even though my son might have been retarded, that still doesn't make me handicapped; I can tie my own damn shoes, really.

I called Cade and told him the whole thing. We're practically separated, but I called him, anyway. I said, "Cade, they actually thought I was retarded."

Cade laughed and said, "You'd make a damn sexy retard."

That's when I hung up the phone.

Entry #23

Zeke's autopsy results came back. I know I should feel better after getting the results, but I don't. We found out he'd turned septic. They discovered large amounts of poop in his blood. The doctor who met with us said Zeke would have died shortly after the thirtieth, even if we had tried to keep him alive.

I had flashbacks the whole time we talked to the doctor. It was crazy seeing him again, and for this reason, like I was stuck in the whole thing again.

When Zeke was alive, I didn't think we'd be here with his doctor, going over Zeke's autopsy. I'm desperately sad, and after the meeting, Cade and I went out to dinner. We talked about things, and Cade shocked me since he feels so much better. He said he's relieved.

"Do you remember driving home after Zeke died?" Cade asked me.

"What about it?" I took a swig of my tea because I'm not a polite tea drinker, not at all.

"Do you remember how we both said how relieved we felt that he was gone and—"

I finished his thought, "—how upset we were for feeling relieved?"

"Yeah," he said. "This whole time I felt bad for being relieved because we wouldn't struggle taking care of him forever. After seeing the autopsy results, though, I don't feel so bad. Even if he'd made it, he would've had a hard life."

"We all would've," I said, thinking about Ruby growing up with a brother who needed constant love and attention.

"We did the right thing."

"Did we, Cade?" I countered. "Should we have let him die on his own?" It wasn't really a question, to me.

"No," he shook his head. "I wanted to be there when he died."

I thought for a minute before responding. "So did I," I said, but still don't know if we did the right thing.

Entry #24

I had a strange night at work yesterday. The owner asked if he could talk to me privately. I got nervous, remembering what his sister said about him having a thing for me.

He took me into the back room and stood too close for comfort. "What do you think of the manager?" he asked gruffly. I could tell he's a man who likes being in control. I tried backing away and bumped into the wall.

"Michelle?" I asked, covering for my crazy nerves.

"Yeah, I'm thinking about firing her. Do you like her?"

"I love Michelle," I said, and forgot about the creep next to me while I defended my manager. "I think she's one of the most honest, hardworking people I've ever met. She's been tough on me at times, but I needed it. She's a good manager and I'd be sad if she wasn't here."

"Really?" he said, took a step closer, and put his hand under my chin. He tilted my face up so I had to look at his baby blue eyes. "I like you, Elisa," he said, and his tone scared me. "You showed a lot of character right now, and I like people with character." I stepped to the side and smoothed my apron. "I'm not going to fire Michelle," he continued, and I gaped. "I just want to find out which waitresses like her, because I'm going to fire the ones who don't."

That made me mad. "You mean," I looked at him defiantly, "this whole conversation was a lie?"

"Well, not all of it," he smiled with lust, and made me all sorts of puked-out.

"Good to know." I bumped him on my way out, as I stormed from the room. I'll never let someone push me around like that again, owner or no owner. He's not God and doesn't deserve my loyalty or respect.

When I worked today, there was a completely new staff. I had to work my butt off because hardly any of those people knew what to do. The owner wants me to train a bunch of them, and I'm not making as much as I was before. I'll look for another job tomorrow. I can't work for that jerk anymore, even if oatmeal is the only option again.

Entry #25

My dad had the surgery, and I visited him today. When I finally found his room, he wasn't there. I went into the hallway and walked in a different direction from how I'd come. I figured I'd ask someone where he was. As I walked down the hallway, I saw this man ahead of me. He hobbled, like he was in pain, and held his IV stand for support. His other hand held his hospital gown closed, in the height of modesty. I noticed his long, curly hair, and I grinned from ear to ear when I realized it was my dad.

"Dad? What in the world are you doing?" I ran up to him. "You're supposed to be taking it easy in your room."

"I'm just escaping from Alcatraz." He smiled and gave me a hug. "I need a smoke."

"But, Dad—"

He gave me a stern look I remember from childhood. "Okay," I said meekly. "But, let me help."

We rode the elevator, then after walking at a turtle's pace, we made it to the front entrance. The people coming in and out of the hospital looked at us funny because my dad was in his hospital gown, leaning on the IV stand, and smoking up a storm. We shot the bull while he smoked, and all of a sudden, he didn't seem well, and needed to get back to his room.

We started the long haul, and I asked, "How long do you think you'll be here for?"

"These pot-lickers wanna keep me in here for a few more days, but I'm gonna see if I can get out tomorrow."

"Dad, you have an eight-inch incision." I cleared my throat. "They just took out part of your liver. Maybe you should stay in here for a while."

"It's not a big deal. I need to get back to work," he said, and glanced out the window.

"You're one of a kind!" I said and smiled at my hero.

Entry #26

Cade got a job today. He's working for another construction company that will work around the band's schedule. Cade seems really happy about it and told me he's hoping I'll be happier now that he's got a job and isn't smoking pot anymore. He's still gone a bunch of nights out of the week, but things are a bit better between us.

We're trying to be nice to each other, and at least that's something, but the fire we had is gone, and our relationship feels dead. I've been pretty depressed about it, and even wrote a poem. That's how damn depressed I am, really it is.

No lock and key are there
No ropes or chains to bind.
The thing that holds me there
Is simply my own mind.

The cage I am held in
I cannot withstand.
I look about and realize
It's fashioned by my hand.

The time has now come.
Tomorrow mirrors fools.
I must find myself,
Deny their lies and rules.

They made them to control,
But I must not comply.
I've busted from my cage.

157

Now it's time to fly.

Entry #27

I got a job at a mechanic shop. I applied to be a diesel mechanic, and they're actually starting to train me. The truckers love it when I work on their trucks. One of them even pulled out his camera and took pictures. That cracked me up!

I honestly don't know how I landed this job, but it's hella fun. I'm still working at the diner, and some days I actually work eighteen hours between the two jobs. I miss Ruby the whole time but am so busy I can't think about Zeke much. The only time I have to think about him is when I'm driving from the mechanic's shop and feel like someone is missing. I constantly look at the back seat, wondering if Zeke is there in his car seat, but then realize I'm just suffering from a sick illusion.

They mostly have me behind the parts counter, but I've already helped with a few oil changes, tires, and stuff. It's so much fun. I don't think Cade's completely thrilled I work there, but it's good money, and even more fun than waitressing. The mechanics are real, and heart-warming, and they aren't gossipy and snooty like some of the people I work with at the diner.

My hands get super dirty, and it's hard scrubbing them clean. It's weird being a waitress and having oily, mechanic hands. A ton of people ask about it. You should see their faces when I tell them I'm training to be a mechanic. It's hilarious, honestly.

Earl is one of the only people who is supportive about me being a mechanic. He brought his old car in a couple of times, and there wasn't anything wrong with it. That made me smile because he was just looking for an excuse to visit.

He's acted differently ever since he found out about Zeke. I still haven't heard his story—the one that made him so bitter about life—but I'll hear it someday, I know I will.

He's not as grumpy as he used to be, and even cracks a smile now and then. I'm glad he's changing because life's not worth being upset all the time.

Entry #28

I drove home from work last night and thought about how life is imperfect. I asked God why it has to be this way, and right in the middle of my thought, I hit a skunk. When I jumped from the car, the creature looked at me, and didn't have a chance. Its body was deformed and made me think of Zeke. I knew the thing must have had a sweet spirit and was deformed as hell now. I cried for it, and decided to have a funeral, a really nice one, right there.

I said, "I know you've probably lived a good life, and I sure hope you don't have a family." I sobbed. "I'm sorry God called your checkout number so soon, and there's no going back." I cried for a bit because the last funeral I'd been to was Zeke's, and a ton of memories flooded back.

But then I stopped crying, because the skunk twitched and moved on its back while its butt faced me. I couldn't figure what it was doing and thought it wanted to be comfortable before it went. I waited, and then I prayed, "Oh, God, please help this—" but that was as far as I got.

My prayer ended because the skunk sprayed me. As it pumped me with its happy juice, I just stood there stunned. I can't tell you how long the damn thing sprayed because I was in shock. It was like a mist that filled the air—all around. The whole time it sprayed, I thought, why? I just tried giving the damn thing a Christian burial. This is like Zeke all over again. I tried to do the right thing, and now I feel like a murderer! A stinky murderer!

So, instead of its funeral ending with a prayer, I said some pretty unholy things. I told that skunk it was a pot-licker, and when it finished spraying me, the damn thing died.

Getting sprayed by a skunk is the nastiest, foulest thing that's ever happened to me. It's like having someone fart on your face, but the fart never goes away, like it's glued there or something.

The smell stays for eternity. I'm embarrassed about what I did next. I don't know why I did it, but I did. I walked to that skunk and kicked it—not hard, just softly. I was mad, that's all, and then felt bad for kicking it, because I'm the freaking queen of regrets right now.

When I got home, my smell must have preceded me, because it woke Cade up.

"What in the hell is—" He stopped talking when he saw me, because I cried and looked horrible. "Elisa! What happened to you?"

I told him the whole story, and although I didn't see anything amusing about it, he laughed and hardly controlled it. "That bad, huh?" he asked.

I grabbed some tomato juice, walked into the bathroom, and slammed the door. Of all the nights for Cade to actually be home, why did he have to see me like that?

I dumped the tomato juice in the bathtub and bathed in the stuff, because I've always heard that's the only thing that will remove a skunk's smell. It didn't do a damn thing, though. I tried everything, and finally I got my skin to smell good, but my hair was another issue.

I washed it in baking soda, hydrogen peroxide, and even vinegar before the damn smell went away. By the time I finished in that bathroom, I smelled better than Aphrodite, and my hair looked a bit lighter. I'd put on so much lotion and perfume you wouldn't believe it. I sloshed from the bathtub, put on a towel, and finished rubbing lotion on my legs, when I noticed Cade staring at me in the mirror.

"You're so beautiful," he said.

"I've had enough of your sarcasm." I turned away from him. "I can't believe you laughed at me!"

"I'm not being sarcastic," he said. "I've loved you since the first time I saw you, and I'll keep on loving you forever."

I blushed, the way he makes me. Before I knew it, he kissed me hard. I was up against the wall, and my towel lay on the floor.

It had been so long since we'd been together, and I missed him. I feel really bad for kicking that skunk now, because it might have saved my marriage. Thank God for that skunk! I hope Zeke can have him as a pet in Heaven.

Entry #29

Cade and I played games today. We're acting like newlyweds, or something. I don't know what's gotten into us, but that skunk didn't die in vain. Cade even held my hand, and we haven't done that since Hawaii. I feel all sorts of shy when I look into his eyes, and he acts love crazy.

Even though we seem completely happy, there's still a weird underlying feeling between us. I can't put my finger on it, but it's there, and it's not good. I guess we're both keeping our guards up, and I wonder if Cade will actually stay the night again. I can't take it how he's hardly here anymore. I mean, aren't you supposed to live with your spouse?

There's something else bothering me, too. When I woke up this morning, our video camera sat on our dresser and stared at me, waiting for some movement. It wasn't turned on, or anything, and I'm sure Cade set it there after he taped Ruby, or something, but I couldn't get over the fact that it stared right at our bed. I want to ask Cade about it, but don't want to make him upset by jumping to any crazy conclusions. It's a silly conspiracy theory because I'm jumpy lately, that's all.

Entry #30

My dad is doing a little better now. Can you believe they actually let him out the next day—the day after the surgery? That man can swoon anyone. I don't know how he talked them into it, but he did. That was the quickest release in history.

He's doing all right, but not out of the woods yet. Surgery can cause the cancer to go into his bloodstream, so he'll start more chemo treatments now. I hope the cancer will leave forever this time, and my dad won't go bald. He loves his long, blond hair, and would go nuts without it; I just know he would.

When I cut my thumb in half on a table saw, my dad offered to give me his big toe. I can give him all my hair. It's not very long, but at least it's something. It'd make a nice wig, for sure, and I'd love seeing him with black cherry hair.

Entry #31

Cade invited me to play with his band. They had a gig at a university, and I played with them. Cade's brother said violin and rock and roll don't mix, but I hope I proved him wrong.

The lead guitarist and I did a special bit together. He played a solo, and then I copied it, note for note. I'm really good at playing by ear and he was impressed, because we didn't even practice beforehand. It sounded pretty damn cool, because he's one of the only people I've ever met who can play by ear as well as I can.

The crowd loved it, and after the concert ended, a ton of people asked me when our next gig is. I didn't know what to say, so I told them to ask Cade.

It was fun watching Cade sing. I've never understood how girls can go all crazy about lead singers, but after watching Cade, I get it. He has a really good voice, and he knows how to perform and get the crowd excited.

Anyway, the lead guitarist and the bassist said they want me in the band, but I can tell Cade's brother doesn't like the idea. I don't think he wants a violinist—especially a female violinist—joining the band.

Entry #32

Cade's brother and the rhythm guitarist don't want me in the band. They said I'd bring drama, since Cade and I have problems, but I know that's not the real reason. I can tell they just don't want a violinist in their rock and roll band. It's not a good idea,

162

anyway, because the lead guitarist wants me down there for practice every night, and I have to work and take care of Ruby.

I finally quit my job at the diner. It's nice not to be working two jobs and taking care of Ruby. I missed her really bad because I hardly got to see her. I see her more now, though, since I'm only working forty hours a week. I make a ton of money at the mechanic shop. I get paid commission, and it ends up being quite a bit. The other day I even took Ruby to the dollar store and let her get a treat. She absolutely loved it, and of all the things she could have picked, she wanted a magnifying glass. I love it when she puts it to her eye and looks at me. That kid is gold, pure heaven-sent gold.

Entry #33

We went to Albertson's. I needed to pick up some cheese because I'm mad about cheese. I could eat the whole block, if I had my way; cheese is bliss, really it is. I thought it would be nice to go to the store as a family but, when we got there, Cade acted like he was retarded. I hate it when he does that because he's really good at it.

He used to work at a place where he helped mentally handicapped people function on their own so they could live in the real world. He's been around them enough to know exactly how they act, and I guess he thought it would be funny to act like them in the store, with a bunch of strangers all around. It wasn't funny, though, and freaked me out. It reminded me of Zeke and the way things might have been if he'd made it, and looked just like Cade, but handicapped instead of normal.

Cade hunched way down when he walked, and his perfectly strong legs suddenly bent in, and he limped and stuttered, "E— E—Elisa."

I looked at him, horrified.

He really looked handicapped, and I thought, *"Is that the same person I slept with last night?"* I wanted to run away from him, but I had to get Ruby. He kept clinging to me and calling me his sister. He even drooled, and I couldn't believe he took the whole thing so far. When no one looked, he gave me a wink.

"H-H-How you doing, Sister?" he asked in a really slobbery voice.

I saw a huge group of people at the checkout line, and quickly walked towards them. I figured he would stop the charade if I got him around a bunch of strangers, but I was wrong.

"S-S-Sister! I don't wanna get shaved, wufus!"

"What in the hell are you talking about?" I asked and gave him "the eye." I couldn't understand what he was doing! He smiled, a horribly pathetic smile, which left spittle coming down his chin, and all of the people present smiled at him. I couldn't figure how he made them so damn happy.

A little boy pulled on his mommy's dress. "Look at that man!" he said.

"Don't point at strangers!" She tore her eyes from Cade.

"Koka Sorus koka tess! Koka Sorus koka tess!" Cade repeated, and I remembered that line as something one of his patients used to say.

Cade gave me a slobbery, disgusting kiss on the cheek, but I had endured enough.

"Knock it off, Cade! This is NOT FUNNY!" I yelled and punched him in the bony part of his shoulder.

"Oh, my," an elderly lady said. She covered her mouth and drew in a breath.

"Did you see what that lady just did to her brother?" The little boy pulled on his mom's dress again.

"Be quiet!" she said.

"He's not handicapped!" I said, trying to get someone—anyone—to see what Cade was putting me through.

"You're not a very nice sister," the old lady said.

"He's not my brother! He's my husband!" I defended myself.

"You are sick!" she said, grabbed her groceries, and stomped, with her big butt jiggling, away from us.

"Let's go, Brother!" I said.

As I drove off, Cade wiped his chin with his sleeve and got rid of the spit. "That was funny," he said. But I didn't talk to him the whole way home, even though he and Ruby laughed up a storm.

When we got home, he said, "Admit it! That was funny."

"Not really!"

"Yeah, it was!" he chuckled. "Oh, man! I thought I would laugh and blow the whole thing when you hit me."

I smiled then. "Did it hurt?"

"Not really." He gave me "the eye."

"It totally did!" I laughed.

"Okay, it hurt," he rubbed his sore shoulder, "for a girl hit." That made me grin.

Entry #34

Cammie is pregnant! She's having a little girl, and the doctor said the baby is healthy. I can't imagine being pregnant again. She's such a strong lady. I can't wait for her to have her healthy little baby. I know she'll be absolutely beautiful.

Cammie seems nervous, but I told her everything will be okay. She already has two other healthy kids. Nothing bad will happen this time. I'm glad she's pregnant. Another child can't replace the one she lost, but I bet it will be nice having another baby.

She's been such a good friend to me. It's nice talking to someone about Zeke, and knowing they actually understand what I'm going through. In an odd sort of way, I think I've helped her, too. Her little girl passed away three months before I met her, and when Cammie first told me, three months seemed like an eternity.

Now, Zeke has been gone much longer, and I can't believe I'm living without him. It's crazy, being on the other side of his death, and having more in common with Cammie than I thought I would. It's comforting, and sad, all at the same time.

I don't know what to think, other than that I'm glad I met Cammie. She's a godsend, and everyone can use one of those. I don't want to talk to her about Zeke right now, though. I don't want her worrying about the darling baby who's on her way.

Entry #35

So, I think Cade is smoking pot again, and lying about it, but I won't accuse him of anything. He's just been so lazy and mean, and the garage smells weird after he's been "just talking" with his brother. I swear, he's constantly yelling at me, and I don't know what to do. Maybe he'll quit smoking if I act nice about it.

He's not doing very well with his job, either. He's playing with the band a lot and been taking too much time off. I don't know what to do. He needs to get his priorities straight.

I worked the graveyard last night, and Marie stayed with Ruby. I had to take a nap this morning. I was so tired, and really thankful she stayed so I could sleep. I didn't sleep long, though, because I woke up and heard my mom and Marie talking.

Marie told my mom thanks for coming. My mom said it wasn't a big deal, before offering Marie a glass of water.

"Sorry I couldn't get here sooner. That's such a long drive," my mom said.

"I know it. You wouldn't believe how many miles I've put on my car," Marie said lightly.

"Me, too!" They laughed for a minute.

"I've just gotta get back to Van," Marie said, and then continued, "I haven't been home the last few nights, and he's really missing me."

"What's going on with Cade?" my mom asked.

"It's that stupid band." Marie sighed.

"Can't you tell him to come home? This is getting ridiculous. He should be the one here watching Ruby, not us."

"I know! I don't know what to say, though," Marie said.

"Phil said I should understand Cade, since I was a drummer in a band, but that was before I had a family."

"That changes things," Marie agreed. "Do you think he's on drugs? He's been acting weird."

"I don't know," my mom said. "I just don't know."

I tried sleeping then but couldn't because I kept replaying their conversation in my head. So, I'm not the only who thinks Cade is acting strange.

I looked through his drawer in the nightstand because I can't stand thinking he's on drugs again. He puts all of his personal stuff in that special drawer, and I never look in it. But today I did.

My hands dug through piles of "Dungeons and Dragons" manuals, pictures he'd drawn, stories he'd written, board games he'd made up, little trinkets he loves, and then I found a big pack of letters. Most of the letters were from "King Arthur," and I really wanted to read them, but Cade told me they'd hurt my feelings. I reluctantly put them back and closed the drawer. I'm glad I didn't find any drugs in the drawer, but that doesn't prove a thing.

Entry #36

I went on a parts run today. I had to drive all of the way downtown, so I called my mom to see how she's doing. I got distracted, and while I talked, I completely passed the parts place. Instead, I kept driving, and before I knew it, I was parked in front of the hospital where Zeke used to be, and I just sat, staring at the entrance. I asked my mom if I could call her back, and absently hung up the phone.

I shuddered and thought about how strange it was I drove there on accident. I don't know how it happened. I guess it was just a big habit for almost three months, and my brain took me there when it was on autopilot, or something.

I thought about Zeke's nurse, Susan for a minute and how much I missed her, but I wouldn't dare go in there again. Just the smell of iodine makes me ill, let alone going back to the NICU. I thought of Zeke: his tiny fingers, his velvety hair, and that soft, baby powder skin. I cried as I sat in front of the hospital when I was really supposed to be getting parts for a semi. Someone behind me honked because I blocked their way. I returned to reality and drove to the parts place as fast as I could. The guy at the counter was extra nice.

"Are you Elisa?" he asked.

"That's me," I said, and tried summoning a disobedient smile.

"I've always wanted to know what you look like. I like talking to you on the phone."

"You, too. It's nice putting a face with your name," I looked at his badge, "Tom."

I waved "goodbye." The door chimed as I walked toward the parking lot, where I could be sad, and there wasn't another person to see my tears.

Entry #37

My parents went out of town and asked if we could watch their dog. We watched my aunt's poodle, too—my aunt who made me like capes because she thought I was heroic. Well, she and my uncle have a little poodle, and it was so sheltered you wouldn't believe it. He had to stay outside, and he thought that was the end of the world.

Last night there was this huge windstorm, and it blew over my parent's fence. We didn't know it until this morning, and both of the dogs got lost. Cade and I spent the last two days searching for them. We found my parent's lab yesterday. She was with five other dogs that had been freed through similar circumstances.

We didn't find the poodle, though, and I think someone stole him. We called everywhere and went door to door asking around for him. He's worth quite a bit of money, and I'm sure someone stole him.

I felt so bad I called my aunt on the phone and told her what happened. She really loved that dog. She said, "That dog was like a child to us. You know we named him Pacho, since that means Frank in Spanish?"

"I'm so sorry," I said.

"Now I know how you felt with Zeke," she said, and she cried on the phone.

Entry #38

I think Cade and I are pretty much separated. We haven't said it out loud, but remember when you'd first start dating someone, and you suddenly knew you were an item? Well, it's like that, but I just know we're not. He hardly ever comes home now. Plus, there's really nothing between us anymore. He seems to be living his dream life. He practices with the band, plays video games all night at his parent's house, and then works, when he's available. I'm trying to be happy for him, but am irate, instead. I can't figure why he's doing this to me. He's dragging me through the mud, and I don't get it. I used to understand the guy, but don't think I will again.

Entry #39

I'm pregnant! I'm only a couple days late, but I took a test, anyway. I can't believe my pee is positive. I'm on the shot and am not supposed to be able to get pregnant! Cade doesn't even want me anymore, and I don't know if I can go through this alone. What if I have another baby with defects, and Cade isn't even around this time. I don't know what to do. My mind is flying a million miles an hour. I wish I could pray about this, but I don't think God would listen anyway.

Entry #40

I saw Cade today, when he visited Ruby. I pulled him aside and told him we needed to talk.

"About what?" he asked, and his eyes were bloodshot. "I think

I'm—"

"What? Would you just finish your damn sentence? You think you're what?"

"Pregnant," I finally said, and held my breath. "What? You're on the shot."

"I know," I said, and my voice sounded far away, "but I took a test from the dollar store, and it said I'm pregnant."

"Oh," he said, and totally changed tones. "It's probably wrong. Hey, I've been meaning to ask, do you want to go to a concert with me?"

"Did you hear anything I just said?" I asked.

"Yeah, did you hear anything I just said?"

"I guess I'll go to the concert, if one of our moms can watch Ruby—again." I looked at little Ruby and smiled; she's so beautiful. "I'm going to lie down." I left the room after that, and rested, because I felt really tired.

Entry #41

I told a girl at work that I'm pregnant, but I don't want anyone else knowing. They'll freak out, I'm sure. I can't even imagine how my mom and Marie will take the news, when I finally tell them, after the baby is born. I just can't imagine.

I'm so tired, and all I want to do is sleep. It's getting crazy, working these long hours, and I'm just realizing how hard it is being a mechanic. I can fit into places the guys can't, and my hands are made for this type of work, but the parts are heavy, and I'm not very strong.

I pulled a ten-hour shift last night, and actually fell asleep on the counter. The night mechanic woke me up by poking me in the side with a dirty dip stick. "What in the hell?" I asked, and then giggled because that guy always makes me laugh, just by looking at him, and my clothes always get dirty at work anyway.

He's such a good guy. He's always pulling funny pranks, and crap. He's this real skinny, tall type of guy, and his girlfriend, who works here too, is huge. She's tall and fat and seems butch if you want to know the truth. It cracks me up, seeing them together, because she bullies him like you wouldn't believe; but he loves every minute of it. I like watching them walk together because they remind me of a couple of evil henchmen, like in the movies, and I'd really like to watch a movie with them in it. Some people are so funny.

Entry #42

I have today off so I can go to the concert, but I've been cramping so bad. It hurts to walk, and I hobbled to the bathroom, all hunched over. The concert is tonight, and I need to get better, but just thinking about it makes me sore and tired.

It's been a rough day. I hurt all night and then, just after lunch today, I bled gushing-blood, and then a dark crimson glob slid out. It hurt like hell, but I've had really bad cramps before, and that's what it felt like. I think I had a miscarriage, and when I called a nurse on the phone, she said that's what it sounds like.

She said I should go to the doctor to get checked out right away, but I don't want to give them any more of my money. We don't have insurance, and it seems like it would be a waste. Everything already fell out, so I don't need to see a doctor to tell me I'm running on empty.

I called Cade, after I got off the phone with the nurse, and told him everything.

He was quiet for a minute, and then asked, "Does this mean you don't want to go to the concert?"

"You can be such a selfish jerk!" I yelled into the phone and hung up.

I don't know if I should go with him. I can't believe how rude he's acting. He must be on drugs. He's not normally like this. I'm feeling crappy, but it would do me some good to leave the house and get some air. Marie is already on her way, and everything.

I'm glad she loves Ruby and hope she won't notice I don't

feel good. She shouldn't know anything's wrong; it would stress her out. But we've gotten so close she can read me like a book.

Entry #43

I went to the concert with Cade. I ran into one of my old friends there. It was hard hearing anything over the music, and the noise made everyone yell if they wanted to hear anything. She asked me how I was doing, and I said I'm okay, and that I have a little girl. She told me all about how she hates our modern culture, and all of the women who feel they have to marry and procreate. She went on and on, and after a bit of banter, I felt weak and cold.

I told Cade I needed to sit down, and he surprised me because he was right there when I needed him. He helped me get away from the fem-Nazi, and when we left the building, he said, "You really aren't feeling well, are you?"

"No crap, Sherlock!" I stared him down. He helped me walk closer to a rock. It was big enough I could actually lean against it, like a bumpy, poorly built recliner. We lay on the rock together and talked. It almost reminded me of the strong mountain we got married next to—the strong mountain I blew Zeke's ashes on— where we saw that scary cougar.

"You can go back in there if you want to," I said.

"No, I'm all right. Are you all right?" He was actually, honest to goodness, concerned.

"I'm fine, if you count blacking out...as fine," I laughed.

"I'll be right back." Cade left, and then returned with a drink in his hand. "You're probably dehydrated," he said. "I always have to keep an eye on you! You never drink enough water."

"Thank you, Mother; I hate water," I said, and laughed as I looked out at the Salt Lake. Its beautiful waters shone in the moonlight. The breeze tickled the waters, rushing past me in its aftermath. "This reminds me of my eighteenth birthday," I said. "Do you remember where we were?"

"Hawaii?" he asked.

"Yeah." I put my forearm under my head. "We didn't have money to eat dinner, so we played for tips that night. We only made a couple of bucks before it started raining."

"I remember." Cade grinned. "We were so hungry, and the only thing we could afford was a loaf of bread. What kind of bread did we get again?"

"Banana."

"That's right." I relaxed to the sound of his voice.

"I remember sitting on a rock and watching the ocean for hours. All we did was eat banana bread and talk." I watched his reaction.

"That's not how I remember it," he said.

"Oh?" I baited him

"I remember a lot of kissing." He leaned on his elbow and looked at me. The concert continued, and we faintly heard the music wafting through the air. "You're still the same."

"I am, huh?" I thought for a minute. "You're not."

"Really?" He sounded shocked, and that pissed me off.

"Really," I said, and harshness entered my tone.

"How so?" he asked, trying to keep the mood light, but I was over his cute little act.

"The old Cade never would have treated me so badly today. The old Cade wouldn't have done these things to me. He would have come home, and got a real job, and been nice, and loving and—"

"I'm that bad, huh?"

"Actually, you are!" I spat.

"Then, why are you here with me?" he asked, and there was something strange in his tone. He sounded weak, just for a split second.

"I don't know," I confessed. "I don't know why I'm here, and why I let you walk all over me. I'm sick of it, Cade! I'm done! My son just died, and now you're doing this to me. My son, Cade! My son!"

"He was my son, too," Cade choked. "You think I don't have

feelings, and can't feel any of what happened. You're heartless and selfish."

"I'm selfish? I'm selfish, and you're the one who dragged me out to this concert when I'm so sick."

"You don't look sick to me!" We both stood.

"You're a blind bastard then, aren't you?" My eyes formed into icy slits. "When will you be a real man, Cade? When? When will you be responsible for your actions?"

"What actions?"

"Starting a family with me because you thought I would leave you!" I hit him at the core. "When will you get off drugs, get a real job and quit the band?"

"NEVER!" he yelled. "Are you giving me an ultimatum? It's either the band—and pot—or you? Is that it?"

I didn't need to think about it. "Yeah, Cade, it is. What's it gonna be? I won't waste my life waiting for you to grow up."

"The band," he said.

Before restraining myself, I cocked back my arm and slapped Cade hard across the face. My handprint surfaced on his cheek within seconds, and I glared into his eyes. "TAKE ME HOME, YOU JACKASS!" My voice shook with rage, and I looked over to see my fem-Nazi friend staring speechlessly at me—the girl she'd nicknamed "Bible Girl."

He took me home, and I slammed the car door when we got to the house. Then I turned back, thinking Cade would jump out and change his mind—just like I'd thought God would heal Zeke, right before he died. But God didn't heal Zeke, and Cade didn't jump from the car. The car door I'd slammed seemed like the final piece of an elaborate puzzle, shifting into place. Something huge closed in a final, irrevocable end.

I watched the car speed away, but I stood strong, as if his leaving was better than the year 1999. I shivered a little because it felt cold outside, and my body ached to sit down. I peered around, though, not wanting to give in. I felt the desert clinging to my lungs. The doctors always said dry air was bad for Zeke's breathing problem.

As I thought of Zeke, I remembered being pregnant, before he came out and died. I thought of that dream I'd had about the fire and the desert.

Cade, Ruby, and I all stood in the fire. It burned everything, even our house, until we stood in the lonely desert. Those crazy-beautiful pansies bloomed around our feet, and even though I still had Ruby, Cade and I had lost each other—and Zeke was nowhere to be seen.

The funny thing is that I hate pansies. My mom practically loves them. She always says how people don't understand those flowers because they're resilient and some of the strongest plants, willing to bloom anywhere. They represent undying love, and a bunch of other things. Well, I think we've been through the fire, or we're still going through it. And those pansies represented our love for our kids, because that's something that will never die.

I'm sad, though, because I wanted Cade to come back and tell me he'll quit drugs, quit the band, and be the man Ruby and I need him to be. I wanted him to hug me tight in those strong arms, and tell me he loves me, even though I'm not perfect, and neither is our life together. But he didn't; he didn't even get out of the car, and I feel dirty, and used, and betrayed by the one person who shouldn't have betrayed me.

When I remember his face tonight, I think of Hawaii....

We swam one day, and an incredibly strong riptide started. We swam and swam as hard as we could, and when we were about fifteen feet from the shore, I felt the sand close to my body. I didn't have to work as hard anymore because I could anchor myself there really easily, but I guess Cade didn't realize the bottom was there, and continued swimming weakly, and exhausting all of his energy.

"Elisa, I can't make it to the shore," he said pathetically. "I can't make it."

"Oh, Cade! Don't say that. Just keep trying," I said, and laughed thinking we were joking.

"I can't," he said seriously, and stopped swimming. It reminded me of an overly dramatic black and white movie where someone dies a tragic death in the name of stupidity. Just before Cade drifted too far away, I stood, and the water was only up to my thighs. I laughed so hard I thought I would pee, but Cade didn't think it was funny as he stood next to me. His face reminded me of when he thought he would drown. I can't help him stand this time. He'll figure that out on his own, and won't pull me back into the riptide, where I might not make it to shore again. I have Ruby to think about now, and we have a bright future ahead of us.

Part IV
Resurrected

Entry #1

Cade and I are through. We've been over for a month, and I'm finding it hard to breathe. I wonder what he did with that brown sack—the one he used when I was in labor with Zeke. I could really use it now. I thought it was hard losing Zeke, but this is hard on a different level. I miss Cade so much, but he's lost to me, like a missing sock, for crying out loud. It's like I'm looking for someone who doesn't even exist anymore. I try being strong, really, but I wasn't hardwired for this. I keep remembering the day Zeke was born, when I still had my husband and my son close. I could hug them anytime, and they'd both accept me then. I wouldn't be accepted now, though. Zeke's ashes are gone, and Cade doesn't want me.

Once Cade and I had a fight when we'd only been together a little while. He went to my parents' house and begged them to let him in, but I told them not to. He sat outside of my window, just talking to my dad for hours. He said I was the only girl for him, and he traveled all the way to Europe looking for a girl like me, but I was back home all the time. That's how bad that kid didn't want to lose me, like I was his perfect match, or some damn thing. Where is that guy now? I'm still here, but he's on another planet, I swear. He's off searching for something, but this time it isn't me. I just wish he would come home and forget about the drugs and the band, and remember what we used to have, and what we still have with Ruby.

I didn't have anyone to talk with today, so I called my grandma. I didn't tell her about the miscarriage or anything. I don't want to tell anyone about it, ever. It's embarrassing, thinking I had a baby with defects, and now I can't even carry a kid. That was God's way of ending the pregnancy before I went through something worse again. I can't handle having a baby with defects; I'd take a miscarriage any day compared to that nightmare! I'm just thankful I have Ruby, and she's healthy and alive.

So, my grandma answered the phone and acted really

surprised I called. Did I mention that the lady is stalking me? Every time the phone rings, it's her, calling to check on me. I used to dread answering the phone because I didn't want to lie and tell her everything's fine, because I hate fibbing if God's listening for once.

But my grandma and I have grown closer since Zeke died. Now I find myself running to the phone, smiling when I answer it. She calls every day, but especially on Saturdays. That's our special day. I answer the phone, and the first one to say "Happy Saturday" wins. We don't win a prize or anything, just loads of respect, and I like my grandma's respect, so I shoot to win. I tell her these super-crude jokes, and she cracks the hell out of me. She acts offended, but I know she really loves them, because she giggles into the phone and all. Today, I told her this wild one about a man farting in church. She laughed so hard I got worried for her health—until I heard her breathing again.

When I talked to her, she asked how I am, and I told her I'm great, but I didn't want to talk to her about my problems because that's not the point of our conversations. I just wanted to shoot the bull with her. There's no one who can shoot the bull like my grandma.

She's full of one-liners you wouldn't believe and told me once I'm the only person she can be like that with. She got my mind off all my problems, and before I knew it, I teared from happiness instead of the sad crap I've boobed over lately. I feel better now and thank God I was named after her. Of all the wonderful things my parents did, giving me the middle name "Beth" is one of the best.

Entry #2

We've been separated for almost two months already! I'm pretty Sky numb, just like Zeke when the lack of oxygen finally affected his brain. I see Cade, and don't feel like smiling anymore. If he had eyes to see me, I'd give him a smile, but he's not there anymore. My ring finger is naked, and when someone asks if I'm married, I tell them, "No." I say it without emotion, and don't give them room to follow up with any words.

I'm working a lot, trying to make the house payment. Cade's giving us most of his checks, but it's not very much money. I pulled a double shift the other day because that's practically heaven on earth, and Cade stayed the night with Ruby.

I got home just before noon, and Cade was still asleep. Ruby cried in her bed, and she was all snotty faced, like she'd practically rolled in phlegm. I cleaned Ruby, and then shook Cade really hard. "SHE NORMALLY GETS UP AT SEVEN!" I yelled, and he seemed totally disoriented as my voice registered.

"Oh, I haven't gotten up for the day yet," he said. He smelled like pot and made me sick. I pushed him from the house and said he should go hang out with "the band," or something. He really pissed me off this morning. Poor snotty-faced Ruby. I gave her a warm bath, the only thing that would remove the damn snot, which was part of her face by the time I got there.

After the bath I wrapped her in a towel and rocked her for a long time. I sang "Hush, Little Baby," and after a while she got the gist of the song and did what the words suggested; she fell asleep in my arms.

Entry #3

A telemarketer called today. I don't know how it happened, but before I knew it, he told me all his problems, and wasn't selling a thing. I sat listening for over an hour. It was actually nice getting my mind off my problems for a minute.

He was a really nice guy and had an Indian accent. I wanted to pass the phone to Ruby, just so she could hear what an Indian accent sounds like, but she was too busy coloring rainbows, and other happy crap. I wished for a minute that he was a Native American so I could ask if he knows what cougars represent, but he was from India, instead, and could have helped me with my chakras instead.

So, I talked to the Indian guy about his relationship

problems, and then told him how I suck at relationships. I said, "I couldn't even work out my own marriage."

"But you sound like a happy little American, like the ones in the movie reel," he said.

I laughed because I liked him, and it drove me wild how he said "movie reel." That Indian guy cracked me up, thinking that being an American could make me immune to pain, and here I am, hardly coping as it is. If only being an American meant that, we'd have even more immigrants, and that's saying something.

Entry #4

I ran into a guy today. Remember "the ex" who didn't make the cut? Have you ever had one of those "the only other person you would have spent your life with if you didn't marry who you did?" Well, this guy was mine. If Cade was the lead actor in my life, this guy was the understudy, the one who wasn't meant to play the lead, but was still a damn good actor. He'll never take the leading role, though, at least not in my life. There's only one man who could take the lead in my play.

Anyway, I went to his nephew's birthday party. I really didn't think that guy would be there, but he was, and when I saw him, my heart went way up into my chest, like it was running for president, or something.

I tried leaving before he saw me, but I wasn't fast enough. He looked at me and his eyes did a jig. It was obvious he didn't recognize me when he introduced himself. Can you believe it? He was as slick as hell, too. I bet he's a real ladies' man now. He never used to be, but I bet he is now. I think getting his heart broken did that to him. He acts so cool because there's not a damn thing to lose.

Anyway, I look really different with this short, dark hair. I could tell he really liked it because he couldn't take his eyes off me. He even forgot to tell his nephew "happy birthday," for crying out loud.

Well, that only lasted until he recognized me. His features

went as droopy as melting wax while his brain registered, but he didn't leave, like he left the church when I saw him a year ago. He just stayed there, even though I knew it was hard for him, and I still can't figure out why.

I had to laugh, because he has no idea how much I used to love him, and it doesn't matter now anyway, because I married Cade, and things are the shambles. I wanted to cry, thinking about Cade, but wouldn't let myself cry in front of "the understudy."

I was a real jerk to him back in the day. We dated on and off for a couple of years. I dated so many people you wouldn't believe it, but it was really all about him. He had real charm, that kid. It wasn't how he acted, or anything, just who he was. He's pretty fun to be with, and I could never get enough.

We kept breaking up because we got too serious, like someone sucked the fun from us with a liposuction machine. I just wanted to know it was only me for him, like it used to be him for me, but I always felt something getting in the way. I guess we weren't meant to be, and tempted fate by dating. It's sad, if you think about it, me being young, and wanting to be with someone, even though it wasn't supposed to be.

Plus, he'd always talk about this girl he dated before, and it got really old. It's funny, though, because I know he ended up doing that with me when he dated girls after we broke up. That guy was the type who always looked to the past, wondering: what if?

He didn't have a car, and I always picked him up so we could go places. It was lame because he was eighteen and couldn't even order food at the drive thru. He has a truck now, and I'm glad he finally got around to getting his license. That comes in handy when he's romancing girls, and crap.

Well, I met Cade during one of my breakups with "the understudy." I was drawn to Cade like a moth to a bonfire, and for the first time, someone plucked "the understudy" from my mind. Cade was everything I ever wanted, and not just part of it, like the other guy had been. But the other guy was still my first love and hard to get over, for some stupid reason.

I guess there's only one way to explain it, and that's 'cause I was a stuffed animal kind of kid. I loved stuffed animals because I could pretend them up to be anything. I had a pink bear named Suzy that was my best friend. She was the kindest, sweetest bear in the world, and always there for me. I also had a prince bear, who was as sharp as hell, too. He didn't always act super kind, even though he was, deep down, but he was real smart and slick, that bear was.

He had all the lady bears, and even some of my dolls, practically drooling over him. They would have done anything just for one date with him. He was the best bear you could imagine, even though you had to look deep to see it. I can't remember his name right now, but I think it was Elvis, or something, and come to think of it, he looked like a Cade.

Anyway, I was a stuffed animal lover because I liked pretending. I think that's what I did with "the understudy." I always pictured him being someone different because I was crazy about him. Somehow, though, we both must have known we weren't meant to be. One time he told me he knew he'd see me with someone else someday, and it would rip him apart.

I asked him today if he wondered what it would have been like if we got hitched like we'd planned back when I was a kid— four years ago. He said he didn't think about it much.

He was as slick as all get out. I know he's thought about it—I could always tell when that kid lied. He rubbed his hands, like he tried getting rid of something, and then said we wouldn't have made it anyway. He didn't sound too convincing, but I was glad he'd said it anyway. It was what I needed to hear, like a subtle "you're forgiven," or something. For the last few years, I've felt like I'd ruined the kid's life, especially after I saw him at church.

We stood next to my car and shot the bull for a while, and I remembered the last time we stood next to a car. We hadn't been shooting the bull, and I still remembered what he felt like next to me. But that memory felt all wrong because, when I thought about "the understudy," I confused him with memories of Cade. When I looked back, I couldn't remember if the memory involved his lips, or Cade's, wrapping gently around mine. Cade must have been a damn good kisser because I realized his kisses wiped all the others away. I just wanted to throw up then, because Cade's soft lips might never touch mine again, and here I was, talking to this guy who didn't give a damn about my marriage. I'd turned "the understudy" into a womanizer, and maybe he hoped to hurt me like I'd hurt him. He had no idea, though, because he hurt me by standing there. He made me miss Cade, and I wanted to leave. Instead, he said he'd tried cocaine for the first time. He said the dealer was really nice and let him have some for free. He swore he wasn't hooked or nothing. I told him the dealer wanted to get him addicted. He seemed distracted then, and the conversation died.

Ruby cried in the car, and I told him I had to get home. He asked me for my number, and I gave it to him. I don't know why; I guess I didn't want to be rude. I don't think he'll call me, but that was nice he asked anyway.

Just before I left, I asked, "Did you really call and talk to my mom after my son died?"

"Yeah, I did. I didn't think she'd tell you," he said.

"That was really nice of you. When she told me you called...it meant a lot."

"No biggie; I just felt bad for you and your son, that's all," he said.

"Well, thanks. You know, Cade had a hard time, too."

"I'm sure he did." He stiffened.

"But you're not sorry for him?" I asked, wondering why he'd only said he felt bad for me and Zeke.

"I do, he's just not you, and I don't really care for the guy."

"Why?"

"Because he's the one who took you away from me, Elisa."

He stumped me with those words, and I felt really bad all

over again. I tried swerving the conversation away from our breakup, as fast as I could, and I asked, "How did you know Zeke died anyway?"

He paused for a minute and looked at the ground. "I ask around...about you, every once in a while."

I didn't know what to say and thought about making a stalker joke before quickly changing my mind in the name of couth. I felt bad for "the understudy," and even worse for myself. I'd thrown a pity party and was the only guest invited.

I almost wish I'd never met him, because then I never would have hurt him. I always end up hurting people, just like Zeke and Cade, and even "the understudy!" I feel like I'm driving a triple trailer semi without my freaking endorsements. That's my life, one that pushes, and goes wherever it wants to, regardless of the wreckage it might leave behind.

It was a clumsy moment, figuring how to say goodbye. I didn't know if I should shake his hand, high five him, punch him in the arm, or what, but he reached over before I could move and gave me a quick hug. "It was nice to see ya."

"You too." I smiled. "Stay off the coke, okay?"

"Yeah, I will," he said, but I didn't believe him because he didn't meet my eyes.

It was really great seeing him and his family. I love that guy's sister and his mom; they're gold, pure gold. I'm glad he looked at me as if he liked me, before realizing who I was. It's nice thinking someone might be attracted to me after Cade threw me away like a used condom.

I still can't get over how handsome "the understudy" looked. He really got cuter with age. He's a good guy, that one. I hope he'll stay away from coke. I can't stand thinking of someone I used to love being on coke. That just pukes me out. I got home, and Cade still isn't here. A part of me hopes he'll come back, but I don't think he will. He's too involved with that damn band, and doesn't want me, anyway, because I don't give him a high, and he's found something else that does.

Entry #5

There's no way I'll sell our home now, so most of our garage is full of boxes and crap. It's sitting in there, waiting until I put it back into our house. It's not that I can't use it right now; it's just that I haven't had time to put it back inside. It's crazy, though, because some of the crap isn't waiting, and a bunch of the things in our garage have gone missing. I don't know where they're running off to, but they don't have legs, and I can't figure out who's taking them.

The stuff that's been taken are things Cade's family gave us when we got married. There was a nice crock pot and some other similar things. Apparently, thieves like to cook. That scares me a bit because I like to cook, and hope it isn't a pre-existing condition.

It's bad, but I wonder if Cade's mom took the stuff. She's taken some other stuff, back before, because she thought other people in the family could use them. She took a T.V., an armoire, and even a couch. It's not a big deal, but it's just the principle that gets me. It makes me feel like nothing is ever mine, not really, and that's why I don't like accepting gifts from her, because she might take them back.

I don't know if it's her, anyway, though, because she's blunt enough she'll ask if she wants something back. That's one of the things I love about her: you always know where you stand with her. She's not like me; I always keep people guessing, since I'm too concerned with being nice.

I'm like the freaking heavyweight feelings champion. I dodge things, and people never know how I really feel, or when I'll knock them out when I finally blow up. I could take a few lessons from Marie because she knows how to handle things when they happen, instead of letting them build up.

Entry #6

Ruby asked if we could go to the store today. She begged and begged until I said "yes." She wanted a balloon, for crying out loud. After we made it to the store, and she finally dragged me to the balloon area, she got so picky I couldn't believe it. Before I could contain myself, I said, "Just pick one, Ruby. Please! Mommy has had it!"

Her perfect little hand grabbed a blue balloon, and she eyed it suspiciously, like it was the lead suspect in a crime, or something.

"This one, Mama! This one," she yelled, because apparently it was innocent.

"Okay, Honey, calm down." I took a deep breath and paid for the balloon.

The minute we got outside, Ruby let go and waved "bye-bye," as the costly thing floated into the sky. "Ruby!" I groaned, but she didn't look at me, and kept waving to her helium friend. "Ruby! Why did you do that?"

She looked at me seriously, and in a toddler accent no one understands except me, she said, "Are there bawoons in Heaven, Mama?"

"I don't know, Honey." The anger vanished from my voice.

"I don't think there are, so I gave my bawoon to Zeke." She smiled up at me, the beautiful smile of innocence.

"Oh, Honey," I sobbed, and hugged her. "Zeke loves balloons." She put her hands on her hips then, and said, "Mama, don't get mad unwess you know the whole story, k?"

"Okay! I promise," I said, and we shook on it.

I can't believe how smart that kid is. I've never heard of a kid her age that can talk so well. She's not as coordinated as some kids are, but she can really talk!

Entry #7

Cade and I see each other often because of Ruby. He's

actually taking better care of her, and that is good, because she needs him to give a crap. We never fight anymore, and I think it's just because we're both so detached.

I'd be lying if I said I don't miss him, because I do, but I've accepted that our life together has passed, just like our son did, and I want to forget and move beyond the pain. We're polite to each other, and it's not unpleasant being around him when he doesn't reek of pot, it's just hard because I want to rewind everything, and freeze time to when we found out Zeke was a boy—before the doctor found the problems. We were so happy, even though I was fat and pregnant.

Now, I feel like the friend who wants "more" from the rewound relationship but will never have it. Things get better every day, though, and I'm glad he is doing well—without me.

He has no idea that I still want him, but I like it that way. I don't need him and make that pretty obvious whenever he's here. He's just my kryptonite, and that's why I feel vulnerable around him. Even though I'm polite, I act coldly, and know he can feel the difference. I don't want him waltzing into my heart again; it hurt too much when we were together, and I'd rather devote my heart to other things, like Ruby.

Entry #8

My mom visited today and moved the kitchen table again. She doesn't like how Marie puts the table, and Marie doesn't like how my mom puts it, either. Every time they come over, they slide the thing back how they like it. I want to throw the thing out the window so no one can ever move it again, because I'd have the final say. But then Ruby and I would have to eat on the floor, and it might suck crap to have a broken window.

So, instead, I try being nice, and don't even say anything when it gets moved. It's almost become a joke, though, because I can tell who watched Ruby just by how the table is moved. If it's lengthwise, my mom was here, and if it's widthwise, Marie was.

I guess it's not so bad. It's their personal seal, or something. I laugh about it, though, because I'm losing control of everything around me. I can't even decide how I want my own table positioned. It'll get moved, anyway, and that's life right now, spinning out of control. God's the only one who completely controls things, that's who, and I hope He won't give me any more than I can handle.

Entry #9

Today is Zeke's birthday, and some of my family met me at his grave. My mom, sister, and sister-in-law were there. It felt nice having them standing by me while I cried over my son. We all bought him some stuff, even though he'll never use it.

My sister said a sweet prayer, and by the time we left, there was an odd assortment of flowers and toys lying by his headstone. I hope he's having a happy birthday, without me. I miss him so much.

Ruby came with us, and I thought about bringing a balloon so she could send it to Zeke. I thought about how that can kill animals, if they find the balloon and eat it, and decided not to bring a balloon, even though Zeke might like another pet in Heaven.

Entry #10

The lead guitarist in Cade's band just called. I don't trust that guy. I know he has a thing for me, and I can tell he wants to catch me on the sly, as if I don't know what he's doing. So, he called and asked to hang out. He's as smooth as hell because he even asked Cade if it would be okay. Can you believe Cade gave him permission to hang out with me!

"I'm not Cade's property," I said, because that guy had real nerve, asking permission and all.

"I didn't mean it like that; I just wanted you to know that Cade's okay with you hanging out with me," he said.

"I'm sure he is." I had to laugh because Cade doesn't give a damn anymore.

"We could make some beautiful music together," he said, and I thought how that line is completely overused in the music industry. "I want my family to meet you. I know they'll love you. Please come to this barbeque with me," he pleaded.

I thought about it for a minute because it did sound fun, and I didn't have anything going on. But I decided non-musical strings were attached, and I only have time for friends in my life now.

"I don't see Ruby very much, and I should probably spend quality time with her—here."

"Isn't Cade taking her this weekend?"

I sighed, trying to get out of it, but that guy knew way too much about my personal life. "Oh, yeah.... I forgot," I said in a slippery voice, and then changed the subject. "How's everything going with the band?"

He talked forever about the band and forgot the barbeque for a minute.

"Are there a lot of pretty girls at the gigs?" I finally asked, wondering if Cade has run into any Piranha.

"Yeah, I guess so. Why?"

"I just wondered if any of the band members go out with them."

"Ty and Chewy have gone out with a few, but I never have," he said. "I'm interested in someone else."

"Is it Erin, that girl you got pregnant?" I asked.

"No," he said. "You know about that, huh?"

"Yeah, I do." I paused and smiled because I'd taken him off guard. "Does Cade ever go out with the girls from the shows?" I put my fist in my mouth and bit it hard, because I was upset with myself for asking such a dumb question.

"It's always about Cade with you, isn't it?" I didn't answer, and he continued. "Cade never goes out with the girls. I wish he would, so you'd get over it, but all that guy talks about is you. A couple of really hot chicks came up to him the other night, and Cade hardly noticed them. He was nice, and everything, but not interested. Everyone could tell."

"Really?" I asked with too much excitement in my voice.

"Yeah, and when they wouldn't leave him alone, Cade's brother walked up to the girls and said, 'He's married; leave him alone.'

The girls acted all butt-hurt and left."

"I always liked Cade's brother. He's a cool guy. That's weird about Cade, though."

"You two really love each other, don't you?" he asked, and I grew quiet, not knowing the answer. "So, will you come to the barbeque with me?"

"No," I said, "but you should ask that chick you knocked up. She sounds like a nice girl." I hung up the phone hard.

Entry #11

Cade watched Ruby during the day today, and I was hella nervous to see him after work. Just before I got to the house, I pulled over and did my makeup so I wouldn't look like I'd just crawled from Zeke's grave. I don't really know why it mattered, but it did. I want him to realize what he's missing out on.

When I got home, Cade was waiting on the couch. His eyes flicked all over me like a searchlight, and I was happy, knowing he still likes what he sees. I held my hands out, and looked down at the floor, scared to meet his eyes.

"How was your day?" he asked.

"Good," I said coldly. Not meaning to, I caught the eyes I'd tried avoiding, and we stared, almost touching each other's thoughts. I hope he didn't hear what I thought, because I'd be embarrassed if he knew how much I miss him. Even though he's hurt me bad, I put on a strong face. I guess neither of us wanted to talk about our thoughts, because things aren't simple anymore, and we've crossed lines we never should have.

"Do you still like your job?" he asked.

"Yeah, it's fun."

"It suits you—I mean, you look real good for a mechanic," he said.

"Thanks," I heard myself say. "I bought a car. You can take the other one, if you want. I just didn't want to drive something you paid for."

"It wasn't a big deal. You know you can keep it. You and Ruby should have a nice car to drive in."

"It's okay." Heat lit my voice. "I don't need handouts. You already helped by watching Ruby. I don't need your car!" Cade stood to leave, and I stayed in the small entryway. I should have moved, but for some reason I didn't. He walked close, and as he tried leaving, our shoulders touched. He stopped and looked down at me.

We were only inches apart and just stood there, quite lost for words. He put his calloused construction hand on my cheek and stared into my eyes. I didn't back away, not wanting him to know how much his touch affects me.

For a minute I thought he would kiss me, but he didn't. Instead, his face fell, and his eyes sunk with tiredness. He opened the front door and didn't even shut it behind him. I stood there, shivering, as I watched him pull out and drive away; all he'd left behind was the cold night air that wafted through the door.

Entry #12

I can't stop thinking about my first kiss with Cade, and I wish I could erase the memory from my mind. When I was in high school, I had these two crazy rules. I wouldn't kiss a guy until I dated him for six months, and I would never shave my legs if I worried the guy might go further than kissing. I knew if I didn't shave my legs, that rule would keep me straight. It was an awesome way to weed out the creeps. Lots of guys wouldn't wait that long—they're dumb like that. So, when I first dated Cade, I told him about my kissing rule. It didn't bother him at all, and that made me happy; he would wait to kiss me.

After we'd only dated a couple of weeks, we sat talking about things. His head rested in my lap, and I asked if anyone had ever drawn on his face.

"What do you mean?" he asked.

"Just close your eyes and I'll show you," I said, and gently traced his features. When I got to his lips, I remember thinking how perfect and full they were. He smiled when I traced them, and I think that's when I decided to break my rule.

I traced his lips again, and his chin for a minute. Then I paused, wondering if I was sure I wanted to kiss him. That rule was a big deal, and I wouldn't break it for anyone—anyone but Cade.

So, I started the whole process again. I traced his eyebrows, his eyes, and before I knew it, I used my lips instead of my fingers. By the time I made it to Cade's lips, he smiled so big; he couldn't help it. I shook my head briefly before diving into that kiss.

He sat up and looked at me for a minute before we kissed again. We stayed locked in that second one for a while. He pulled away, then bent his head so just our foreheads touched. He closed his eyes, and softly said, "I love you...I always will."

"I love you, too," I replied, like I was the dumbest kid in the world, love struck at seventeen. That was the first time we kissed, and the first time we said, "I love you."

But I think he lied that day, because I don't understand how he can possibly love me and not want to be with me. If he wants me, why isn't he here? Why can't he come home, choose us, and leave everything else. I don't understand.

Entry #13

Did I mention that my sliding glass door is broken? It locks, but if you yank it really hard, it comes right open. It's not very comforting, thinking about when Ruby and I are alone at night. Our house creaks a lot, and when I don't think it's the "disappearing act," I think robbers are in the house. It's loads of fun, since I don't have a gun or a baseball bat, and I keep wondering what I could defend myself with. I should buy a bat; I was always great at hitting balls—all kinds of them.

When I was a kid, I had a romantic image about how a bad guy would attack me, and right before he'd make his move, I'd say, "Stop. What would Jesus say?" And then the guy would stop and look at me like the thought never struck him. Then he'd leave and change his lifestyle by becoming a priest.

Well, Zeke happened, and I don't have that romantic image in my head anymore. If a creepy guy comes in here, I should count on more than my words as weapons. What I wish is that I had a pet skunk, because there is no better weapon than a skunk's happy juice. That would rock it like the 80's, if I had a skunk juice gun. No one would want to attack us because I'd spray them, and then I'd give them the Jesus talk. It'd be the ultimate "double no-no."

Anyway, I came home today, and there was a bunch of baby powder all over the black futon, the floor, and everything else, like it'd been raining baby powder in the living room. I love baby powder, but not that much.

I looked around and noticed the back sliding glass door was wide open. I don't know who got in here, but I wonder if it's the "cooking stuff bandit." I want my stuff back from the garage! All I know is, the person loves cooking and baby powder, and that doesn't tell me a whole lot, other than that I should get my door fixed.

Entry #14

My dad isn't feeling well. I don't know what to do. He's sick, and I hate seeing him like that. The chemo is helping, and he puts on a happy face for everyone, but when I'm at the house alone with him, he tells me how things really are. He's always sick from the chemo and having other problems since part of his liver is gone. I wish I could help him, but there's nothing to do except pray.

So, I got down on my knees and prayed for the first time since Zeke was born, and since the skunk's funeral. I told God,

"Hi," and I'm sorry I haven't prayed in a while, but I didn't want to bug Him.

"God," I said, "I'm not here to bargain or bribe you, like I did when I first prayed for you to heal Zeke. I'm just here to say 'mercy.' We've been playing a game of bloody knuckles, and it's a game I can't win—'cause Godly hands are bigger than mine. I just wanted to let you know I can't take any more. I don't really have control over my life, but I know you do, and I trust you with that power. But I need You to know I can't handle it, if you take my dad. I don't think I'd survive since You already took my son. Please help my dad, God. Please, because he's a really good guy and he's not done living yet, and I couldn't take it, if you took my dad and my only son. Oh, and I hope Zeke likes his balloon." That was how I ended my prayer. It wasn't a fancy prayer, but it sprouted from my heart. I hope God heard it and knew I didn't mean to be sacrilegious (just in case I came off that way). Hopefully, He won't send me to Hell for it. It's just that He didn't listen to my super stuffy prayers before, and I figured I'd try a more friendly style, and He'll listen this time.

Entry #15

Cammie had her baby! She's beautiful and healthy, just like the doctors foretold. I'm so happy for them. I held her today. I can't believe how tiny she is. She's got the cutest little nose and the most gorgeous eyes.

Cammie just beamed when I visited them. She's so happy, her joy affected me. Isn't it wonderful, knowing most babies are born healthy? She really is perfect, and the best part is that Cammie gets to keep her.

Entry #16

I got up this morning, and I heard a loud knock on the front door. It was only about six-thirty, and I couldn't figure who would come over so early. I answered the door. Standing in the cold was a darling little boy, wearing nothing except a diaper. He held a note in his hand and gave it to me as soon as he entered the house.

"What's this?" I asked, but he cried. So, I read the note aloud while trying to make sense of things.

"Thomas," I read, "I'm going to the city. I'll be back in a few hours. Please eat some cereal, and I'll see you soon. Love, Mom."

"Mama?" he whispered.

"Yeah." I looked at the note again.

"Mama?"

"She's gone to the city," I said. "It's a place, like where we live, but about one-hundred times bigger."

He nodded.

"So, your name is Thomas?"

"Yeah."

"How old are you?" He held up three fingers. "Really?" I feigned amazement. "I used to be three. We've got a lot in common!" I paused. "Thomas, do you know your mommy's phone number?"

"No."

"Can you read?"

"No," he whimpered. He took the note from my hands, looked at it upside down, and splashed it with tears. I smiled then because I liked the kid; he wasn't a member of the snotty-nosed kind. I thought about calling the cops then, because I couldn't imagine what kind of mother would leave her child. But then I waited and gave her the benefit of the doubt. Sometimes people have emergencies, and they have to do crazy things. I don't want to call the cops unless I absolutely know why she left.

"I'll tell you what. I'll leave your mom a note saying where you're at, and you can stay here and play." I smiled at him.

"I'm hungry," he said.

"That's awesome, because I just hoped a cute little boy would come over and eat some breakfast with me!" I pulled some cereal from the pantry and poured him a big bowl. As soon as he started eating, I got him a blanket so he wouldn't be so cold. I couldn't figure out where his mom was.

I watched him eat, and looked away for a minute, because he reminded me of a dream I had about Zeke. In the dream, Zeke is healthy, and spends the whole day happy with me, Ruby and Cade. We're at the park and we wear smiles all day long.

After Ruby woke up, she and Thomas had a ball together. The whole time they played in the backyard, a mentally handicapped girl (who lives behind us) kept sneaking over the fence to play with them. She's a cute little girl who cracks me up.

There are eight kids in her family, and the mom has a hard time watching them. So, her mom put a tracking device on the handicapped girl, and it beeps loud if she goes farther than a two-block radius. I've never heard the alarm go off, but her mom said it's pretty loud. I like my neighbor, but she's a good form of birth control; I don't want eight kids.

Anyway, I had fun watching them play, and it struck me strange that Thomas looks like the "disappearing act" I saw after Zeke died.

I imagined Ruby and Zeke were playing, and blinked back tears when Ruby waved to me. I thought again about how no one will take Zeke's place. I shook the thought off like dandruff, or something, and I went about cleaning the house again.

Thomas' mom finally burst in a few hours later. She looked super nervous and almost shook. I wanted to ask if she was okay, but after what happened with Zeke, I don't feel right prying into things that aren't my business.

She told me she was sorry for the inconvenience, but she'd lost her house and was in the middle of a bad divorce. I told her it wasn't a big deal, and wanted to tell her Thomas can't read, and he is too little to be left alone, but I didn't want to upset her, because she looked flustered, and I can tell something really bad just happened in her life. I told Thomas he's welcome anytime. He grinned and even gave me a hug goodbye.

Entry #17

"The understudy" called me tonight. I was super surprised when I heard his voice on the phone. He was really sweet, and I found myself laughing and actually enjoying the conversation, like I'd been drinking happy juice, or something, but not the kind that comes from a skunk. He said he stopped messing around with drugs and got a good job. That made me happy.

While we talked, I remembered some of the fun times we'd had together. There was a park I went to whenever I needed to think. A huge canopy of trees hid it from the world. A tiny stream ran through the little clearing, by a long, bony bench.

I'd go there, and we'd somehow show up at the same time. We'd sit on that bony bench and talk about all sorts of things, for hours, even though we hadn't planned on meeting there at all. After a while we'd forget our problems and laugh together. The echoes of our laughter are stuck in my heart, for crying out loud, because whenever I think about it, the voices still laugh at me now.

He was a good friend for a couple of years, and I still feel bad I broke his heart. That's why I was shocked he called; I didn't deserve a call from him, not after I took his ring, and then left with Cade, instead.

It got quiet for a moment on the phone, and he said, "You know, Ruby is the prettiest little girl I've ever seen."

"I love that kid," I said.

"So how are you and Cade doing? Are you still together?" he asked. I knew he was interested in me again and looking for more than friendship.

I don't know why, but I lied, "We're doing okay." I clenched my teeth. "He's the best husband I could ask for."

"Oh...that's good," he said, and I wondered if he knew I had lied. He'd known me pretty well, and I bet he saw through me like a piece of cellophane. As I talked to him, I couldn't believe I'd lied, and couldn't figure out why. Maybe I still am in love with Cade? Maybe?

"Does Cade know that you're talking to me?" he asked like Pinocchio's cricket-conscience.

"Oh yeah," I said, even though I knew Cade couldn't give a crap less. "He doesn't care. You should go to one of his gigs sometime. I bet he'd love that." I laughed at the thought of Cade seeing "the understudy." Those two guys really don't like each other. They could have been best friends in an alternate universe, but will never be in this one, because I'm here, that's why.

Entry #18

I talked to Cade tonight. We stood outside the house, and our breath circled around like halos. I frowned as I thought about that, because my boy's the one who's an angel, not me. Cade looked at the stars and rocked back on his heels as he stood in the snowy driveway.

"What are you thinking about?" I asked him.

"You wouldn't understand," he said.

"Try me." I stepped toward him.

"I was just thinking," he paused, "about how good it feels...not being high."

"Oh," I said, and didn't really know what else to say. "Well, that's good."

"Yeah, I guess," he said.

"Cade, why is it such a big deal for you to be in the band?"

"It's my way of coping," he said, and I grew quiet as he got into his car.

I wonder if he'll quit smoking pot. I hope he will. The last thing that guy needs is a damn crutch.

Entry #19

Thomas comes over every day. His mom is a sweet lady, but I think she's on drugs, because she doesn't have any fingernails, and I wish I had called the cops the first day I met her. Have you ever seen someone without fingernails? It's weird, but not as weird as seeing someone without eyebrows. It's like looking at the bottom of someone's hands, just without the callouses, and all. Once I had a sleepover with a girl who drew on her eyebrows. Her forehead looked like eternity when she washed her eyebrows off. It was the weirdest thing, going on forever, like an alien from Venus or something.

Anyway, the lady who has no fingernails used to be a stripper, and she said she moved out to this small town, hoping no one would know who she was. She's sick of dirty men coming up to her in the grocery store and telling her how good she was at wearing tassels. I guess they tell her that right in front of her kids, and everything. She's fun to be around, and I really don't mind watching her boy. Ruby likes the company, and I feel responsible for him somehow. It's just nice, knowing he's being taken care of when he's with me.

I want to call the cops on his mom, but don't have any proof she's doing drugs, and I know Thomas needs his mama. Plus, I've heard foster parents are really crappy, and I'd hate seeing him go there, just in case they're worse than his mom.

I garden with his mom all of the time and have so much fun talking with her. She's really blunt and says things I didn't know women could say without getting their mouth washed with soap. I must be a pretty innocent girl, because I don't understand half the stuff she jokes about. But I laugh, anyway, just like I'm super educated about stripper humor.

I've told her all about Cade, and she said I should hurry and divorce him. She said it's not very hard after you leave your first husband; she's done it about fifty times, and even left a woman once. I wish I could fix her somehow, not that she's broken or anything, but it would be neat if she'd get off the drugs and magically turn into a mother, or something. Stripping must be hard; I get naked twice every day when I change. I can't imagine wrinkly, prying hands all around. She needs to see that people really care about her. Plus, it might be an extra bonus if she got her fingernails back.

Entry #20

When I got home from work, Cade was waiting in Zeke's room. He sat in the rocking chair. After I walked into the room, I told him about my conversation with the "the understudy." It wasn't a very nice thing to say, especially since I knew he was thinking about Zeke, but I wanted to make him fume. Cade's face practically lit on fire, and his body tensed visibly.

"Oh yeah," he said as he stood, and I found it funny how he couldn't remain calm.

"You okay?" I asked, but he didn't answer. He paced around the room I'd decorated for our dead son.

"What'd you talk about?"

"Just old times, mostly." I fake smiled at the memory, and Cade caught the smile on my face.

"Are you gonna hang out with him?" Cade asked, acting like he didn't care whether I lived or went to be with our son.

"Maybe," I said, even though I knew I wouldn't, and was satisfied when Cade turned pasty white.

He jumped in my face before I had a chance to back away and was so close my chest touched his body. "Don't you know how hard this is for me?" he asked in a shaky voice. Then, for the first time in months, he decided to talk about things now that it's too late. "Can't you see how much I want to be with you, but I can't, can I? I can't have everything, and God's playing a joke on me! Just like Zeke! I couldn't keep my son, and now I'm losing you, too! Why did you make me choose between you and the band? Why? This is your fault, Elisa. This time, it's your fault!" Rage carved his face.

"I—" but I didn't get to answer. He kissed me like I was necessary oxygen, and he crushed me against him. His hands ran over my body, blindly searching for the light. I wanted to be with him then; for some stupid reason, I really wanted him back.

I trembled from his touch, and part of me said I should turn away because I can't stand being hurt by him again. I kissed him back, though, and dug my hands through his hair as I pulled him closer, hoping he'd never leave me, because I knew it'd be a sad, lonely life without him.

But then I leaned against Zeke's baby crib, and I felt his hands release me so they could feel the hard wood of the crib. He pushed himself away then, and it ended as fast as it had started.

"I've got to go," he said; harshness drugged his voice. I leaned against Zeke's crib and slid down in a heap of misery.

"Why, Cade? Why?" I rested my face in my hands. "Why are you doing this?"

"Because you won't be supportive, and that just shows.... You don't really love me."

"But I—"

"And because I can't stop loving you—even though we're through." His eyes drifted to Zeke's crib. "Zeke was just a sign that we shouldn't be together!"

"Cade, don't go!" I sobbed the words out.

"I'm leaving! I can't stand seeing you night after night and knowing how happy you are without me. I never suffered like this," he looked at me contemptuously, "until I met you! And now you might go see Johnny again?"

"If you were in my shoes, you would do the same damn thing!"

Cade turned. "I would have supported you in anything you wanted to do!"

"Even if I was always gone, and you had to work, and find a babysitter for Ruby?"

"That's different!" Cade spat. "Like hell it is!"

"I'm leaving!" He left the room, even though I wanted him to stay. I just want him to see my side, but know he won't, because he's being a sexist man, and I loathe him for that: for thinking he's so much better than me, that he deserves to be selfish, and leave all responsibility behind.

"But, Cade," I rasped as he left the room, and he didn't hear me. I lay on Zeke's floor and cried. I cried for a long time because I'm in the world's record book for being the biggest boob. Plus, it seemed like the only thing to do since Cade had left.

I realized, though, I'm not the only one going through pain. He acts like he's over Zeke, but he's not. I've been in survival mode, and don't have the energy to help someone else through this—anyone but Ruby. I wish I could help Cade, but I can't. I'm having enough trouble just helping myself, and I'll be damned if I ever let him do this to me again.

Entry #21

Remember the lady who talked to me after Zeke's funeral? You know, she said he'd still be here if I just had enough faith. I talked to her on the phone today, and she's still chock full of Bible thumping power.

"Do you miss him?" she asked.

"Who?" I didn't know if she had referred to Zeke or Cade.

"Your son," she said.

"Yeah, I do." I tried keeping the annoyance from my voice because it was a silly question to ask.

"Maybe you'll have more faith next time," she said in her sweetly prudish voice.

"What?" I asked and couldn't contain my anger because she'd pushed me too hard. "Hopefully, there won't be a next time! Sometimes crap just happens."

She drew in a stunned breath when I said "crap," because that just bought me a ticket to Hell.

"My son was meant to die. That's the only way I can look at the situation, and when people, who have no idea what it's like to lose a child, preach their inexperienced views, and tell me what I should have done to save my son, it just makes me sick!"

"Some people can be so inconsiderate," she said, and I couldn't figure if she was agreeing, or talking about me. I was tired of getting walked on by her holier-than-thou views, and it felt nice lashing at her, just once! "I'm sure you would know," I said.

"Please tell your mother that I called."

"I will," I said, but she'd already hung up, and I'll never wake her from her self-righteous world, not in five-hundred years. I wonder if she even heard a word I said, and what she'll tell my mom.

Entry #22

Ruby is finally potty trained, and I think potty training is harder than crossing the Red Sea, even with God's help. Potty training is a messy business! Ruby used to freak out when I'd put her on the toilet, and it reminds me of when I had to poo in the pan before I had Zeke. It didn't feel natural; maybe that's how Ruby felt when she sat on the toilet for the first time. Anything is better than pooing in a butt sack though, honestly.

We ate at McDonald's today, since Ruby graduated from my potty school. I got her a burger, and let her play as long as she wanted, which was about two hours. By that time, I'd already gone down the slide two hundred times, and was dying to go home. All of the other moms looked at me like I was nuts. But I thought they were the ones missing out; ignorance isn't always bliss, not really, at least not when you miss out on the kids' slide at McDonald's.

They aren't making those slides like they used to. They're not as steep, and not as big as they were when I was five. You have to scoot down the thing like they made it practically horizontal, but Ruby thought it was great, anyway. My voice echoed in the slide, and I told Ruby we came just because she's potty trained now. I'm still pretty slap-happy about it because I'm so proud of her. She even used the bathroom there, no kidding. That kid's better than conventional cooking, she just is.

I'm glad Ruby's doing so well. She's even made a new friend, and everything. The only weird thing is that he's invisible. I guess that's what makes him imaginary, and all. He never hangs around until just before I go to work. Whenever she sees me getting ready, she walks into the closet and finds her friend, because that's where he lives.

She calls him "Prince," and is crazy about him. It's a funny thing, a prince living in a closet, but she thinks it's pretty normal. I can't figure why he always comes out just before I leave, because I'd like to see her interact with him sometime. I'm a little worried about her having an imaginary friend, though. I'm sure she's okay, but it still makes me nervous.

Entry #23

I work with a hella cool lady. She's one of a kind, for sure. She's a mechanic and a parts manager, but her skills don't stop there. She's also the hunters' safety teacher for our little town. I love her because she's so real; she has nothing in common with the Easter Bunny. One of my other co-workers says the "hunter lady" is nothing but white trash, but all I can see is the good in her.

The "hunter lady" asked if I would hang out with her. I said, "Yes," and thought how fun it would be, even though she's three times my age. So, I met her at her house and her oldest son was there.

I was surprised she had such a good-looking son and wondered if she'd wanted me to meet him. He asked Ruby if she would like to feed the chickens, and Ruby was happier than crap on a shingle. We each held one of her little hands as we walked over to the chickens. I thought it was strange, how natural Ruby and the "hunter lady's" son seemed around each other. I wanted to tell him that we'd just met, and I didn't feel comfortable with him holding her hand—even though he's a good-looking cowboy, he's not her daddy—but I kept my mouth shut in the name of politeness.

Ruby fed the chickens and picked an egg like it was a flower. We brought it in the house, and the "hunter lady" fried Ruby a super-organic egg. It made me happy just looking at Ruby's yoked-up face. She told me she wants to visit those chickens every day.

Anyway, we went to an expo, and I don't know how it happened, but her son, the cowboy, ended up riding with me and Ruby. We followed his parents to the show. I shot the bull with him, and I had to smile a little when I saw how scrunched up he was in my car. He sat contently in accordion style, and he's the biggest oxymoron I've ever met. I still can't figure how that could make a tall, lanky sort of guy so damn happy.

I didn't even fill in the blank parts in the conversation, because they just vanished, and at one point we laughed so hard I forgot to keep a good eye on where his parents drove. They weren't in front of us anymore, and when I looked at the car next to us, all I saw were two huge, saggy boobs. They hung out the driver's window, swaying in the wind and they were bigger than Milwaukee!

"Mom!" "the cowboy" yelled, and turned green, like he needed Cade's paper bag.

"Is that—?"

He looked at me, begging me to stop confirming the truth. I giggled, and it must have been catching because he and Ruby started laughing, too. I accidentally snorted, and I covered my face, totally embarrassed. But he didn't mind, and I smiled wider, knowing I could be myself around that guy and his crazy mom, whose chest had been naked like Eve in Eden.

We finally made it to the expo, and "the cowboy" was excited that the rest of the ride didn't involve any more of his mom's bare nipples. We walked around, and I couldn't believe how much Ruby took to him.

An old lady told us what a cute family we are. I just smiled and said, "Thanks," because I didn't want to go into the whole story about how I'd lost my son and my husband, all in the same damn century, and how I hardly knew this guy. "The cowboy" blushed when she said it, then he grabbed Ruby and threw her onto his shoulders. I saw his arms flex, and I realized he's a man used to hard labor.

I couldn't believe how much he loved the comment. He must

206

be one of those "damsels-in-distress" types of guys that look for a woman to save. Too bad for him; I don't need saving. He'll have to look somewhere else because Ruby and I are fine on our own.

It was a nice day, and I'm glad Ruby had such a great time, but when I close my eyes, I keep seeing those big saggy boobs swaying in the wind, like the things are carved into the backs of my eyelids. I never knew God made boobs so crazy-long like that. I guess I'm glad I'm so flat. On the way home I accidentally whistled "Do Your Ears Hang Low."

"The cowboy" heard me, and asked, "You still thinking about my mom's boobs?"

I considered lying, and then realized God might be listening. I said, "Yeah.... you?"

"Yeah, I'm scarred for life—again," he said, and I tried changing the subject, just to be nice.

But I don't think I should call his mom "hunter lady" anymore. I think I'll refer to her as "big sag."

Entry #24

Cade called me today. He doesn't want to watch Ruby at the house anymore because it's not working out, and I need to ask one of our moms to tend on the nights he usually comes.

"That's really putting our moms out! Are you sure?" I asked.

"I need to be at band practice. The guys are mad because I miss so many practices. Plus, it's better than making a fool of myself again," he retorted, and I knew he remembered the night he kissed me.

"You didn't—"

"I have to go."

"Yeah, you do have to go, don't you! You have to play in your precious band while I struggle making ends meet, and while I do the right thing! Don't you know that I wanted to do music for a living, too?

"Then why don't you?" he asked.

"Because I have obligations, and I won't turn my back on them and be a selfish jerk like you!"

"I'm the selfish jerk? You're the one who can't stop nagging me, even when we're apart!"

"If you'd stand up and be a man, then I wouldn't have to nag you!" He was quiet, and I went on, "I'm applying for state assisted babysitting. Tomorrow."

"Have fun," he said, and hung up the phone.

I plopped down on the couch because I felt too weak to stand. I can't stop thinking about the other night, and I really wish I could. When I'm not thinking about that, I'm thinking about how Cade is driving me toward the insane asylum—I'll be making balloon animals before I know it—and I can't figure out why he's doing this to me. I've never seen a nut house, and it might be interesting to look at, just not be admitted into, that's all. I don't know if I hate Cade or love him. I just want to hit him really hard, and then maybe he'll understand how much he's hurting me!

I did hit a guy once when I was in junior high. I never wore dresses to school because I was a tomboy, but this one day I wore a sundress. I cut my hair in this cute short style, and I wore makeup for the first time. I think I did it because I sat next to a really cute guy in my history class, and I wanted him to think I looked good in a dress.

Well, in my history class, this crazy-nerdy kid dropped his pencil, and then touched my legs. After dropping his pencil, he grabbed my shoe and threw it to the front of the class. He said he wanted me to get it just so he could watch me walk. I fumed, but he had no idea as I walked to the front of the class.

I tried being as cute as hell when I fetched my shoe because the really cute guy was watching me. I had a serious limp working for me since I only had one shoe on. It had a three-inch heel made of pure wood, and I'm sure my hips swayed worse than a sail in a double wind. I looked pretty gimpy, if you want to know the truth, and I laugh about it now. I wasn't one of those prissy girls and didn't have much experience trying to be attractive. By the time I got my shoe, all of the boys in my fourth period class gawked at me. They noticed me for the first time, even though I'd just looked like the biggest dork ever.

I glared at the guy who'd taken off my wooden shoe, and I said, "You wanted me to get my shoe? Well, here it is," and I hit him across the face with the clog's heel.

It wasn't to be mean; it was just the only sensible thing to do. He ran like a little girl and went straight to the boy's bathroom. There was a tiny bit of blood on the floor next to where he'd been sitting, and I thought how weird it was that the jerk's blood pooled red, just like mine would have. I thought it would be black, or something.

Anyway, my teacher grabbed me by the arm, and said, "Elisa! I never would have expected that from you!"

"The creep touched my leg!" I said back and watched as all of the boys in the class leaned away from me.

The teacher took me to the principal's office, and I acted innocent. I had to meet with the leg-toucher, too, and he didn't even think of touching me that time. He looked at me like I was a rabid dog, and I liked it that way, feeling feisty.

So, I'd dislocated his jaw, and the principal didn't call my parents or even make me pay a doctor's bill, since I didn't break the jerk's jaw, or anything. It was funny, too, because, as we sat in the principal's office, I didn't get the reprimand, the leg-toucher did, and at the end of the thing, he apologized. I laughed after leaving that office, but not too loud because I didn't want the principal hearing me. I guess sexual harassment is worse than a dislocated jaw.

Entry #25

I went to the state building and qualified for assisted babysitting. I'm nervous, though, because I've never had a stranger take care of Ruby, and I hope they'll do a good job. I just need to find a good place to bring her, and then the state will pay a portion of the bill. There's a sweet girl who lives behind me. She's the oldest kid out of all of those kids in her family. She's offered to watch Ruby a few times, and I might see how much she would charge, and leave Ruby with her. She's a cute girl, and I'm sure she'd do a good job, but the state will only pay if they're certified.

Plus, Ruby's going through enough as it is. I can tell she's having a hard time, and it's strange because she's still so little. She bawls every time I go into another room, and holds onto my legs, so I do a gimp walk.

"Holden? Mama, please give me holden?" she asks, because it's her way of getting hugs. I hold her tight and rock her. After a while, her little sobs fade into my shoulder, but I can't figure what's wrong.

She's still been hanging out with "Prince" when I'm gone. I know he's just pretend, but I hope he's a nice imaginary friend. I don't know how to help my little girl. We're both going through so much together, and I'm too young to go through this. If I feel like that, I can't imagine how she feels, because she's eighteen years younger than me, and that's quite a bit.

Entry #26

I told my mom and Marie that I qualified for assisted babysitting. They said they don't care what they have to do, but they don't want Ruby going to daycare. That kid sure is loved. I'll have the neighbor girl watch Ruby when my mom and Marie can't. It will work out really well, and Ruby's as happy as a lark about the whole thing because she loves the neighbor girl.

My mom and Marie don't know what to think about it, though, because they said the neighbor's too young to watch Ruby. But they've put me in a corner, and that girl watches her siblings all the time. If our moms don't want me taking Ruby to a daycare, and Cade won't watch her, then I have to do something. I can't just sit around and wait for the bills to pay themselves, and I'm not going to let life get me down, not when I can do something about it.

Entry #27

I went through Cade's drawer again. I still didn't find any pot, but I did read one of "King Arthur's" letters. I just couldn't help it. They sat in there, begging me to read them. I've never been good at resisting temptation like that. Whenever I have a chance to know what someone really thinks of me, I jump, like a dog on hot coals. I want to know, even if they hate me. It's not the best trait, but at least I'm honest.

I had to smile after I read "King Arthur's" letter. I'm glad I didn't read it back when Zeke was alive because I would have maimed the author. He wrote about the day I saw him at my in-laws' house.

He said he tried putting a curse on me, and I laughed when I read that, because now I know why he stared at me. I can't believe he didn't think having a son with birth defects would be bad enough, and that I needed to be cursed, too. He wrote that he envisioned a spider on my belly, because evidently spiders are the ultimate bane for pregnant women. I stopped, stunned when I read that part. "King Arthur" hates me so bad, but I don't care anymore. Something childish and stupid died in me, and I learned another life lesson as I read his cruel words. There's no point in caring what people think about me because I should just care what God thinks of me, and what I think of myself.

His words were prideful, arrogantly written, and as I read the end of the letter, I flew into a haze of laughter and fog. He'd written a part about being intimate with sheep, and other crazy things. I called Marie and told her all about the letter, since "King Arthur" is her nephew and all.

"He's not related to me by blood," she said, after I told her the whole story. "He's related to Cade's dad!" It felt nice telling her the whole thing, and after I got off the phone, I took all of those crappy letters, crumpled them up, and threw them in the garbage. I didn't read any of the other ones, there wasn't a need to. I'd read enough.

I don't care if Cade gets mad, and honestly, I'm upset he's still talking to "King Arthur" after all the mean things he said about me. I can't figure why he saved all those letters, unless he wants to turn the guy in for animal cruelty. But I guess "King Arthur" is Cade's best friend. Why would he try to put a curse on me and my unborn son, anyway? Wouldn't that end up hurting Cade, too?

I'm glad he was "King Arthur," and not Merlin, in a past life. Otherwise, I might have been in serious trouble!

Entry #28

I called my sister today. I needed to hear advice about Cade. After I finished talking, I felt bad for calling. She got mad when I told her what's happened with Cade and said I should get away from him. She even offered me a place to live, but I had to smile then, because I'm making my own house payment, and everything. She said I should attend college so I can get a good job to support Ruby. She'd willingly baby-sit Ruby while I'm in school, and we wouldn't be a burden.

I didn't know she would get so mad about Cade, and when I talked to her, I noticed that I didn't stand up for him anymore; I just listened to everything she said. But I shouldn't have pushed my problems on her like that.

We don't talk a whole lot, and I feel bad, calling her about my problems. At least I know how much she loves me. It meant a lot that she offered me a place to stay, even though I don't need one. I couldn't believe how protective she got, because half of the time I don't even know if she really likes me. I mean, if I weren't her sister, I don't know if she'd even want to be friends with me. I know I'd want to be friends with her, though. She's one of those people everyone loves and asks for advice. She has it all together, and even strangers can tell.

I wish I could talk to my brother about things, but I know he'll want to beat the crap out of Cade. The last time I talked to my brother about things, he said he would make Cade bleed from every orifice. I still don't know what an orifice is, other than that it bleeds, but I do think it would make a cool name, for a dragon.

So, instead of unburdening myself on my grandma, who never hears any of my problems, or on Cammie, who hears too many of them, I called Cade's sister. Cade's living with her right now, and I don't know why I felt possessed to call her, but I did, and it ended up being the right thing to do.

She listened, and told me not to worry, that everything will work out the way it's supposed to. She said Cade still loves me; I wanted to laugh but didn't because whatever he's experiencing for me right now, it's not love. She was very sweet, though, and I'm glad she talked to me, even though I'm on the outs with her baby brother.

Entry #29

Ruby has nightmares about Zeke. I sing his song a lot, and maybe that's why she has bad dreams. I don't mean to sing about him all of the time. I just catch myself singing to him, and then I see Ruby in the corner of my eye. She's crying from the music, like she's trained to sob when she hears that song.

Every time she dreams about Zeke, she wakes up soaking wet because she's peed the bed. I don't know what to do for her. I don't want to put diapers back on so she thinks it's okay, but I also don't want her peeing the bed. Poor kid, I wish I could take away the dreams. She won't tell me what they're about, and says she misses her baby. I'll quit singing Zeke's song around her.

Cammie's oldest girl has had some problems since their baby died. I guess she talks about her sister at school, probably because she doesn't completely understand why she's gone, but knows just enough that it bothers her. I'm so glad they have another baby. Her oldest daughter wanted a little sister so badly. I

213

just feel bad they had to lose one.

People say Ruby can't remember Zeke, and she's fine, but they're wrong. I know she remembers and can tell someone is missing. I wish I could explain things to her, the things I don't understand, myself. I hold her a lot and say how much I love her. She always asks if I'll leave her. I say, "No, Honey, no. I'll never leave you."

Entry #30

Cammie visited me today. She cried, and I worry for her.

"What's wrong? Is everything okay?" I asked, hoping things were okay.

"We're moving, and I'll miss you so much!" I felt some more pieces of my world come crashing to the ground, and my heart wanted to float away like Zeke's balloon, because then maybe it wouldn't hurt so badly.

"You can't move," I said, and hugged her. She's been such a good friend.

"Blake got the U. S. Marshals job. He'll be one of the youngest U.S. Marshals around."

"That's awesome," I said, trying to be happy for her, and wanting to understand why she's leaving.

"We're leaving really soon."

"How soon?"

"As soon as we sell the house."

"Oh." I felt a little deflated. I've gotten so close to her over the past while. It's going to be hard when she leaves.

Entry #31

My sadness reaches out, trying to claim another victim. I want someone to stand by me, to tell me they know how I feel, but no one knows enough, not really. They look at me, but their eyes don't see. They're too narcissistic—more worried about looking in a damn mirror. My friend visited today, and it was all about her. She laughed her sweet, kid laugh, and her words paraded around my sorrows, trampling over what makes me most sad in the world.

"Isn't it crazy that I'm the only one, out of all of our friends, who had a boy?" she asked me, as if Zeke never happened, like he'd been smudged from the world by some huge eraser. And I'm irate, because his life should never be erased from her mind, because she knew him.

"I had a son...once," I said, and my eyes tried to be sweet, like hers, but I felt them turning to slits instead of saucers. I wanted to remain light and nice, like I usually am. She apologized over and over until I wished she would simply apologize for even being there, but she didn't, and stayed, trying to cover up her crap.

Finally, she left me in the silence of my living room, and its walls seemed bigger, and the ceiling was higher, as I sat there feeling all alone, because today it seems like everyone has forgotten Zeke. Everyone but me. Smiles play the leading role on the faces of everyone around, as if Zeke wasn't in my belly last year.

When they talk about mothers and children, they seem to forget the one I lost, and it hammers me to pieces. I sit here, thinking his suffering was so great, and he suffered for nothing but my sadness.

I wonder how she forgot such a strong little soul, who wouldn't give up, even though his body wasn't perfect and refused to work the way I know his brain told it to. So, I'm depressed because there's no one to talk to, except you.

I sat down and wrote this poem since it was practically the only way I could cope:

It Was You

Walking down a desolate hallway,

215

not knowing what's about to come,
Wondering every step...
why did you need to take my son?

The day he was born—
one of the best days of my life—
His little hand held mine.

It just felt so right.
I'm thankful for every day
that I spent with my baby boy.
Now, you're holding him tight,
just how he likes.
You're taking care of him for me.

Yet, you're holding me right now,
and you're telling me how
you love me.
You're seeing me through;
without you, what would I do?

I love you more,
I need you more than before.
You're everything to me.
Help me be the person that you want me to be.

My baby waits in Heaven.
Joy fills his little heart.
His pain has now ended,
but it still hurts me to be apart.

God help me live right.
I want to see my son's face

when he sees me up in Heaven
because of your amazing grace!

I know you have a reason,
and I know you understand.
I'll put my faith and trust in you;
without you, how can I stand?

Entry #32

I talked to Cade's mom today. She invited me to a family lunch.

"But I'm practically not family anymore," I said.

"You'll always be family to me," she said. "You gave birth to my only grandchildren, and you'll always be welcome around the family, as far as I'm concerned."

I told her I would give Cade a call and see what he thought about it, but when I talked to Cade, he acted completely indifferent.

"You can do what you want," he said, "So, my mom asked you to go?"

"Yeah. That was nice of her to think of me," I replied.

"You wouldn't believe what she told me the other day." Cade paused. "She said she doesn't want me to be mad, because she'll talk to you, no matter what happens between us. She said she loves you, and that you'll always be family to her."

"I love your mom," I said.

We didn't talk about much after that because the conversation was lacking, and Cade's never been much for talking on the phone, anyway.

Well, I guess we're going. Ruby is super excited. It's next weekend, and I'd love to see Cade's sister. I really like that girl. She's fun to talk to, and such a sweetheart.

Entry #33

I got home today, and my neighbor's handicapped little girl was dancing with baby powder. I guess I know who's been breaking in. I sure wish her incredibly fertile mom would keep a better eye on her. I brought her back home, and her mom didn't act surprised at all. "Oh, I'm sorry," she said.

"You might want to keep a better eye on her," I said. "This isn't the first time this has happened."

"Don't worry about her, Hon," she said. "I'm a good person, and I know Heavenly Father wouldn't let anything bad happen to my family."

I don't know what overcame me, but my anger took control. "If my faith was only that strong," I said, and stormed off, thinking I should fix my sliding glass door. I'm glad God gave me a brain—and wish that lady had one, too.

I took Ruby back to the house, and after a few hours of cleaning, the scent of baby powder finally left. I got ready for work. When Ruby saw me getting dressed, she ran right over to the closet, and said, "Prince.... Prince, it's time to play!"

"Ruby! Honey!" I said. "Prince isn't real! Why do you keep playing with something that isn't real? You've got to face life. This," I pointed all around, "is real."

She cried after hearing my raised voice. "Mama?" she sobbed. "Mama! Zeke was my prince." Her words knocked the wind out of me. "And he was real!"

"Oh, Honey." I ran to her and hugged her. We stayed locked together in our sadness. I kissed her on the forehead and brushed my hand through the back of her hair. "Hush, Baby. It'll be all right. I'm here. I'm here."

"Why did Zeke go, Mama?" her face tilted toward mine.

I wanted to give her some reliable line she could play with and think about, like, "He had to be with Jesus."

But I decided to be honest, and instead told her, "I don't know. I just don't know."

"Will you leave, too, Mama?"

"No," I said. "I'll never leave you. I need you so much, Ruby. Will you ever leave me?"

She laughed her happy, childish laugh. "No, Mama. Course not."

As I held my little girl, all hunched on the floor, I pulled out my cell phone and called the diesel shop. I told them I couldn't make it because something very important had come up. I never call like that, ever. I rocked Ruby awhile, and then we played with a ball for a few hours before I put her to sleep.

I decided to write before going to bed. It's nice to get things out. I think I'll sleep on Ruby's floor tonight because I'm better than any imaginary friend, and I want her to know I'll always be here for her, as long as I'm alive.

Entry #34

A new guy started working at the mechanic shop. He's a good-looking guy and seems all right. He told me he just got divorced and has a little boy. He showed me a picture of him, and I about melted, right there on the floor. We talked for a while, and then he asked me out. I couldn't believe it, but before I realized what I was doing, I said, "Yes."

I really don't want to go on a date with him because I know I'll just think about Cade the whole time, but maybe it will be good for me to get out. I haven't done something fun in weeks since Cammie moved away. And he does seem like a pretty nice guy to hang out with, as friends. I'll just have to tell him I'm only interested in friendship, that's all.

Entry #35

I couldn't find a babysitter today, so Cade actually watched Ruby. I'm really glad he helped, even though he hates seeing me. He didn't look very good, and I could tell he hadn't gotten a lot of sleep. He gauged me with sad, careful eyes, and kept his distance. I wondered if I had B.O., but then realized he acted weird because of the night way back, when he kissed me.

I tried starting some small talk, even though he only replied with one-word answers. Thomas knocked on the door, and Cade lit up like Christmas in the suburbs. Thomas is practically a member of the family now. His non-nailed mom has been gone a lot, so I watch Thomas all of the time. He keeps Ruby company, and he's a good little boy.

I left after Thomas got there, and when I arrived at work, none of the mechanics saw me walk in. They were all huddled in a circle, talking about something interesting.

I decided to sneak up on them and tease them, but then I heard their conversation.

"She'll never sleep with you, man, not unless you marry her!"

"You probably won't even get to first base."

"I'll get her to sleep with me within the first week," the new guy said. "Make your bets if you want, but this is one I know I can win."

I waited until they placed their bets, and then said, "Hey, you dirty Pot-licker." I said it as smooth as ice, like it was the best thing in the whole world to lick pots. "If you're talking about me, I think you just lost a bunch of money."

All of the mechanics betting on my side laughed. "Serves you right," Wayne said. "That's the easiest money I've ever made."

I gave the new guy "the eye" Cade taught me about. Then I walked away and thought about Cade, and how much I missed him, and how he'd never place a bet on a girl, just to try making a dime.

"You just lost out on a good woman," Wayne said "That's the kind of girl you can bring to meet your ma, and it's hard finding one of them these days."

The new guy ran up to me. "I'm sorry," he said. "We were just having some fun. I've never met a girl like you, who's not afraid to mechanic, and all. Please, give me another chance?"

"No," I said sharply, and he knew I'd never change my mind.

His face got sly as he stepped out of my punching range, and he said, "I'll even split the money with you...if we win." He winked at me, and I wished I could clock him in the nose with a brake drum that leaned against the wall.

"You jerk!" I said, before stomping from the laughter of the guys in the second bay.

Entry #36

I went to the "family lunch" today. It was more of a small picnic, but everyone was nice, and it was great seeing them. Cade kept his distance, but I caught him staring at me a few times. I wore the same tank top I had on the day Cade and I played music together for the first time. I wonder if Cade noticed. I don't know why it matters, though, since Cade inspires me to make balloon animals in a nut house.

At one point his nephew asked us if we brought our instruments. I don't think he knows we're separated. Anyway, I surprised everyone when I said that I'd brought my violin. Cade reluctantly borrowed his dad's guitar, and we played a few songs for everyone. He didn't sit very close to me, and I thought about how fun it would be to jab him with my bow. But I didn't, since the guy is going through enough as it is.

It shocked me how I'm not even wearing his ring, and we can still play so well together. I knew exactly where he went with the chords and rhythms, and it sounded perfectly rehearsed, even though it's been months since we've performed together.

Our last performance was at a gay coffee shop. You wouldn't believe how much we made. Gay people must be loaded, and I figure it's because they can't have kids. Cade hated it, though, because a bunch of the guys came up and hit on him. I remember laughing, before a girl asked for my number.

I said, "I'm so sorry; I don't swing that way. We're married." I pointed to Cade and me. After she walked away, Cade had a fit of happiness. He thought that was hilarious, seeing me take my own medicine for a change.

So, after we played at the lunch thing, I noticed Cade smiled, and even talked to me. We talked more like old friends than old lovers, but, by the end of the thing, he said he'd come over and watch Ruby again.

"I'm sorry about what happened that night," he said, talking about the night he kissed me and ran away.

"It's okay," I said, and actually meant it, because something strange happened between us while we played music together. It's like we're tied together in freaky-musical strings, and when we play, they make us move and smile like marionettes— brainless and obedient.

We gave each other an awkward hug goodbye, and for a minute it reminded me of the last time I saw "the understudy." Cade patted me hard on the back, like I needed the Heimlich or something. I noticed Cade's mom watching us from the window and had to groan. "Cade, I think your mom is trying to set us up."

"Nice," he said, and we both waved to her like a couple of teenagers past our curfew.

Ruby giggled when I got into the car. She loved seeing Cade and me hugging. It wasn't a bad hug, as far as hugs go, and even would have saved my life—if I'd been choking.

It was weird, though, because there was no emotion behind the hug, and I feel like we've moved beyond being angry, and now maybe we don't care. What I'm trying to say is that Cade would make a good rock, because he doesn't show me emotions anymore, and that's good for me. It makes it easier to move on and be the mom Ruby needs, the strong mom who doesn't need a guy bringing her down.

Entry #37

Ruby isn't potty trained anymore. She refuses to go potty in the toilet and is stuttering really badly. I don't know what to do. I wish I knew what went wrong. I want to talk to Cammie, but I can't get ahold of her since she moved. It's weird; she's just gone, like Zeke and Cade. I feel like nothing is permanent in my life, nothing but Ruby. For some reason I don't ever worry about losing Ruby. I feel like she'll always be with me, like a sidekick.

Ruby keeps talking about her baby, and she wants to know where he is. I don't know how to explain death to a toddler. She doesn't understand, no matter what I say. So, I'm telling her a story. It's about a cute little boy named Zeke, the same Zeke who used to be her baby. In the story he takes a trip across the ocean and saves the one he loves. I figured that was a good reason for him to leave, since I can't think of the real one.

I don't know how much of it Ruby understands, but she sure likes it. I think I might try turning the story into a book someday. Then she'll always have it and will see the symbolism and hidden meanings throughout every inch of the story. I hug her tight and rock her in the rocking chair. I know she can feel how much I love her. Every night I add more to the story, and I know she's just waiting for the day when Zeke will be reunited with his family. I feel like part of me is waiting, too, but I know he never will, at least not on Earth.

Entry #38

I got really sick, and Cade rushed over to help me take care of Ruby. Things swirled around me, and I had a fever. I think I got so sick because I'm run down from working so much. Cade seemed worried, and that surprised me. He never cooks, but he actually made me some interesting soup. It wasn't too terribly bad, and I ate all of it, just to show him I appreciated the thought.

I went to sleep and woke up four hours later. I had the chills, even though I had sweat from head to foot. My blanket was secured around every inch of my shivering body before I ventured from my room.

I trudged down the stairs and was shocked because the house was spotlessly clean. I'm not a slob, or anything, but the house was pretty messy, because I hadn't felt good enough to clean it.

"Cade?" I gaped. "Did you clean all of this?"

"Yeah, it only took us a few hours. It's not a big deal."

"That was so nice of you!" Ruby hugged my leg, and I

smiled at her. "Did you help, too?"

"Yeah, Mama. It was fun." My fingers fell into place stroking her curly blond hair.

"I know how much it bugs you when the house is dirty. I even did your laundry—and none of the clothes are pink." Cade laughed.

"Well, aren't you a laundry ninja." I paused. "Once there was a guy who taught me how to do the laundry—"

"Was he ruggedly handsome?" Cade's brow arched.

"Ummm." I smiled, and then a chill hit me. "It's so cold in here."

"It's seventy-five degrees in the house, Babe, and—" He stopped after realizing he'd called me "Babe." He cleared his throat. "You better go lay back down. Do you want some more soup, or tea, or something?"

"No, I'm good. Thanks, though." I turned around before walking up the stairs. My blanket was still tightly around me, and the bottom dragged like a soft, fuzzy tail.

Entry #39

Earl drove into work this morning. I worked the graveyard, and he came in a little after six. He's almost stopped going to the diner with Sam, and comes to the mechanic shop, instead. It's always slow in the early morning, and he loves visiting with me and the other mechanics. He doesn't bring his car to get checked out anymore. He stopped doing that a while ago, when we told him it's okay if he just wants to piss the time away with us.

"Why do you keep coming here?" I asked because my balls finally came in and I was man enough to ask.

"You need someone to look after you," he said in his grumpy voice, which made me sound like a burden. Steam went up from his coffee.

"Like hell I do." I laughed. "You're the one who needs some looking after."

"I did once, but I'm doing okay now."

"Once?" I pried.

"Yeah, once." He smiled and took a sip of his coffee.

I grabbed the necklace hanging around my neck and held it close to my heart as I waited for Earl to tell me more. My necklace has a little ring on it, one of the rings Zeke had on his finger when he died. Susan put two of them on Zeke a few hours before he passed. She said Cade and I could keep them to remember. I always wear that necklace because I'm that busy remembering.

"Well?" I lost patience.

"Well, what?" he asked.

I let go of my necklace and held up my hands in exasperation "Will you tell me the story, or not? I know you have an interesting story, and I want to hear it."

"You knew that?"

"Everyone knows it." I nudged his heavily coated elbow.

"It's a long story." He sat and patted a spot next to him. "You might as well have a seat." I plopped my butt down faster than a bullet train delivering cargo. I didn't want to jinx the moment because I'd waited forever for old man Earl to tell me his story.

"I was eighteen when I got married," he started. "She was a beautiful girl, and she looked a bit like you." I blushed from the compliment and diverted my eyes to the sky. "Everyone loved her, everyone!" he continued. "She would go places, and folks would be better off just for being around her. We'd only been married for a few months when I found out she was pregnant. I'd got a good job, and she was as happy as a lark. We loved each other, too; I mean, we really loved each other. Her family disowned her because they were rich and didn't want her marrying a nobody like me. I thought that was hard on her, but she said it wasn't.

"Well, some time passed, and I was able to feel the baby kick. I couldn't believe she was carrying life like that, inside of her. I'd always hurry home from work so I could be with her, and we would talk about the baby and what kind of future he would have, 'cause we thought the baby was a boy. We didn't have much, but she never complained about a thing, even though she'd been used to having a lot, growing up. Once I asked her if she wished she could have fancy clothes and a big house. She said she was happy to be with me and have my baby, and that was all she wanted." Earl got teary eyed, and he sniffled, just to keep his nose from running and his eyes from overflowing.

"My mom died then, and she left me some money. I bought us a small, run-down house, and fixed it up real nice. After that, things went quick 'cause we were getting ready to have the baby. There was less than a month to go. But, when I got home one night, she wasn't there. I kept calling her name over and over, but she didn't answer, and then the phone rang, and the police told me she'd gone to be with my mother. They told me to hurry to the hospital because my wife had just been hit by a car, and even though she'd already passed, they were trying to save the baby." Earl stopped and looked across the parking lot. I could tell he focused on every detail of a semi parked out in the boonies. He tapped his coffee cup, and a shadow overtook his face.

"What happened?" I asked after a minute.

Instead of answering, he pulled a faded black and white picture from his wallet and handed it to me.

"What a good-looking couple!" I said. "Is that you?" He nodded. "You're so handsome, and she's beautiful." I passed the picture back, and he tucked it into his wallet.

"The baby didn't make it. They got her out pretty fast, but she was in worse shape than her mother. They told me I didn't need to see her, but I did, anyway, and I'll never forget wondering how she'd been a baby, once." We sat quietly, neither of us breaking the silence, and both thinking hard. "I hope I'll be with them again, someday," he said, and tears jumped down his cheeks and into his whiskers.

I hugged Earl, and for some crazy reason I cried, too. One of the mechanics walked out and saw us hugging and crying like the apocalypse had come. He raised his eyebrows at us before he left.

"We must look funny," Earl said, wiping the tears from his scruffy face.

"I guess so." I chuckled, and my laughter started replacing my sadness. "What do you think happens after we die?"

"I don't know," he said. "And I don't think any honest living person does."

I smelled some exhaust coming from a nearby semi and wrinkled my nose. "I wonder what it smells like in Heaven," I said. "I've always thought it smelled like baby powder, or cherry taffy, or something like that."

"Cherry taffy?" Earl grinned thoughtfully. "You're a funny kid sometimes." I gave him "the eye," and he went on, trying to appease me, "I don't know about Heaven, but I've heard Hell smells like brimstone."

"Nope," I said seriously. "It smells just like iodine. Believe me; I've been there." I paused. "I wonder if your wife and daughter met my son."

"I bet they have." His eyes studied the sky. "Maybe they're watching us right now."

"Maybe. I hope I'll make it to Heaven, Earl." I choked down a silent tear. "I'd love to see my boy again."

"I hope I'll make it, too, seeing as how it's not too far off for me."

"Now you're just begging for compliments," I joked. "You know you're not that old."

He snickered. "Close enough," he said. "I'll be riding on eagle's wings."

Earl likes to talk about animals. He makes extra money by collecting pine nuts, and he's always running into all sorts of strange wildlife. So, if he found a bright side to anything, of course he'd think it had something to do with animals. I thought about Zeke, and how I'd let his ashes rest in that place where nature runs rampant, and a cougar almost killed me. The thought suddenly hit me: Earl thinks animals always represent something—maybe we'd seen that cougar for a reason. After all, I've never seen a cougar in the wild before, it must be fairly uncommon.

Then, for some reason, instead of talking about vicious cats or deeper symbolism, I told Earl all about my problems with Cade. I left out all of the really bad things Cade has done and made him sound pretty perfect. I couldn't stand talking bad about Cade, because I told my family about what's really going on, and they got super upset. Plus, I didn't want to upset Earl with jerk or cougar stories, not after he'd spilled his guts; but I still wanted his advice about Cade.

"You love him?" Earl asked.

"I don't know, but I think so. No matter how hard I try, I can't get him out of my mind." I leaned back on my hands.

"Then you need to win him back and make him realize what he's missing."

"How in hell can I do that? He doesn't even want to be around me, for crying out loud."

"Yeah, he does," Earl said. "Trust me. He just needs to get his priorities straight and see that you love him like he loves you."

"I don't think he loves me. He'd be home if he loved me. I can't imagine him acting like this if he's in love."

"That's 'cause you can be real stupid sometimes," Earl said.

"Wow, that was blunt." I slapped Earl on one of his skinny legs. "Someone's got to be stupid sometimes, because that's what makes the smart moments so damn cool." I laughed. "I don't see why I have to make the first move."

"Someone needs to make the first move, and it might as well be you," he said.

"But—"

"But nothing! If you really want him back, you might need to make the first move."

"He's the guy!"

"It doesn't matter. Listen, if I had a chance to get my spouse back...I would! But I can't, and you can. End of story." Earl stood. "See you tomorrow, Darlin'." He walked away, leaving a trail of muddy footprints behind him.

Entry #40

The "big sag's" son called and asked if I would go four wheeling. I went because the guy is hella cool. We brought Ruby with us, and had a ball. We drove for awhile, until stopping in a desert-looking area. It was still cold, but seemed the perfect place to bring four-wheelers, because sandy hills rippled for miles around. We hung out there, and I couldn't believe he'd even packed us each a lunch. We sat on the sand and joked about life.

"Hey, Cowboy?" he looked at me, and I smiled because there was a little bit of jelly in his mustache. "Why do you think God lets so many bad things happen to good people?"

He swallowed. "Because of Eve. Wasn't she the one who ate the forbidden fruit, and brought evil into the world?" he said. He's either very knowledgeable, or he's visited church too many times.

"Eve? What about Adam? He's the one who didn't stop her, and he was right there. Talk about sins! He turned her into a guinea pig, for crying out loud. He took a bite after he saw that she didn't die!"

"Better than taking the first bite and being responsible for the Fall," he said.

"At least Eve wasn't the biggest victim of peer pressure in the history of the world!"

"Adam was a smart guy." He leaned on his elbow and smiled at Ruby drawing in the sand. "Every man knows he should do what his woman says, if he wants to be happy."

"And you would know this from experience?" I asked and rested back on the sand as Ruby came over and snuggled into the crook of my arm.

"No, but my dad says—"

"He would've made a great Adam," I spat.

"Probably." He chuckled because he likes making me mad. It

229

was quiet then, and I enjoyed the feel of the cool sand underneath Ruby and me; it made me feel numb to the pain in my heart. Ruby snuggled closer, my only warmth in a cold world, and I thought about how "the cowboy" hadn't really answered my question at all.

I can't imagine how some forbidden apple—from over two thousand years ago—could be the reason why my son died. If that's the case, then I hate apples. It's like some stupid Snow White story come to life, and I can't stand it. Why did God take my son? Maybe He doesn't think I'm a very good mom.

Entry #41

Is death just another form of change, or is it the end? I wonder what Heaven will be like. I try thinking about it, and when I close my eyes, all I imagine is complete whiteness: no imperfections, and no chaos. It's all white because it's sterile so there won't be pain or sickness. If there were colors then someone might get sick, and I might lose my son again. I sure hope Heaven isn't boring, but I can't imagine how it wouldn't be.

I imagine myself sitting at a table with Cade, playing checkers for the millionth time, and neither one of us can decide who should go first. Of course, we sit on a cloud in my picture, and don't fight about silly crap, like our son dying. No, we just sit there, deciding who goes first, because neither of us really wants to start the game...again.

Zeke is next to us. He's sitting on a cloud, too, and he's fishing with that handmade pole my uncle brought to his funeral. I can't figure out what he's fishing for, because I've never heard of colorless fish being way up in the clouds. He's not a kid when I imagine him, though. He's a grown man, happy and healthy, wearing ripped overalls and a straw hat, and he can hold his own, because he's my boy. Ruby isn't up here with us, though. She's alive when I imagine things. I can't stand the thought of her dying, too.

Heaven does sound boring, though, really it does, but if

Zeke's there, it won't be too bad, I guess. I always dream about Heaven, but I never see Zeke in my dreams. I swear I want the dream to go on forever, just in case I might see Zeke, but I never do. I just bump into people who I know, that have died. They're always very pleasant, and everything, but they're not Zeke, that's all.

It would be cool to sit down and visit with God. I wouldn't want to ask Him anything. I'd want to play Him a song I've written for Him, then stare at Him, because I can't imagine how amazing He must be since He created everything. It would feel so great to have Him all to myself for just a minute. I can't imagine anything more awesome.

It wouldn't be boring if God's in Heaven, but I wonder if He'll have time for me when I'm up there. If I make the cut, and He does have time for me, He might stare into my soul and show me my sins. Then, He'll replay my entire life, or something, just so I can see all of the bad things I've done. That doesn't sound too great, but at least it doesn't sound boring.

When I was in Hawaii, my sister told me I was going to Hell. She said I wasn't living right, and now, after Zeke died, her words play in my head, and I wonder, will I go to Heaven? Going to Hell is my greatest fear, because I love God, and want to spend eternity with Him, and see my boy again.

I hope I won't go to Hell, because fire has never been my thing, and I burn easily. I wish I knew how to get into Heaven. I asked Cade about it once, and he said Heaven only exists in our minds. I thought that was lame but didn't say so. I nodded politely, even though I can't see where he's coming from. I know I'll find out about Heaven after I die. I just hope that loving God with all my heart is enough for me to get in, even if He does want to look into my soul and show everyone my sins.

Entry #42

The ex-stripper visited my house this afternoon. She said she kept feeling like she should give me a statue. I saw the statue and was speechless because it looks just like Zeke. Its ears are a little different from each other, and I wondered what type of sculptor would purposely create something so imperfect, yet beautiful.

Apparently, the ex-stripper is closely connected with the Almighty. I thought about asking her to pray for my dad, but changed my mind fast, and said, "My son died last year, and this is exactly what he looked like." I stared at the statue again. It's of a little baby who's sitting down with a bird resting in his lap.

"He must have been a beautiful little boy," she said, and gave me a hug. I saw that she cried, pretty sober at that moment. I thanked God for thinking about both of us, even though she used to strip, and I had a kid with defects. I'm so glad she gave me the statue. I'll keep it forever!

"Wow, this must have cost a fortune!" I said.

"More than you know. I made good money stripping."

"Really, was it worth it?" I asked because I was curious and had lost all common courtesy.

"No, not at all," she said, then left me alone with the statue of Zeke.

Entry #43

I went to church last week because I'm in serious need of counseling. I just can't get Zeke out of my mind, and figure I should move on now, like Cade has. I met with this really nice Asian counselor. She gave me a packet the size of Milwaukee, and then made some tea. The tea was better than the packet, which seems like a bunch of crap. It's filled with activities for me to do. The first activity in the packet said, "Write down things your family members have done to hurt you."

She had me write down everything on that paper. I had a rough time at first, but, after a few minutes, my hand flew into a blur of gossip. I went on and on, and most of it was about things that had happened while Zeke was alive. The counselor told me to take the paper home, read it tomorrow, and then burn it tomorrow night. I'm super surprised that the church hired a gossiping pyro, but I guess that's okay if it'll help me.

Entry #44

I set the crap list by the fridge, and when Cade left, I noticed the table was turned widthwise. His mom must have been there earlier and seen the paper with all of those horrible things. The packet sprawled on top of the table, just waiting for me to see it. I didn't really care if Cade saw it, because he needs to read those things and grow up, but a couple of the things on the paper were about Marie. I cried when I read it, because I never wanted her knowing those things, and I got really mad at the gossiping pyro. I grabbed the table and shoved it against the wall. I put it exactly how all of us hate it, but at least it's how I put the damn thing!

I read how I wondered if Marie had taken the stuff from the garage, because I saw a crock pot and blanket at her house. They looked just like mine that went missing. I guess I wondered about it, because Cade and I might get divorced, and I figured she might have taken it back, since they both looked like the ones that ran away.

It wasn't a very nice thing to write, though, even if it does seem true. I'd never confront her about it because that's just mean, and it doesn't matter, anyway. I love Marie, and those things in my garage are just stupid, lifeless items. Nothing could ever replace her, nothing.

The other thing on my list was about Zeke. It was about how I'd come to visit him so many times, and she'd been there, instead. I would have to wait to see my boy because lots of times she would have someone with her, and they would only let two people in at a time.

Cade said I was selfish and needed to learn to share our son, because everyone wanted to see him. I guess he didn't understand what I went through, because he's not Zeke's mom, and I am. I just wanted to be with him every minute I could, and I lost out because so many family members wanted to be with him all the time.

Marie wasn't the only one, and it was wrong of me to target her, but for some reason I target the people I'm closest to, and that means I target her a lot. It was just weird that Marie would be there when I would go see him. I finally started going at night because I knew I was guaranteed time with him. I would do anything for my boy, my baby.

So, I know Marie saw the crap list because of how she'd turned the table, and I feel horrible. As soon as I saw the list on the table, I picked it up and threw it into the garbage. I found the packet and brought it back to the gossiping pyro who had suggested it. I told her how dumb the idea was, and then I left. I'll never make a list like that again because it brought back old times, and I have enough on my plate now, without digging up the past and messing up my future.

Entry #45

I had to run some errands today and didn't have time to make Ruby lunch. So, I went to a drive-thru, and let Ruby eat some fries in the car. I didn't think it was a big deal until I heard her choking in the back seat.

"Ruby? Ruby?" My heart stopped. "Ruby?" I turned around and panicked. "Ruby!" She changed colors like a freaking chameleon, but nothing in her background was blue and I knew something was wrong.

I swerved off the side of the road and almost hit a car in the process. I ripped Ruby's door open, then yanked her from her seat faster than I knew I could. Before my brain even registered, I had her upside down with her tummy lying on my leg. I beat the crap out of her back, just how they taught us in the NICU class I'd taken. I remembered the class, where they teach you how to help the baby you think you'll take home, but never do.

Ruby still didn't breathe, and I held my breath, too. I flipped her over and tried clearing her airway but couldn't get a damn thing. I flipped her over again. "God! Don't do this! You can't." I hit her on the back again. "Don't take my baby girl! You already took my son." (Slap.) "Isn't that enough," (slap) "for crying" (slap) "out loud?" (Slap.) On that last slap, I hit her extra hard, and a huge fry flew from her mouth like it was a baby airplane.

I held her up at arm's length and stared at her for the longest time. I stood there, on the side of the road, taking in the utter beauty which constantly surrounds my kid. I felt ashamed because I'd lost one child and had still taken Ruby for granted. The sun shone just beyond her little head, and its extra light glowed around her face while she looked at me.

I pulled her close and buried my head into her fluffy baby hair. "I love you, Honey! Please don't ever leave me! I need you so much. Don't leave me." I cradled her, knelt down in the dirt, and cried.

"God, thank you for Ruby! Thank you for my beautiful baby girl!" I held her tightly until she finally stopped crying. She turned to me. Her eyebrows pointed like a question mark, and I wondered what she was thinking.

"Mama, that was a mean fry," Ruby finally said. I laughed at her wonderful simplicity as another car whooshed by us, and both of our hair danced in the dusty wind.

Entry #46

Cade got a gig close to the house and asked if I would like to go. I didn't want to be rude, so I brought a bunch of friends. Some of my girl friends came along with "the cowboy" and a few other guys I know. They were super impressed with the band and had fun playing pool while we listened to the music.

At one point I watched Cade and saw the lights perfectly highlighting everything about him. I had to laugh because the scene reminded me of a painting of an angel I'd seen as a kid. Cade sang, and his voice echoed all around me, and I couldn't pull my eyes from him. He completely outshone every other guy in the room, and that said something.

I listened to the words he sang, and realized he'd written the song about us. He sang about how he'd seen a girl and made her his, but in the end, it wasn't meant to be, and he couldn't move on because she was his one and only. I wanted to scream at him and say I'm still his, and he should come home and tell me he needs me, but I know he won't, even if I ask him to.

Just then, I heard a girl next to me turn twitter pated about him. She was a Piranha if I've ever seen one! "He's so hot!" she said, and her friend practically drooled on the floor as she agreed. I wanted to deliver a marital message to them, but my ring wasn't on, and that meant it would hurt a lot less if I threw a punch.

I ran up to the bartender and got a couple of shots. I'm not much on drinking, but I took those shots like water in the desert, and a couple of the guys standing nearby smiled and said they'd never seen a girl take hard whiskey straight. I thought for a minute about how the lining of my stomach didn't exist anymore and got worried God had punished me for underage drinking. Then I went back over to "the cowboy," so I could play pool. I overheard a guy talking.

"See those girls hitting on Cade?" the guy asked. "I'm sure he's got enough balls, but he's only got the one stick."

"Nice!" I said sarcastically and hit the pool balls with such force everyone around backed away. I asked one of my girlfriends to bring me home, but "the cowboy" insisted on taking me.

"You've got to calm down, Elisa," he said as we got into his big truck. "Everyone's coming over to your place after the concert. Did Cade say something to upset you? I swear if he did anything to hurt you—"

"I'm fine, really I am," I said, and we were quiet as the truck drifted over the bumpy dirt road.

"I need to talk to you about something important," he finally said.

"Like what?"

"I think I'm falling in love with someone," he said.

236

"Yeah, well, love sucks."

His face turned sad, and he seemed to struggle seeing through the darkness ahead.

"I'm sorry to be so negative," I said. "I don't want to talk about love right now. I'm too upset. Can we talk about this later?"

"If you don't want to talk now, when can we talk about it?"

"Maybe you can come over sometime next week." I tried sounding like my normally happy self. "I'm not a good person to talk to about love. I couldn't even make my own marriage work."

"Okay, next week works," he said thoughtfully. I looked toward the bar's lights that faded into the distance—the bar that held Cade inside. I wanted to go back and see him again, but couldn't stand knowing he isn't mine anymore, and has a bunch of Piranha around to hit on him.

I finally turned my thoughts back to my buddy and said, "She's a lucky girl."

"Who?" he asked.

"The girl you're in love with," I stated, and "the cowboy" smiled slightly.

Everyone did come back to the house; well, almost everyone. The lead guitarist didn't want to come over, and I don't blame him after the last conversation we had on the phone. I think everyone had a good time at the house.

I acted like everything was fine, and by the time Cade got there, I was ready for him. He wanted to know why I'd left so early, and I told him it was because I was a little bored at the bar. I was surprised he even noticed I was gone. I acted nonchalant, but still hung around him at all of the right times. Cade and "the cowboy" didn't get along, though, and I'm bummed. I thought they would end up being great buddies, or something.

My best friend came, and we ended up talking forever.

"How are you?" she asked.

"Things have been so rough," I finally said.

"I didn't know you're having a hard time. You've always

seemed like you have it all together, even in high school and junior high. You're always so happy."

"Things are hard right now, but I'll make it through. There's always a bright side." I stopped talking and traced the lip of the beer in my hand. "I'm glad I have you in my life. You're a good friend," I said, getting all sappy because the liquor made me grateful.

"You know, you're the only kid who was really nice to me in junior high."

"Yeah, right." I laughed.

"No, really, you were. I'm glad we're still friends." I gave her an awkward high-five before turning to walk up the stairs. I took the first couple of steps like a pro before slipping and coming right down again. I laughed so hard it hurt, as the room spun like crazy.

"Casey?"

"Yeah?" she asked.

"Is the room spinning? Why is it spinning?"

"Elisa, you're drunk."

"Don't ever let me do this again, okay? I don't like spinny things."

"But you're so much fun when you drink." She laughed.

"Because I fall down stairs, and crap?"

"Yeah, something like that."

Anyway, a bunch of people stayed the night, and in the morning, I overheard a couple girls talking about how Cade and I were never meant to be, and how we wouldn't have made it, anyway. I love how their voices carried all of the way through the house, just like a couple of bad spirits. I wonder if they're right, and what else they say when I can't hear them. I don't really care, though, because it's not like their words can send me to Hell, or anything.

So, it was a good party, and the house was fairly clean, other than a couple of cigarettes I found, having a party in the stove's left burner. I thought that was crazy because I don't even allow smoking in the house, but I guess I had other things on my mind last night, that's all.

Entry #47

I visited my dad today while he was suffering from a chemo treatment. It didn't look how I'd expected it to. I guess I thought he'd be in a space contraption, and would be hooked to a spinning wheel, or something. He was attached to a bunch of stuff, but none of it was from an 80's flick. I felt disappointed—how in the world can they save my dad with a load of IVs?

There were a lot of other people there, too. They were completely different, even though they were all doing time for the same thing. It hit me strange that cancer doesn't give a crap who you are, or where you've come from. My dad had all of those people laughing, just like I knew he would. An outsider would've thought he was a doctor, not a patient.

I had a great time visiting with him and my mom. Ruby kept us smiling when my dad wasn't cracking jokes. She pulled funny faces the whole time, and an old lady next to us said Ruby is as cute as a button.

I hope my dad will get better soon. That last prayer I sent may be as good as a message in a bottle—in a sea of endless bottles. I hope God heard it, and that He'll fix my dad fast. I can't stand losing my dad because I love that guy.

Entry #48

I'm going to take Earl's advice, even though I haven't seen him since he gave it to me. It's like he's dropped off the face of the earth. I just realized how little I know about him. I don't even know how to find out if he's okay. I feel like he's all right, but I can't figure why he hasn't come back.

Anyway, I'll take his advice. I can't live without Cade. I'll get him to fall in love with me again. I don't know how I'll do it, but I will. It might take a ton of planning, but it'll be worth it if he realizes how much he loves me and sees my side of things. I'll swoon him this Friday. I hope my plan will work.

Entry #49

He showed up just after dark, and you should have seen his face when he walked into the house. I wore a dark blue dress, and it accented all my good parts. I'd turned the lights in the house off, but lit candles everywhere. A fancy dinner sat on the table, just waiting for us to eat it. I put Ruby to sleep early, and then waited for Cade to arrive.

Cade looked around confused, and then his eyes widened when he saw me. "What's going on?" he asked, as I helped him take off his coat. "I feel a little underdressed."

"Just a little, huh?" I laughed. "I thought it would be fun to have a fancy dinner together—as friends."

He nodded his head. "Just as friends?"

"Yeah," I said. "I thought I'd try making up for how hard things have been. What's wrong with that? You know, just a couple of lonely people, having dinner together...alone." I teased, and I hoped he would keep the mood light because I was trying really hard.

"Nothing, I guess, but where's Ruby?"

"She's asleep." I smiled and pulled his chair out for him.

"Thanks, this looks good," he said as he sat down. "What inspired this, anyway?"

"Nothing, it just sounded fun. Eat up."

As we started eating, the mood lightened, and it almost felt like old times. "Do you remember when you saved my life?" I asked.

"When we were climbing by those waterfalls?"

"Yeah," I said.

"That was a close one. I remember looking back, and suddenly you were slipping."

"Then you grabbed my wrist, just in time. That would've been a good way to go, though, don't you think? Falling down a couple of waterfalls is better than dying in a fire, or suffocating, or something."

"Probably." Cade looked thoughtful, and I found myself clutching the tiny infant ring that hung just between my boobs, which actually looked like they existed. I went and bought two water bra pads from Walmart the other day.

"You still have Zeke's ring?" I asked before I could shut my mouth. The words darted as an accusation because I didn't think Cade had the ring anymore—like he'd thrown it into the same dumpster where he threw his feelings for me.

"Yeah, I do," Cade said, and pulled a chain that hung under his shirt. Then the ring at the bottom of his necklace twirled dimly in the light. Cade lowered it to his palm as if it was as precious as life, and I could tell he didn't want to hurt the ring, which now slept in his hand.

"It looks so small in your hand, and it's a different color than mine is." I noticed he'd practically sanded all the coating from the thing.

"Yeah, it is." Cade put it back into his shirt. I realized he must have held Zeke's ring more than I could imagine, and he must miss Zeke just as much as I do.

For the next few moments, I knew Cade and I both thought about Zeke and the twin rings hanging around our necks. I almost wanted to laugh, and cry, thinking about how neither of us wear our wedding rings, and how we're still connected through two tiny infant rings. No matter how hard we try to run away from each other, we'll always be connected.

Suddenly I wanted to say so much to Cade about how we'll always be held together, by everything, by our kids, by our music, by our memories, and maybe even by our love. But I looked at Cade's sad face, and wanted to kick myself, or Cade, for somehow saying the wrong thing, and bringing the conversation around to the death of our son. Zeke's ring slowly warmed under my fingers as I sat there, and Cade finally cleared his throat.

"What were we talking about before?" I asked.

Cade paused. "We were talking about that time when I saved your life?"

I tried to smile. "Of course, you would remember that conversation. I know you loved saving my life."

"Actually, I did." Cade smiled. "That was really crazy though."

"Especially since I was pregnant with Ruby, and I didn't know it," I said, trying to take his mind off Zeke.

"I never knew that." Cade looked surprised.

"Well, consider it your fun fact of the day," I smiled at him.

"That was a good day." Cade stroked his goatee and smiled.

"What? The day you got me pregnant with Ruby?"

"Well, that too." He turned red. "But I was talking about the day I saved your life. I still can't believe we climbed up tree roots, just because they were hanging from the side of a mountain."

"What else would we do?" I winked, lightly brushed his leg under the table, and acted like it was an accident.

"Elisa, you've got something up your sleeve. Is this poisoned or something?"

I acted offended, and then sweetly said, "I don't have any sleeves." As he looked at my bare shoulders, he missed the bite he tried taking, and poked himself with the fork.

I laughed. "Are you okay?"

"I'm fine," he said; his pride was hurt, though. "I just wasn't expecting that!"

"What? The fork to stab you in the face?" I giggled really hard.

"You think you're so funny!" He scooted to my side of the table, and I practically fell from my chair. "That was such a girly thing to do. Playing footsie. You are a girly girl."

He knew that was below the belt. I am not a girly girl, never have been, never will be. "Am not!" I tried composing myself. "I am not a girly girl!" I feigned sophistication.

A smile dimpled his face, like he'd realized Zeke was back from the dead. We sat so close to each other I felt my heart beating nervously, and I didn't dare say a word. Then, before I knew it, he held me in his arms, and I laughed because I suddenly felt happily complete for the first time in forever. I leaned down so our foreheads and noses touched—just like he had after the first time we kissed.

But, before anything else could happen, confusion sprinted across his forehead. He scooted away, and then stood. I couldn't understand why he acted like that, but I didn't want him seeing my pain; so, I smoothed out my dress as he tried acting like my enemy.

"I can't do this!" Cade said.

"Do what?"

"Be here with you, and act like everything's okay, when it's not! I need to think about things."

"Like what?" I asked, but he wouldn't tell me. Instead, he left the house and half of his dinner, which still steamed on his plate.

Entry #50

I got a call yesterday. A guy wants to pay Cade and me five-hundred dollars to play at his daughter's wedding in Colorado. He said he would pay our traveling expenses, and everything. I told Cade about it, and he's stoked. I'm nervous to travel with Cade for all that time. It will go really well, or really badly, and I'm hoping it will go well.

I called Marie and asked her if she can watch Ruby so we can play at the wedding. She was nice on the phone, and still hasn't said a word about the crap list I wrote. I wonder if she'll ever say anything. She's one of the most amazing people I know. It's like the crap list never happened. How weird is that?

Entry #51

It's been a year since Zeke died, and can you believe only a few people called me? Today is much harder than his birthday. I was happy to talk to all of them, but it really shocked me more people didn't remember. After all, hundreds of people attended the viewing and funeral. I sound ungrateful, and I don't mean to. I'm just shocked, like a fat bird on a wire, that's all.

I went over to Marie's house because she's really good at getting my mind off things. She made some hash browns, since they're my favorite, and I had a hard time not crying when I ate them. She made them just for me, even though I'm a filthy crap list writer. I tried calming down when I ate them, though, and looked around for something to take my mind off boobing. Then I spied the blanket that looks like the one that vanished from my garage.

"That's a beautiful blanket," I said. "Didn't you get me one just like it?"

"Yeah," Marie smiled, "I bought us matching ones," and it was then that my throat refused to swallow. I knew she hadn't taken my blanket. I felt dirty and sick, like I was some sort of vermin—like I should be stepped on and put out of my misery.

"I'm sorry about the crap list," I finally said, and she looked at me sadly.

"The what?" she asked and refused to talk about it anymore. I don't know if she even saw the thing, but I have a hunch she did, and doesn't want to talk about it because that's her silent "I'm forgiven."

I left soon after that, and Marie gave Ruby and me a huge hug before we went. I took Ruby to Zeke's grave. Cade went with us, and it was really cold. We had a hard time finding his grave because all of the headstones were covered in snow. We finally found it, though, because his grave is right under a little sapling planted just a few weeks before he died. I loved that idea at the time because I thought I could watch it grow to be the same age Zeke would have been. It's a sad looking sapling now, though. It's tiny and hunched over. It can hardly handle the weight of the snow.

We took turns watching Ruby in the car, so both of us could have a moment alone by Zeke's grave. When my turn came, I cried while I knelt in the snow. I sang Zeke his song, and my tears dropped into the snow and made vertical tunnels that went straight to the ground above the grave. I shook when I sang, and it wasn't from the cold.

While I stared at his icy headstone, I noticed someone moving in the corner of my eye. Snow danced around both of us as if it wanted him to come closer to me. I recognized him as the man with the cleft lip who had shoveled dirt onto Zeke's casket.

I didn't say anything because I didn't want to break the magic of the moment. I found it strange that we were both there, in the same places we'd been exactly a year before. He gently touched the sapling and wiped the snow off its tiny branches. He smiled at me, and the snow stopped falling around us. I smiled back and felt like time quit existing in that moment. We stared at each other, quiet understanding written between us, before he turned and walked away.

The sapling stood brave and strong after that, daring the snow to try and conquer it again. It reminded me of Zeke and his little life, and I beamed when I looked at it. It's going to grow into a nice, mighty tree, and I'm glad it will be the one to shade Zeke's resting place.

It's amazing how things happen. I don't believe in coincidence. God must be watching out for all of us, and if we'd just pay better attention, we'd understand that. That makes me think about that cougar again. I don't think we saw it by chance. I need to find out what it meant.

Entry #52

When I got home from work, Cade was waiting for me. He looked well rested and happy for the first time in months.

"I'm excited for the gig in Colorado," he said.

"Me too, it'll be great."

He grabbed my hand, and then squeezed it softly, just like he used to. "I miss you," he said, and he left. I was really confused as I went into the house. I couldn't figure what had happened to Cade. He's acting so strange. As I looked at the kitchen table, I had to grin because it was lengthwise, and there was a glass of water on the counter. I knew my mom had been on the first babysitting shift. A beautiful, white, wooden box sat on top of the table. It had a piece of etched glass as a window on it, and a little note rested in the bottom of the box.

The note said:

> *Dear Elisa,*
> *Every time I'm here, I'll leave you a special note to tell you how wonderful you are.*
> *Love- Your Cade*

There was another, smaller piece of paper folded inside the first one, and the smaller paper said:

> *Note #1*
> *You are a great mother.*

My heart warmed when I read the words, and I realized I held the note to my chest as I looked at the gorgeous box on the table. I can't tell you how much that little note meant to me. I'm really mixed up, though, and don't know what is going on with Cade. Did he think about things and decide he wants to be with me?

I wish he would just make things easy and talk to me. We'll get things figured out on the way to Colorado. We'll be stuck in the car together for over twelve hours each way. That ought to be enough time to sort things out, I hope.

Entry #53

Today, when I gardened, Ruby wouldn't stop staring at the statue of Zeke. I have it on my front porch, and I love seeing it there.

"Mama?" Ruby's voice cheered the air. "Mama?" she asked again.

"Yeah," I said, and pulled up a big dandelion. "What is it, Honey?"

"Mama, was Zeke really turned to stone?" she asked, and I laughed and laughed. That kid is better than life!

Entry #54

Cade watched Ruby, and I got another note in the box. It's like Christmas every time he comes over now. He didn't stay long, but kind of glowed when I talked to him. I can't figure out why he seems so happy. He's a different person or something. The note said:

> *Note #2*
> *Living life with you made me the happiest man in the world. I'll never stop loving you. You are the only one who has my heart.*

I stopped short after I read the note. Does he really love me? If he does, why isn't he home?

Entry #55

"The cowboy" came over tonight to talk with me about his girl problems. When he got here, I was surprised because he was dressed extra nice. Right after work he's normally in his construction clothes. He's a superintendent of a huge construction company and makes a lot of money; but you wouldn't know that by the way he dresses.

He walked into the house, and smelled really good, too. "What's gotten into you?" I asked. "Are you going to see that girl tonight, or something?"

"Yeah," he said, and smiled down at me in a strange way. I'd never seen him smile like that and should have known what was coming.

"You look really nice," I complimented. "She'd be an idiot to turn you down."

"Where's the first place you were kissed at?" he asked.

I got nervous then, because I only like "the cowboy" as a friend, and didn't want him talking about crappy feelings, so I said, "On the lips," and he laughed hard.

"No, I mean where, as in a location."

"In a picture booth. I was fifteen." I cringed at the memory.

"Was it Cade?" He tried sounding like he didn't care, but he wasn't a natural born actor, and I could have punched him for reminding me of my first kiss with Cade.

"No," I said. "It was my first boyfriend, and he had a butt the size of Milwaukee. It kept going, and going, and going, just like the energizer bunny!"

"Oh, so you like big butts?"

"No," I smiled. "I just like to make fun of them, if they belong to my first boyfriend."

"Yeah, note to self, don't get on your bad side."

"It's great when you talk to yourself like that," I said. "Very GQ."

I didn't want to talk to him anymore, though, because I'd hate to break his heart, and can never give him mine; it's already taken, and it's probably laying in the mud somewhere, wherever Cade left it.

My phone interrupted us, and it was one of my old friends from high school. I liked to call him "The Boarder" because he'd been the best snowboarder in school. Anyway, he just heard about Cade and me. He felt really bad and wanted to come talk to me in about an hour. "The cowboy" heard the whole thing and didn't seem too thrilled when I got off the phone.

"Who was that?" he asked in this really possessive way, but I shook his tone off, and thought he was just nervous or something.

"Just my buddy from high school. I haven't seen The Boarder in forever. We used to do the craziest things together." I chuckled at the memory. "Have you ever been sand jumping?" I asked.

"No," he said.

"You'd love it! We should go next weekend." I sat down on my couch and felt really comfy because I was in some fleece pj's, and life looked up. In less than twenty-four hours I would leave with Cade for Colorado, and I thought things would be better between us.

"Elisa, I need to tell you something. It's been killing me for weeks now."

"What?" I asked, worried I'd done something wrong, and he didn't want to be friends anymore.

"I've met a lot of girls," he cleared his throat, "and I've never felt this way about one, until now."

I breathed a sigh of relief then, because he wasn't mad at me. "I'm so happy for you...for the two of—" Then my phone rang again, and I saw that it was Cade. "Hang on; I've got to get this."

"Hello?" I said and stood.

"Hey, Hon. What's going on?" Cade asked.

"The cowboy" scooted to the edge of the couch. "Maybe I should go."

"No, it's okay. I'll be off in a minute." I held my hand out and motioned for him to stay.

"Who's that?" Cade asked with a bit of acid in his tone.

"A friend."

"I don't want you and Ruby alone in the house with him," Cade said, and he actually sounded worried for some silly reason. "I know who they are. His family is total white trash, and he gives me the creeps"

"What? Why?"

"Because he has a thing for you," Cade spat.

"Um, no," I waved the thought away like it was a bad fart. "The Boarder's going to be here soon, anyway."

"The Boarder? Elisa!" He paused, and I heard jingling keys. "I'm on my way to the house, right now," Cade said before hanging up the phone.

"What was that about?" I watched "the cowboy" ball his fists as he asked the question.

"Oh, just Cade. I guess he's coming over, too. He sounds kind of mad at me."

"He doesn't really have a right to get mad at you anymore, does he?"

"I guess not. I can't figure that guy out lately." I tossed my phone onto the loveseat next to me, crossed my ankles, and practically threw my feet on top of the coffee table. We were quiet for a minute, and the silence felt good. "Oh, sorry. So, when are you going to make your move? I'd be happy to help you with anything. I'm really good at knowing what girls like since I am a girl, and everything."

He took a deep breath. "It's you, Elisa. I've never met someone like you, and I know I never will again. I'm a good guy for you, and I know—somewhere, deep down—you know that."

I was speechless and shocked, really. "Me?" I asked, "But you can't mean me. We're just friends, right?" I looked at the guy next to me and knew there was no way I would ever love him, even though he adores Ruby, and might be Dr. Laura's choice. I didn't know what to say. His face paled, and my eyes drifted to the beautiful, white box and the sweet notes it held inside. I knew my emotions were as naked as his mom's saggies that day on the highway. "I—" and I didn't get to finish because there was a knock on the door.

The Boarder was completely oblivious to anything going on and bounded into the room like a playful tomcat. He picked me up in his arms and gave me a hug. "I'm so sorry to hear about you and Cade. It's been way too long." Then he turned to Dr.

Laura's choice and said, "Hey, man," and "the cowboy" gave him a halfhearted wave that looked like a mock salute. The Boarder sat way too close, and I found it odd, how I could be so uncomfortable in my own home.

"What's new?" The Boarder asked, trying to clear the air with his words.

"We were just talking about love," he said rudely; that "cowboy" was getting under my skin.

"Oh yeah, love, man." The Boarder nodded and laughed his big, happy laugh. "I was in love once, back in high school. I didn't try to get the girl, at least not hard enough."

"That was a smart move," the deflated words left "the cowboy's" mouth just before someone knocked. The door didn't even wait for me to open it, and Cade burst through like lightning in a storm.

"How are you doing?" Cade asked in his gruff base, and looked at "the cowboy," and then The Boarder, in turn. "Are you having a nice visit with my wife?"

"Yeah, just catching up, Man," The Boarder said, acting guilty as he picked up the coat he'd taken off a few minutes before.

"I've got to go." My eyes flitted from "the cowboy," who'd just spoken, to Cade, because he sat glaring. Cade's eyes must have been like a mesmerizing bug-zapper because he caught The Boarder's eyes, too.

"Man, it's getting late. I better get going, too." The Boarder looked at his wrist, which didn't have a watch on it, and with that they both left the house, and I was alone, with my heavily pacing husband.

"What were you thinking?" Cade asked me. "You planned this whole thing, didn't you?" He paused. "Didn't you?"

"No, I didn't!" I said and ran upstairs. I shut the bedroom door but tried not slamming it because Ruby was sleeping, and I didn't want to wake her.

I had to come and write everything down because my mind is

going a million miles an hour. Cade is lying on the couch downstairs, and I want to go scream at him, and tell him to stop being so confusing and so damn lovable, all at the same time.

Entry #56

Cade finally fell asleep on the couch, and I tip-toed downstairs, just to check on him. He looks handsome in the moonlight. His shirt is off, and the blanket he got is hardly big enough for him. It partially slipped off him, so I got our best blanket and covered him up, since he looked cold. After covering him, I noticed there was a new note in the white box. I took it out and brought it upstairs. It said:

This letter is to the most beautiful person in the world.... You

First, I want to say I'm sorry. I know I haven't been myself lately and haven't taken care of you and Ruby like I should. Life has been hard these past months. I feel like I am a failure, in work, financially, to you and even myself. Why I have been into music (the band) lately is because it seems that it is the only thing I'm not failing at. It makes me feel important to myself and even those around me.

I know this is one of the hardest dreams to pursue in life, but it is what I need and want. Also, what I need and want is you. You are still my life. You make life worth living, Elisa. I love you and always will. It may not seem like it, but the thought of losing you kills me. I cannot pursue my dreams without you because you are the only person who makes me whole. I wish you knew how beautiful you are to me and understood that without you I am dead inside. You have given me more than "the band" or my dreams ever could, in an eternity. You are my one and only.

You may not see it, but I miss you terribly when we are apart. That is why I'm putting my dreams on hold until I can get our lives in order and support you like you deserve. I'm going to get a better job, or a second job. I'll even do it on my own.

All I ask from you is patience, love and support until things get back in order. It means the world to me when you support me, my dreams and when you tell me I'm doing a good job. Thank you for putting up with me and always pushing me to better myself. Thanks for providing for this family where I could not. I am proud to call you my wife and to be married to someone as amazing as you. I love you Elisa and always will, no matter what.... I'll see you in the morning.

Love,
Cade

Entry #57

It's still the middle of the night, and I can't stop thinking about how sweet Cade is being. So, I did something for him. I hurried to my room and wrote a bunch of nice things about him. I wrote about who he is now, and sweet things I remember from our past. I put them all on yellow sticky papers. Then I tip-toed from the house and put them all inside his car. I stuck them in the glove box, the mirrors, the steering wheel, under the seats—everywhere.

After I walked back into the house and checked on Ruby, I rested on the couch with Cade. I don't know if he completely noticed me, or if he still slept, but he held me tight as soon as I lay down. There wasn't much room on the couch, and we had to snuggle close. His warm chest felt nice against my cold arms, and I slept really well, for once in about five-hundred years.

I woke up as soon as I heard Ruby. The first thing that hit me after her squeal of delight was the smell of sausage and eggs in the air. I got Ruby, and we both ran into the kitchen, where Cade was making omelets.

"What in the world?" I asked, and he said he couldn't sleep in, and it must have been the first time in his life. So, he made some breakfast for us. Ruby grinned like a creature that never stops smiling, and we had a ball for breakfast. Cade didn't say a word about last night, and it was nice to be together as a family.

I'm really excited to go to Colorado. I think it'll be good, spending time with Cade alone. I can't wait for him to see all of the notes in his car. As I walked away from breakfast, I noticed that there was another note in the white box.

It said:

You're the most beautiful when you're happy.

I read that and decided he should write for a fortune cookie company.

Entry #58

We're on the way to the wedding now, and Cade thinks I'm nuts for writing while we're driving. "Won't that make you sick?" he keeps asking, but I just laugh in reply.

You should have seen Cade's face when he saw all of the notes in the car. He found them everywhere, and then he beamed and almost blushed while he read them. He's so cute when he's embarrassed. They've made for some good conversations, though, and I'm so glad he likes them.

It's been a nice trip so far, and we're almost to the wedding now. I can't believe how much we've talked about, and we haven't fought once. We've talked about Ruby and the last few months, but mostly we've been talking about Zeke. I remember the last time we drove to Colorado, the time I held Zeke's ashes in my lap, back before we let them go, and saw a cougar.

By the way, I finally found out what cougars represent. It makes me want to bawl as I write this, because I remember how hard it was, letting Zeke go. When his ashes drifted, I wanted to jump after them, gather each one, no matter if it meant falling to my doom. But I stayed on top of that mountain. Cade stayed with me, and the wind swept Zeke's ashes away. But then that crazy cougar marred the whole experience. It stared at me with those big golden eyes, not even making a sound when it left me in my fears. I wanted to talk to Cade, reminisce about Zeke, but instead I ran down the mountain. And every time I've thought about Zeke's ashes, all I really remember are those golden eyes.

But they have a new meaning for me now, because cougars represent something amazing; the will to live; strength in adversity; justice; compassion to watch and protect those they love. They're special animals, and if I had to think of one person who embodies what they mean, I'd pick Zeke.

As I sit here, I can't help wondering if I didn't completely lose Zeke the day I blew his ashes off that cliff. Maybe he's still watching me, just like that cougar was, before I knew it was there.

I don't know why Zeke was born the way he was, but I do know that God is taking care of us, and that cougar was a sign.

"Why do you think God allows so many bad things to happen?" Cade asked, trying to see my point of view. I found irony in his question because I'd asked "the cowboy" the same thing.

"So, we can learn from them, I guess," I said.

"Who's to say they're really bad, anyway?" Cade rhythmically patted the wheel as we drove along.

"Yeah, exactly," I said, and then we were quiet for a long time. I thought about how Cade is the only person in the world who truly understands me, that's what he tells me in the silence anyway.

"Elisa?" he finally asked. My eyes rose at the sound of my

name. "I'm sorry."

"For what?" I looked out the window, and worried about broaching the subject. We were in the middle of a beautiful Colorado canyon lying just beyond the Utah border. I marveled over the outdoors.

"For everything, but most of all for letting go. I tried so hard to let go of Zeke that I let go of you and Ruby in the process. I didn't know how to handle things, and I'm sorry for what I put you through."

"It's okay," I said, still studying the landscape, the steadily blurring landscape.

"Did I ruin your life—" he paused, and tears stained his voice, "—when I got you pregnant with Ruby?"

"No," I said, and took a deep breath. "That was when my life truly began." I leaned over and put my cheek against his right arm.

"You, Ruby, and Zeke are the best things that have ever happened to me. I'm so happy right now."

"Me, too." He smiled. "You make me happy."

"I'm scared, though, because things seem too perfect," I said.

"I know what you mean. The last time that happened, we found out Zeke had problems."

"It's hard letting myself be happy. I don't want something bad to happen. I think life tries to balance itself out, somehow. I guess I should be glad I'm happy now and stop worrying."

Cade laughed. "Happy now? But you seemed so happy when we were separated."

"I'm a good actress."

"Yeah, right. You didn't miss me for a second."

"I wanted you back the entire time," I said, and kissed his arm lightly.

"I didn't know! I thought you were fine without me. I would've been back in a heartbeat if—"

"Well, now you know," I interrupted, and Cade pulled the car over.

"And I'll never let you go again; you're all I've ever wanted," he said, drew me close, and kissed me.

Entry #59

The wedding was amazing! It was the most beautiful wedding I've ever seen, but it was pretty weird, too. It was a pagan wedding, and the man and woman who performed the ceremony had long, dark-purple hair, and they looked like pale twins, who were a little bit too friendly with each other. But they're not twins. They just happened to marry someone who looks exactly like them, and they must be experiencing too much self-love to go that route.

Anyway, we played music the whole time, and it went perfectly with the nature theme. I always love playing at weddings because I like watching when the groom sees the bride for the first time. It's one of the most magical moments on Earth.

While they stood, taking their pagan vows, Cade grabbed my hand and held it tightly in his. We both remembered the vows we'd taken when we got married, and I thought about how happy I was being next to him. I knew, then, I'd follow those vows forever, because Cade's the only one for me, and tears tumbled in my eyes.

The father of the bride smiled at me, and I'm sure he thought we were really worth the money, but I didn't cry about the gorgeous wedding; I cried because I knew I was getting my husband back, and because I knew we'd just made it through the storm. I can't help remembering my dad's speech at Zeke's funeral. "At the end of a storm is a golden sky. Walk on, walk on, with hope in your heart, and you'll never walk alone."

After the ceremony ended, the couple released a bunch of doves into the wild; they were white, instead of the black theme which hovered over the rest of the wedding.

The newlywed couple stepped onto a flat wooden raft, and the groom used a huge staff to push them to the middle of the lake they'd just gotten married next to. They ate dinner on the raft, in the moonlight, and it really was a magical moment. Cade and I continued to play, and at one point, when everyone danced to the music, I broke a string on my violin. I'm good enough that it didn't mess me up too badly, and I just went up an octave if I needed to hit certain notes.

After the song was over, I said, "Cade, I just broke my G-string."

"That sucks! Do you have another one?" he asked.

"I'm not sure, but I think—" I said, and then a little old woman, who had a very loud voice, interrupted me.

"Where I come from, the young folks don't talk about G-strings in public! I can't believe you'd say such a crude thing in front of all these people," she fumed, and everyone stared at me.

"I was talking about the G-string on my violin," I said, and the woman hobbled away as everyone laughed until they couldn't laugh anymore.

We took a break so I could restring my violin. Cade went over to the bar and got us some drinks.

When the party ended, the father of the bride gave us a key, and told us where our room was. I felt a little nervous, sharing a room with Cade, like I was the one who'd just gotten married.

I took my time walking back to the room. The pathway was strange, where the desert blends with a vibrancy many places can't claim. I stopped walking and turned to Cade. The moment felt so familiar, like I'd been there years before.

I remembered:
We stood in a desert, an amazing desert. Crazy-beautiful flowers bloomed on the path next to our feet. They were pansies—aqua and purple, all mixed up, and they were so intriguing I couldn't pull my eyes from them. I bent to touch one of the flowers. I didn't want to pick it, but I couldn't keep from feeling its beauty.

Tears came to my eyes as I remembered those flowers. I'd

had a dream once about those crazy-beautiful pansies. I cleared
my throat and said, "I always hated pansies. I thought they were
weak. But my mom was right; they can grow places other
flowers can only dream of. They pop up, even after a fire takes
everything else away." I chuckled softly. "That's why they
represent undying love: that's the only thing that can make it
through a fire."

I looked at Cade, and as I stood, he grabbed my hand and
held it like he'd never let go.

We got to our room, and as we walked in, it reminded me of
the time I'd given birth to Ruby. I was so worried to have a baby,
because then my mom would know I wasn't a virgin. It didn't
matter that she'd heard Ruby's heartbeat, or practically seen
hundreds of my ultrasounds. The fact was, she knew I didn't have
the same gift as the Virgin Mary, and I was embarrassed about it.

We walked into the fancy hotel room. There were a bunch of
nice things waiting for us, including a five-hundred-dollar check.
Next to the check sat a bottle of wine and some beautiful glasses.
We each drank a couple of glasses full, and then Cade sat close
to me and put his hand gently behind my neck. He kissed me
softly, and I felt my heart beat faster and faster. I smiled then,
because I remembered that I'd shaved my legs that morning, and
I guess I knew all along how far I was willing to go.

Closure

It's been almost two decades since Zeke died, and as far as I know, the people I wrote about in my journal are doing well. Here they are in order of appearance:

° Cade and I are no longer married. We had three more healthy children after Zeke died. Every day is an adventure with these hilarious kids, and I see life through grateful eyes because of Zeke. My three little girls get more darling with each passing day, and my son (who looks a lot like Zeke and was born on Cade's birthday) is a gift beyond words.

Cade quit the band shortly after the last entry in my journal, and although we tried for nearly 13 years, we both knew we needed to go separate directions with our lives.

We played music together until our divorce in 2013. Now, Cade is remarried with a child from that marriage. I am also remarried and living life to the fullest. (To read more about my current adventures—and battle with stage 4 melanoma—visit my blog: *www.ECWrites.net.*)

° Ruby is a beautiful adult—older now than I was when I wrote this journal! She's absolutely stunning and enjoys working at a tattoo shop where she is one of the four main artists on staff.

People come from all around Idaho and Utah just to see her artwork and unique designs.

❀ My parents and siblings are still in the Western states, and they all are very happy. Cade's mother (and my mom too) stopped moving our table when I turned twenty-three. That was a serious day of rejoicing, and they are a credit to mothers everywhere. My dad recovered from cancer and has been cancer free for several years.

❀ Both of my grandparents have passed on to be with Zeke, and I hope they are taking good care of him for me.

❀ I still talk to Cammie. She's doing awesome, and her kids are grown up and just about the cutest people around. She worked as a single mom for quite a while, and I'm so proud of her amazing example and strength.

❀ "King Arthur" is currently writing several self-help books.

❀ The "experts" who helped us with Zeke will always be around, giving endless amounts of information to those willing to listen, and I'm thankful I no longer cling to hear their words.

❀ I visited Zeke's nurse, Susan, and she is as spicy as ever. She looked genuinely happy to see me, and I hugged her hard because I miss her, too.

❀ The "Understudy" became a very successful musician and electrician. I ran into him a while back and told him I wrote a book, and he's in it. He asked, "Wow, what's it about?"
    "Zeke," I replied.

"Who's that?" he asked and was all sorts of stumped.

"My son who died."

He took in a deep breath. "I am so sorry!" he said. "I had no idea you had a son who died."

How strange that he'd called me years before to talk about Zeke. How could he have forgotten so easily? I guess it's true that sometimes life does just go on for everyone else....

❀ My aunt still misses her dog, and I feel bad he went missing.

❀ I only saw Earl once more after the last time I wrote about him in my journal. He saw Ruby, Cade, and me eating at a restaurant. He gave me a bear hug, and his eyes sparkled when he saw Cade and Ruby sitting next to me. "I'd know you both anywhere," he said. "I've heard so much about you."

Can you sit with us?" I asked, and he smiled. "I just finished my coffee, and I need to get going."

"Of course." I laughed. "I should have known you were only here for the coffee."

He winked at me and waved as he left. After we finished eating, we went to pay for our food, but Earl had already taken care of it for us. That was the last time I saw him, but when I look back and think about it, I still catch myself wondering if he was an angel.

❀ The "big sag" keeps her bra on now; it's quite a feat if you ask me. She's still living the good life, working at the mechanic shop.

❀ I ran into "the cowboy" a few years ago. He said he just bought a house and was living with a lady named Barbie. She had three kids, who were a few years younger than me. She was quite a bit older, but he seemed pretty happy. It was nice to see him, and I wish him well.

❀ I saw Thomas a couple of years ago. He didn't recognize me, even though I helped raise him for two years. At the time, his mother was going to church, had gotten off drugs, and grown her fingernails back. Last year I heard she got back on drugs, had another baby, and lost her home again. I can't find a way to get ahold of her, but I pray for them often. I hope Thomas is okay, and that his mom is doing all right.

Reflections

One of my best friends inspired me to reread my journal in 2009. The whole experience seemed so far away (Zeke was born in 2002 and died in 2003). Reading my words felt so painful at first, but I made myself push through. After finishing, I finally came to peace with Zeke's death. Thank God I wrote everything down! It is interesting, looking back at my past and seeing things through new eyes. Cade has read my journal, as well, and when we were still married, we had many late-night discussions regarding our memories and the lessons displayed in my journal.

I love all my children, and Zeke will never be forgotten. My time with him has been pushed into a special place in my heart. Nothing can take that away, and those memories will always be here to keep me strong and help me be the person I know Zeke would want me to be.

Other books in this series...

Book 1 in "The Golden Sky" Series: "One Wing in the Fire" by EC Stilson

Elisa has unending faith until a group of religious zealots in Utah decide to perform an exorcism on her. Feeling her foundation crumble, she begins to rely on a mysterious stranger. But will he help or make things even worse than they were before?

"One Wing in the Fire" is the prequel to "Homeless in Hawaii," the true story of how author EC Stilson became a homeless street fiddler on the Waikiki Strip.

"EC Stilson" on Goodreads!

Book 2 in "The Golden Sky" series: "Homeless in Hawaii" by EC Stilson

Running away from her past, Elisa finds herself homeless in Hawaii. The streets aren't what they seem, though — even in paradise — and cops make her stay in "homeless park."

She's only seventeen and with a man she hardly knows, but they must learn to work together if they expect to survive as street musicians.

"If you are in search of an enlightening tale to scratch an intellectual itch, 'Homeless in Hawaii' will not disappoint. The literary style is descriptive, intelligent, and sometimes downright hysterical."

–Peter Greyson
Author of "Dear Lily"

About the Author

EC Stilson (Elisa Magagna) has authored nine novels and one children's picture book. All three of her memoirs, in "The Golden Sky" series, have become No. 1 bestsellers on Amazon for women's memoir. Since 2011, through fundraisers, book donations, and national radio interviews, EC Stilson has helped raise thousands of dollars for organizations such as Angel Watch, the Pregnancy Resource Center, the American Diabetes Association, and Primary Children's Hospital. When she's not editing, parenting, or fiddling, she is speaking at events or going on hilarious adventures with her husband (who happens to be her very best friend).

As of this latest publication, Stilson is currently battling stage four melanoma and continues to share her journey through her blog, The Crazy Life of a Writing Mom: *www.ECWrites.net*.

Made in United States
Orlando, FL
28 December 2024

56654470R00161